AF736805

More on Risk and Energy Infrastructure

Value Chains, Stakeholders and Black Swans

Consulting Editors **Thomas Dimitroff** and **Troy Edwards**

Consulting editors
Thomas Dimitroff and Troy Edwards

Managing director
Sian O'Neill

More on Risk and Energy Infrastructure: Value Chains, Stakeholders and Black Swans
is published by

Globe Law and Business Ltd
3 Mylor Close
Horsell
Woking
Surrey GU21 4DD
United Kingdom
Tel: +44 20 3745 4770
www.globelawandbusiness.com

More on Risk and Energy Infrastructure: Value Chains, Stakeholders and Black Swans

ISBN 9781787420670
EPUB ISBN 9781787420687
Adobe PDF ISBN 9781787420694
Mobi ISBN 9781787420700

© 2017 Globe Law and Business Ltd

All rights reserved. No part of this publication may be reproduced in any material form (including photocopying, storing in any medium by electronic means or transmitting) without the written permission of the copyright owner, except in accordance with the provisions of the Copyright, Designs and Patents Act 1988 or under terms of a licence issued by the Copyright Licensing Agency Ltd, 6-10 Kirby Street, London EC1N 8TS, United Kingdom (www.cla.co.uk, email: licence@cla.co.uk). Applications for the copyright owner's written permission to reproduce any part of this publication should be addressed to the publisher.

DISCLAIMER
This publication is intended as a general guide only. The information and opinions which it contains are not intended to be a comprehensive study, nor to provide legal advice, and should not be treated as a substitute for legal advice concerning particular situations. Legal advice should always be sought before taking any action based on the information provided. The publishers bear no responsibility for any errors or omissions contained herein.

Table of contents

Setting the scene

Thomas Dimitroff
Infrastructure Development Partnership; Roland Berger GmbH
Troy Edwards
Allen & Overy LLP

Risk and Energy Infrastructure: Cross-Border Dimensions (Vol I) was published by Globe Law and Business in 2011. That book provided an inter-disciplinary perspective on project-specific risk factors that apply to the implementation and operation of cross-border oil and gas pipelines, together with best practice risk allocation and mitigation methodologies. While much of the analysis provided by the various authors in Vol I is generally applicable to other types of energy infrastructure, the specific focus of Vol I naturally invited a second volume that would expand upon that analysis.

Accordingly, *More on Risk and Energy Infrastructure: Value Chains, Stakeholders and Black Swans* (Vol II) looks beyond oil and gas pipelines to consider energy infrastructure more broadly in several important dimensions. First, this book seeks to examine energy infrastructure within the current macro-economic, technological and geopolitical context. The 2008–2009 global financial crisis dampened enthusiasm for capital investment in greenfield conventional energy infrastructure projects. Notwithstanding this, investment in US energy infrastructure to support shale oil and gas production proliferated thereafter and has endured the subsequent 2014 downturn in global oil pricing as a result of the drop in services costs and technological advances in fracking. With the United States now requiring fewer imports of crude oil and gas, and indeed exporting liquefied natural gas (LNG) and crude oil, Middle East low-cost production will have difficulty preserving market share. Additionally, rapid technological advances in, *inter alia,* renewable energy, battery storage and transportation have opened the prospect for dramatically reducing the cost of renewable energy. From a geopolitical perspective, these technological advances both alleviate US dependence on the Middle East and shift oil demand growth to Asia, Africa and the Middle East. China's 'One Belt, One Road' strategy ensures that, among other things, the infrastructure is in place to support the transportation of oil and gas from the Middle East and Africa. Combined, these developments promise profound and disruptive structural shifts in global energy markets in the coming decades.

Second, this book examines risk factors associated with broader societal impacts that arise from several interrelated policy failures, including in particular:

- governments prioritising the production and export of crude oil and natural gas over the completion of the domestic infrastructure needed to link key power and product production value chains back into the domestic economy. This book considers the risk factors and opportunities where this situation prevails across many parts of the Middle East and sub-Saharan Africa;

- governments failing to master plan infrastructure projects properly, giving rise to gaps in otherwise interdependent projects, redundancies in projects with overlapping services, technological obsolescence and consequential adverse socio-economic impacts. These risk factors, as well as opportunities to structure properly master planned infrastructure, are examined across a number of concrete examples in sub-Saharan Africa, South Asia, Australia, North America and the Middle East; and
- governments and businesses failing to take proper account of the rights and interests of indigenous populations when developing and operating projects across indigenous lands or where projects otherwise adversely impact indigenous communities. Once again, numerous concrete examples are examined and innovative solutions – including community investment – are elaborated and considered.

A comprehensive understanding of energy infrastructure cannot be gained by looking at individual infrastructure components alone. A third dimension therefore involves examining conventional oil and gas infrastructure as well as renewable and nuclear energy infrastructure within the context of their respective full value chains. In the case of oil, this will include production, transportation and product refining. In the case of gas, renewables and nuclear, the whole value chain that delivers feedstock to power plants, regulatory support regimes for renewables and electricity market issues will be examined. The multiplicity of risk factors shared and distinctive to these sectors is considered.

Fourth, in the wake of the global financial crisis, the traditional role of banks as the providers of long-term capital to infrastructure has been overtaken by institutional investors. Pension funds, insurance companies, international institutions, private equity and sovereign wealth funds and, in the developed world, in addition to the foregoing, bond markets are now seen as the primary financiers of infrastructure. However, the overwhelming bulk of this capital is limited largely to brownfield infrastructure investments and greenfield projects in the developed world. Risk in the developing world is often perceived as being too high for the long-term steady state requirements of institutional investors. Adding to the array of risk factors is the potential impact of climate change on the value of investments and the willingness of banks and institutional investors to finance long-term infrastructure projects that support the relevant hydrocarbon value chains. A chapter on financing energy infrastructure will therefore consider both how a shift from bank financing to bond market financing in developed markets, as well as how new approaches to risk allocation, may minimise the impact of global warming on banks, investors and society.

Fifth, as technology advances, the need for sophisticated master planning to enable interconnected 'smart infrastructure' will intensify in tandem with increasingly intimate collaborations between the public and private sectors to protect communities adequately against physical and cyber security threats. Accordingly, a chapter is dedicated to examining the topics of physical and cyber security risks to critical energy infrastructure. Risk assessment and evaluation methodologies are offered in respect of physical security threats including point assets (those located at a particular site – eg, a production facility, refinery, tank farm or power station), linear assets (eg, pipelines, power grids and communication networks) and remote assets (eg, buried midstream assets or upstream assets). With reference to cyber security threats, hacking, cybercrime, cyber espionage and cyber warfare are considered, as well as the interaction between physical security and cyber security.

Finally, *More on Risk and Energy Infrastructure* also asks each of the authors to engage in 'out of the box' thinking. This is the exclusive focus of the last chapter, written as a dialogue between two of the book's authors. On the one hand, recent technological advances, environmental impacts and social developments are examined and we are invited to consider whether they together represent 'disruptive change' to the way risk and energy infrastructure has been assessed to date. On the other hand, these advances, impacts and developments can also be seen as the latest manifestation of a form of 'groupthink' that has prevailed among communities throughout history and which is a constituent part of our very human nature. Is risk in this context a function of how, and to what extent, these advances, impacts and developments may transform the nature and role of energy infrastructure, or is risk a function of our collective perception of such transformation and when markets assess that it has in fact occurred?

Delivering sustainable energy infrastructure solutions: The Middle East and sub-Saharan Africa

Thomas Dimitroff
Infrastructure Development Partnership; Roland Berger GmbH

1. Introduction

Ideally, the implementation and operation of an energy infrastructure project involves the alignment of business objectives to government policies. Those policies should be targeted to deliver key societal benefits that outweigh adverse social and environmental impacts on particular communities. Where adverse impacts are inevitable, consultations and grievance processes should be engaged to enable appropriate remedies. In addition, individual projects that are implemented in accordance with an overarching master plan that takes into account broader infrastructure and societal needs will enhance the opportunity concurrently to deliver business objectives, avoid redundancies and enhance community interests.

Achieving a sustainable balance among these objectives, goals and interests has never been more urgent. This is especially the case within many parts of the developing world, including, in particular, sub-Saharan Africa and parts of the Middle East.[1] Geopolitical, macroeconomic, climatic, conflict and population dynamics are converging with speed to place strains on people, communities and the environment. Africa's population is projected to more than double from 1 billion to 2.5 billion between 2015 and 2050,[2] with certain sub-Saharan African countries more than tripling in population – for example, Niger will grow from 19.9 million today to more than 72.2 million, and Nigeria will become the third most populous country in the world.[3] A similar situation prevails across many parts of the Middle East where populations in certain countries, especially in conflict areas such as Syria, Yemen and Iraq, are projected to more than double. For example, Iraq's population is projected to grow from 36.4 million to 83.6 million by 2050.[4]

1 It is important to note that some Middle Eastern governments have managed the challenge of attaining a sustainable balance better than others (eg, Qatar and the United Arab Emirates). Indeed, Qatar boasts the fifth highest *per capita* GDP in the world and UAE has sought to diversify its economy by developing nuclear power to satisfy 25% of the country's domestic power generation requirements and to free up additional oil production for export. See www.enec.gov.ae and www.imf.org/external/pubs/ft/weo/2017/01.

2 https://esa.un.org/unpd/wpp/Graphs/Probabilistic/POP/TOT/.

3 https://esa.un.org/unpd/wpp/Publications/Files/WPP2017_KeyFindings.pdf.

4 https://esa.un.org/unpd/wpp/Publications/Files/WPP2017_KeyFindings.pdf.

At the same time, a number of man-made factors are placing increasing strains on the natural environment in these regions. Climate change is raising temperatures to intolerable levels in parts of the Middle East – for example, Basra, Iraq and Kuwait City recorded temperatures of around 54C (129.9F) during the summer of 2017, and these temperatures are now becoming the seasonal norm.[5] The combination of high temperatures and increased populations is causing an accelerated reduction in arable land and water resources, and thus increased desertification. Across sub-Saharan Africa, the pace of urbanisation, the intensification of farming on agriculturally degraded land, deforestation, mining, conflict and illegal poaching are dramatically reducing the amount of arable land and the habitat available to sustain the diversity and sheer quantity of wildlife.[6]

In order for governments in these regions to ensure that *per capita* gross domestic product (GDP) growth maintains pace with population growth, massive investment in infrastructure is required. For example, there is a strong correlation between power generation and *per capita* GDP growth with "energy use [considered as either] the cause or facilitator of economic growth".[7] Unfortunately, while the Middle East and sub-Saharan Africa account for more than 20% of the world's population,[8] 35% of global oil production and 20% of global gas production, these regions account for only 4.5% and 3.2% (respectively) of annual global power generation.[9]

The World Bank estimates that sub-Saharan Africa will require $95 billion in annual infrastructure investment to 2030.[10] Of this total amount, the largest sub-sector requirements are for transport and energy infrastructure – primarily power generation and grid capacity, but also gas processing, transport and liquefaction and oil refining. Investment in infrastructure in war-torn parts of the Middle East is also urgent. For example, as Iraq ramps up its oil production, it will need to reduce the flaring of associated gas which currently places Iraq second among countries in the world by the amount of gas flared.[11] The investment needed in gas separation and processing, pipeline transportation, power generation and related projects required to address this problem adequately is alone estimated to total $80 billion to $90 billion.[12]

This chapter will examine the 'triangular relationship' between government, business and local communities and how the roles of government and business have morphed, and the challenges and opportunities this presents to achieve a sustainable balance in this relationship. A series of case studies – flare gas reduction in Iraq, power sector master planning in Lebanon, oil sector master planning for South Sudan, and increasing refining and power generation capacity in Nigeria – will be

---

5 https://weatherspark.com/y/104337/Average-Weather-in-Basrah-Iraq-Year-Round; see also, www.vanityfair.com/news/2017/06/extreme-heat-global-warming.

6 For example, the populations of giraffes, elephants and antelope in South Sudan have dropped 99.7%, 97% and 92% respectively since the 1970s. See https://ss.usembassy.gov/pr-03032017/.

7 www.cdcgroup.com/Documents/Evaluations/Power%20economic%20growth%20and%20jobs.pdf.

8 https://esa.un.org/unpd/wpp/Publications/Files/WPP2017_KeyFindings.pdf.

9 www.bp.com/content/dam/bp/en/corporate/pdf/energy-economics/statistical-review-2017/bp-statistical-review-of-world-energy-2017-electricity.pdf.

10 www.brookings.edu/blog/africa-in-focus/2017/01/17/foresight-africa-viewpoint-unlocking-infrastructure-investment-across-africa/.

11 www.worldbank.org/en/news/press-release/2016/12/12/new-data-reveals-uptick-in-global-gas-flaring.

12 Study undertaken by author and Roland Berger GmbH, June 2017.

considered. Each constituent in this triangular relationship will be examined to evaluate the extent to which its interests may be better aligned to address the challenges presented in these case studies. Specifically, policy recommendations will draw upon conclusions reached in other chapters of this book to suggest that:

- all energy infrastructure implementation must be undertaken in accordance with well-formulated and integrated master plans;
- oil and gas value chains are implemented to deliver refined products and power locally and not simply to deliver oil and gas export revenues;
- there is an expansion in the use of public private partnerships (PPPs) across the regions better to align finance, technical capability, stakeholder incentives and operational excellence over the life of the projects;[13] and
- consideration is given to opportunities for community ownership in projects, where appropriate, better to align project objectives and interests.

The chapter will conclude by noting the elevated perceptions of political risk to infrastructure investment that currently prevail among strategic and financial investors (particularly private sector investors) when considering projects in the Middle East and sub-Saharan Africa. In order to address these perceptions of political risk, and thus to unlock the vast amount of investment required to fill the growing gap between population growth and infrastructure, a pragmatic solution in the form of greater utilisation of PPPs and carefully crafted government guarantees is suggested.

2. Regional challenges, case studies and energy infrastructure

2.1 The roles of foreign states, state-owned enterprises and business

The engagements by foreign states and business interests with local governments in the Middle East and sub-Saharan Africa have historically been troubled. Foreign conquest of large parts of these regions has longstanding roots that in some instances extend back into antiquity.[14] The principal relationships established have been exploitative and targeted principally at raw commodity production and export. After World War II and decolonisation, western business interests stepped more visibly into the role previously played by government – that is, to produce and export raw commodities and principally crude oil, and thus to provide secure access of energy supply. Nevertheless, western governments, and in particular the United States, have remained assertive in pursuit of regional objectives, including being involved in 'regime change'.[15]

---

13 Countries across these regions are well advised to adopt and fully implement appropriate PPP laws and regulations. Indeed, failure to do so may place countries at a competitive disadvantage as competition for capital investment increases.

14 Following the Macedonians, Persians and Romans, the Arabs conquered the Middle East and North Africa in the 7th century and Islam quickly spread into large parts of sub-Saharan Africa from the 10th century. Western European states commenced colonisation of large parts of sub-Saharan Africa in the 15th century and the Ottoman Empire stepped into large parts of the Middle East and North Africa in the 16th century.

15 This started with the overthrow of Mosadegh in Iran (1954), involved multiple interventions in parts of sub-Saharan Africa during the Cold War, including in Angola and Congo (Zaire), and, more recently, has involved no less than nine 'regime change' operations in the last 15 years. See, www.globalresearch.ca/overthrowing-other-peoples-governments-the-master-list-of-u-s-regime-changes/5400829. While the United States provides large-scale aid support to sub-Saharan Africa, it also remains involved in large-scale conflicts in Iraq, Afghanistan and Syria.

China has more recently emerged as the largest trading partner for sub-Saharan Africa[16] and one of the most significant funders of infrastructure development projects in the region. Chinese government, contracting and banking interests have deployed a variety of trade finance and engineering, procurement and construction (EPC) solutions to deliver infrastructure projects across the continent.[17] Unfortunately, most of China's earlier trade finance engagements in sub-Saharan Africa were also targeted at raw commodity export and secured through, *inter alia,* forward commodity sale arrangements (eg, in Nigeria and Angola).[18] Moreover, most infrastructure projects virtually ignored local content and dispatched Chinese labour to fulfil even unskilled roles.[19] More recently, infrastructure projects funded and implemented by China have been in the transport and power sectors – for example, between 2010 and 2020 China has, or is projected to, implement 96 power projects and 49 transmission and distribution projects.[20] In addition, sub-Saharan African exports of manufactured goods to China have grown from 5% to over 20% of the total since 2012, signalling a shift in approach to its engagement with the continent of Africa.[21] Whether these developments are entirely benign or seen, with hindsight, to have been targeted principally to entrench China's own long-term strategic objectives (via its 'One Belt, One Road') policy remains to be discerned.[22]

With much of the oil and gas industry in the Middle East and North Africa (MENA) now under state ownership, the largest oil and gas production companies operating globally (including across MENA) are state-owned national oil companies (NOCs)[23] not private sector-owned international oil companies (IOCs). However, approximately 35% of global downstream trading is dominated by seven private companies (only two of which are publicly listed).[24] In the case of the Middle East, almost all export revenues are generated from the sale of crude oil, natural gas, liquefied natural gas (LNG), liquefied petroleum gas (LPG) and related hydrocarbon

16 http://wits.worldbank.org/countrysnapshot/SSF/textview.

17 www.brookings.edu/wp-content/uploads/2017/04/global_20170417_africa-energy-infrastructure.pdf.

18 www.kwm.com/en/uk/knowledge/insights/made-in-china-financing-nigerias-infrastructure-20160719.

19 www.ictsd.org/bridges-news/bridges-africa/news/china's-infrastructure-development-strategy-in-africa-mutual-gain.

20 www.ictsd.org/bridges-news/bridges-africa/news/china's-infrastructure-development-strategy-in-africa-mutual-gain.

21 www.imf.org/external/pubs/ft/wp/2015/wp15221.pdf.

22 The policy initiative is targeted to enhance trade and capital deployment between China, South East Asia, South Asia (Pakistan and Bangladesh in particular), Africa and the European Union, and will involve $1.7 trillion in investment by 2030 (with $1.1 trillion already committed). See www.business.hsbc.com 11 May 2017.

23 The largest global oil and gas companies are NOCs and two of these are Middle Eastern (Saudi Aramco and NIOC (Iran)), although IOCs are significantly present in parts of the Middle East (eg, in Iraq) and sub-Saharan Africa.

24 Vitol, Glencore, Noble Group, Arcadia Petroleum Limited, Trafigura, Gunvor and Mercuria. Interestingly, of these seven trading companies, only two are publicly listed (Glencore and Noble Group). The combined consequence of having a very large percentage of global oil reserves and production controlled by NOCs and traded by privately held trading companies is that information about this important commodity sector remains notoriously opaque. Sector analysts are left to discern market conditions primarily by implication based on a multiplicity of factors including, in particular, storage data.

25 For example, in 2015, of approximately $600 billion in exports, only $15 million involved non-hydrocarbon based products http://wits.worldbank.org/CountrySnapshot/en/MEA/textview.

26 For the purposes of this chapter, the Middle East will primarily include Iraq, the Levant, the Saudi Arabian peninsula and MENA, recognising marked disparities between, for example, the Gulf Cooperation Council countries and Yemen, Syria, Libya and Iraq.

products (2015).[25] Specifically, the Middle East as a region[26] produces in excess of 30 million barrels per day (Mbpd) of crude oil, of which 21 Mbpd is exported. The regional daily consumption of oil products is approximately 9.57 Mbpd, yet the region still has a shortage of installed refining capacity of 7.93 Mbpd.[27] With reference to power generation, notwithstanding the abundance of natural gas reserves (the Middle East holds 41% of the world's conventional natural gas reserves), many countries in the Middle East, including Iraq, Syria, Lebanon and Yemen, suffer power generation deficits. For example, in Iraq, peak demand often exceeds installed generation capacity by nearly 50%.[28]

In the case of sub-Saharan Africa, the overall regional trade imbalance is significant, with the region running a deficit in excess of 25%.[29] The top six export categories are comprised of raw commodities, and of these, less than 10% (by value) are non-hydrocarbon commodities (eg, cocoa beans, textiles, agricultural produce and gold).[30] As a region, sub-Saharan Africa produces 8.35 Mbpd of crude oil, of which 5.43 Mbpd is exported.[31] With only 2.07 Mbpd of installed refinery capacity, 1.7 Mbpd of refined products are imported back into the region to satisfy regional demand of 3.88 Mbpd (primarily from refineries and crude oil traders based in the European Union and the Middle East). This is particularly alarming as the region collectively expends $36 billon per year of hard currency to procure the import of refined petroleum products at the same time that it is running a $55 billion trade deficit.[32]

With reference to power generation, notwithstanding an abundance of hydrocarbon resources that could be used as feedstock, the World Bank estimates that 25 countries in sub-Saharan Africa face acute power generation deficits.[33] Nevertheless, these deficits exist in hydrocarbon-rich economies, such as Nigeria, where electrification rates currently stand at 56%,[34] as well as in other parts of sub-Saharan Africa given the absence of significant intra-African transportation infrastructure and related trade.

As noted above, an important key to generating increases in *per capita* GDP growth for emerging markets lies in the successful transition from economies dependent on raw commodity exports to manufacturing,[35] the export of finished products and electrification.[36] Access to affordable power not only boosts manufacturing capacity and creates jobs, but also enhances human development.[37] Unfortunately, the lure of quick access to petrodollars too often overshadows the

---

27 www.bp.com/content/dam/bp/en/corporate/pdf/energy-economics/statistical-review-2017/bp-statistical-review-of-world-energy-2017-full-report.pdf.

28 See www.iberglobal.com/files/2016/iraK_eia.pdf, p. 13.

29 http://wits.worldbank.org/CountrySnapshot/en/SSF/textview.

30 http://wits.worldbank.org/CountrySnapshot/en/SSF/textview.

31 www.bp.com/content/dam/bp/en/corporate/pdf/energy-economics/statistical-review-2017/bp-statistical-review-of-world-energy-2017-full-report.pdf.

32 http://wits.worldbank.org/CountrySnapshot/en/SSF/textview.

33 http://web.worldbank.org/WBSITE/EXTERNAL/COUNTRIES/AFRICAEXT/0,contentMDK:21935594~pagePK:146736~piPK:146830~theSitePK:258644,00.html.

34 https://assets.kpmg.com/content/dam/kpmg/pdf/2016/05/kpmg-sub-saharan-africa-power-outlook.pdf.

35 http://ycsg.yale.edu/sites/default/files/files/wtr_2014.pdf.

36 www.mckinsey.com/industries/electric-power-and-natural-gas/our-insights/powering-africa.

37 www.undp.org/content/dam/india/docs/human-development/Energy%20access%20and%20human%20development%20IC4HD_Session%204_Iyer.pdf.

longer-term process of master planning, financing and implementing the individual energy infrastructure projects that together create the value chains required to generate more fruitful impacts on domestic economies. This is exacerbated by the fact that the attention span of government, as in the developed world, is often no broader than the next election cycle.

In the case of sub-Saharan Africa, these temptations are easily exploited by the international oil trading community. Trading margins are captured by exploiting the need for petrodollars and the absence of local and inter-regional refining, transport and power infrastructure, thus completing a vicious circle rather than a value chain. This situation is exacerbated by perceptions of instability and political risk that foreign investors associate with these regions. Seven Middle Eastern governments and 35 sub-Saharan African governments are ranked in the 'Highly Corrupt' and 'Corrupt' categories by Transparency International (2016).[38] Moreover, 20 contiguous sub-Saharan African countries are ranked in the two most fragile 'Alert' state categories (2016 Fragile States Index),[39] and the lowest levels of investment in research and development globally are found in the Middle East and sub-Saharan Africa (2.3% and 1.1% of the global total respectively).[40]

While the roles of government, business and their respective engagements both domestically and internationally have merged and morphed, the principal exports from the Middle East, North Africa and sub-Saharan Africa remain raw commodities. Clearly, in order for benefits to the local populations in these regions to be maximised, and adverse environmental and social impacts minimised, greater attention to integrating oil and gas value chains delivering power and refined and manufactured products to these regions is needed. The following sections will briefly examine four case studies, two from the Middle East and two from sub-Saharan Africa, to illustrate the challenges and potential solutions that they may present.

(a) *Gas flaring and gas-to-power in Iraq*

While Iraq has the fourth largest reserves of oil in the world, it has only the 12th largest reserves of conventional gas,[41] and yet it is the second highest gas flaring country in the world (16 billion cubic metres (bcm) per year).[42] Similarly, the country is plagued with power brownouts and is currently paying to import more than 20 bcm of gas per year (ie, an amount equal to over 75% of what the country is currently flaring each year) through two new-build pipelines from Iran. When the annual cost of importing gas from Iran ($3.7 billion per year) is added to the losses represented by flaring gas ($2.5 billion per year), the annual losses to the Iraqi budget exceed $6 billion per year.[43] With oil production projected to more than double over the next 15 years, the foregoing imbalances will be further exacerbated. On the power

38 www.transparency.org/news/feature/corruption_perceptions_index_2016.
39 http://fundforpeace.org/fsi/.
40 www.iriweb.org/sites/default/files/2016GlobalR%26DFundingForecast_2.pdf.
41 www.bp.com/content/dam/bp/en/corporate/pdf/energy-economics/statistical-review-2017/bp-statistical-review-of-world-energy-2017-full-report.pdf.
42 www.worldbank.org/en/news/press-release/2016/12/12/new-data-reveals-uptick-in-global-gas-flaring.
43 The problem is particularly important to address as the comparable costs for generating a megawatt hour of power from natural gas is $15 as compared to $173 for heavy fuel oil and $200 for gasoil.

demand side, the country will need to treble its gas utilisation to balance properly power supply to projected demand.

Key existing bottlenecks are large and found in all three streams of the gas value chain. Upstream, proper commercial incentives for industry producers to capture natural gas production and development of new exploration plays are needed.[44] Midstream, existing pipeline infrastructure is ageing and requires replacement, and capacity is, in any event, inadequate. Gas separation and processing facilities are also grossly insufficient. A promising move, however, was made in 2013 with the establishment of the Basra Gas Company, a joint venture between the Iraqi state-owned South Gas Company, Shell and Mitsubishi to develop 5 bcm of new-build gas processing infrastructure.[45] While much more gas processing infrastructure is needed, the Basra Gas Company has secured significant private sector investment in exchange for the ability to export LPG and gas condensate. Downstream, gas supplies to existing power generation facilities are grossly insufficient, requiring use of more expensive oil products (heavy fuel oil (HFO) and diesel). In addition, the absence of large-scale creditable power off-takers renders investment by independent power producers (IPPs) more difficult without offtake guarantees.

Sadly, in addition to the absence of investment capital, the level of skilled employment available within Iraq to implement adequately the foregoing infrastructure projects remains extremely low. While engaging local technical capacity-building is a requirement for foreign oil company operators, implementation has remained a challenge due to competing political/sectarian interests that control the various ministries responsible for regulating the training. As a consequence, rather than building training centres in Iraq, smaller numbers of capable locals are often sent abroad, thereby limiting the actual impacts.

Rectifying the foregoing imbalances will require first and foremost the mobilisation of significant external (most likely private sector) financing. A key factor to enable the mobilisation of the requisite investment is the preparedness of the government to offer various guarantees and undertakings to developers. In addition, the following actions will need to be addressed:

- a comprehensive and well-integrated master plan providing a clear roadmap to enable inter-ministerial cooperation between, among others, the ministries of oil, electricity and finance, thereby mitigating the implications of political/sectarian biases and allowing the challenges to be more pragmatically addressed;
- a complete legal and regulatory framework properly to enable commercial risk allocation mechanisms to guide private sector investment;
- the use of PPPs, modelled on the Basra Gas Company, and the mobilisation and support of IPP projects;
- the provision, by the Government of Iraq, of, *inter alia,* appropriate feedstock supply and power purchase agreement (PPA) guarantees to enable investment; and

44 Iraq is one of the least explored large-scale hydrocarbon producing countries in the world.

45 The Basra Gas Company is owned by the Iraqi (state-owned) South Gas Company (51%), Shell (44%) and Mitsubishi (5%). Data compiled by Roland Berger GmbH.

- proper funding and institutional support (including appropriate inter-ministerial coordination) for larger numbers of local Iraqis to be trained at technical institutes and training centres within Iraq.

(b) *Power supplies for Lebanon*

At present, the Republic of Lebanon suffers from an acute deficit in power generation capacity, and the national fuel feedstock supplies are overwhelmingly concentrated in imported liquid hydrocarbons. As a consequence, the country experiences chronic power shortages, is vulnerable to security of supply disruptions due to the lack of diversity in its fuel supply, and suffers the consequences of poor air quality due to the fact that it must combust liquid hydrocarbons, in particular heavy fuel and diesel.[46] The foregoing challenges are exacerbated by the fact that the country is deeply sectarian, with ties that directly link the key Sunni, Shia and Christian divisions found across the Middle East and North Africa into the country's main governing institutions. Lebanon is also currently hosting 1.5 million refugees – primarily from the war in neighbouring Syria, placing enormous strains on the country's finances.[47]

In order to address the power sector challenges referenced above, the Ministry of Energy and Water has pursued a power strategy targeted to migrate its power sector towards gas feedstock.[48] While this makes some sense, especially given the proximity of Lebanon's offshore exploration acreage to large-scale gas discoveries in Israeli, Cypriot and Egyptian waters, Lebanon does not currently have a domestic supply source or proven gas reserves. While in theory IPPs can be mobilised to invest, it is unrealistic to expect that they would do so in the absence of government guarantees over long-term gas supply and power off-take. Moreover, Lebanon would still need to finance the domestic gas receiving terminal and associated domestic gas transportation infrastructure.

Unlike Iraq, Lebanon is looking ahead to ensure that its future gas supply resources will first and foremost be linked to a domestic gas-to-power value chain to address its power generation challenges. Moreover, while Iraq has massive unproduced wealth in the form of its existing proven oil and gas reserves that can be secured to unlock investment, Lebanon is altogether lacking in proven oil or gas reserves and will therefore need to be more creative to attract foreign investment to address its immediate funding and technical capacity constraints. Nevertheless, both countries will need to be prepared to offer various forms of government guarantee to developers to de-risk the infrastructure projects and thereby unlock the requisite investment. Fortunately, Lebanon has taken the following steps to address its power sector challenges:

- it has already commissioned an integrated power sector master plan;

---

46 Polluted air can also cause disease and chronic health conditions. Interestingly, the neighbouring Republic of Cyprus also has analogous power generation challenges. While Cyprus has proven gas reserves (9 trillion cubic feet), it is unable to convince the upstream investors to invest large amounts upstream in the production of gas to service such a small market. Consequently, like Lebanon, Cyprus is currently utilising imported liquid hydrocarbons to fuel its power generation and will also need to look for an interim solution to address existing challenges.

47 https://ec.europa.eu/echo/files/aid/countries/factsheets/lebanon_syrian_crisis_en.pdf.

48 *Policy Paper for the Electricity Sector*, Ministry of Energy and Water 2010.

- the master plan involves an analysis of the full gas-to-power value chain, including:
  - current and alternative (natural gas) import supply sourcing;
  - development of 1–2 floating storage and regasification units and associated gas transportation infrastructure, including a trunk line and spur lines to main power off-takers and power sector master planning; and
- the power master plan also proposes that the Government of Lebanon is prepared to enter into arrangements with IPPs as well as PPP arrangements with strategic private sector investors.

Further to its power master plan, Lebanon also appears to be considering long-term gas off-take arrangements and in turn to be offering back-to-back gas supply guarantees, which gas transporters and power producers will need in order to proceed to implement the required infrastructure projects.

(c) ***Petroleum sector master planning for South Sudan***

The Republic of South Sudan became the newest member of the United Nations on 14 July 2011.[49] It is well endowed with oil reserves (P1 and P2 reserves of 1.179 million barrels and an additional 1.5 million barrels of additional recoverable and 'yet-to-find' oil resource potential). In addition, South Sudan has vast blocks that remain under-explored (Block B) and vast areas of the country altogether unexplored. Since 2000, a number of foreign oil companies have been producing and exporting oil through two pipelines currently located in the Republic of Sudan and terminating at Khartoum (the Petrodar Pipeline) and Port Sudan on the Red Sea (the GNPOC Pipeline).[50]

South Sudanese oil production might have afforded a very substantial revenue base from which the country could eventually accumulate substantial foreign currency reserves. The reserves could have been deployed more strategically to guarantee the investment activities of foreign investors to develop the badly needed transport, refining and power generation infrastructure. This may also have enabled the country to diversify its economy into mineral extraction and agricultural production and export.

Instead, the country descended into civil war on 15 December 2013 and oil revenues have been used to procure weapons and otherwise to fuel a conflict which remains unresolved. The problems facing this young country are vast and of an emergency nature, with at least 50,000 dead (some estimates place the number of dead at as high as 300,000),[51] a displaced population of 2 million people, a famine involving an estimated 6 million people and more than 50% of the population living in poverty. Oil production and export remains virtually the sole source of government revenues, constituting over 97% of the country's GDP.

---

49 www.un.org/apps/news/story.asp?NewsID=39034#.WajMC9N97q0.
50 Based on analysis undertaken by Infrastructure Development Partnership between 2011 and 2015.
51 www.news24.com/Africa/News/south-sudan-is-dying-and-nobody-is-counting-20160311-4.

Sadly, South Sudan remains without any refining or on-grid power generation capacity. As a consequence, the country is currently exporting all of its crude oil production, approximately 130,000 bpd. Prior to the war, South Sudan was exporting in excess of 380,000 bpd, and oil production had peaked in 2009 at over 500,000 bpd. Since secession, South Sudan has continued to export oil production via the Republic of Sudan, albeit subject to punitive transit payments ($15 per barrel). Concurrently, South Sudan is importing approximately 13,000 bpd of refined products (including gasoline, kerosene and diesel), with a large percentage of these products coming back into the country from Republic of Sudan refineries.[52]

The Republic of South Sudan urgently needs to take the following actions:

- commission and agree an integrated petroleum and power sector master plan;
- prioritise the implementation of an upstream production rehabilitation plan to stabilise and boost production from existing fields using water flooding and other forms of enhanced oil recovery;
- the Ministry of Petroleum and Mining, in coordination with other ministries, needs to commission and implement a comprehensive programme to attract inward investment into the exploration and development of additional upstream reserves;
- renegotiate with the Republic of Sudan an arrangement to enable transit payments to be changed from a per barrel 'flat fee' arrangement to a mechanism more appropriately indexed to oil price, thereby enabling South Sudan (as producer) and the Republic of Sudan (as transporter and transit state) more equitably to allocate market risk;
- commission an appropriate market assessment to locate, design and implement one or more simple (topping) refineries capable of producing approximately 30,000 bpd;
- commission the implementation of a domestic road and/or domestic pipeline transportation system to move 'white products' produced by the refinery(ies) to support the country's transport sector;
- plan for the utilisation of residual HFO yielded by the refinery(ies) as feedstock for the development of the country's power sector;
- design, finance and implement power generation capacity (95 megawatts (MW)) to be installed proximate to principal demand centres;
- plan for off-grid solutions (ideally solar) to be implemented for more dispersed rural communities;
- propose funding and finance solutions for the implementation of the foregoing infrastructure projects; and
- finally, an oil fund should be established to ensure that sufficient allocations are set aside for future investment in the requisite infrastructure. The oil fund should be used to backstop government undertakings to private sector strategic investors who may be prepared to enter into PPP arrangements to implement and operate the foregoing infrastructure.

---

52 The foregoing data is based on work undertaken by Infrastructure Development Partnership in the Republic of South Sudan between 2011 and 2015.

(d) *Oil refining and power generation for Nigeria*

As referenced above, the United Nations projects that Nigeria will be the third most populous country in the world by 2050.[53] While endowed with abundant natural resources (Nigeria has the 11th largest reserves of oil (second largest in Africa) and the 8th largest reserves of gas (largest in Africa)),[54] Nigeria imports more than 80% of the oil products[55] it consumes and suffers acute power generation deficits.[56]

In terms of crude oil production, available refinery capacity, refinery runs and imports of refined products, Nigeria remains significantly out of balance. Currently, Nigeria is producing 2.053 Mbpd and exporting 1.738 Mbpd, and while it has nameplate refinery capacity of 446,000 bpd, it produces only 53,500 bpd of products,[57] consumes 317,000 bpd and imports approximately 80% of all oil products consumed.[58] While Nigeria earns substantial foreign currency through the sale of its crude oil production, the country is expending a very substantial portion of those proceeds to procure refined products and to supply these to its domestic market. Moreover, until 2016 the Nigerian government subsidised the price of oil products sold domestically. This, together with the theft of 150,000 barrels of crude oil every day (representing a loss of approximately $5 billion per year) and the precipitous drop in the price of crude oil since June 2014, has greatly exacerbated the country's foreign currency crisis.

In terms of Nigeria's respective oil and gas-to-power value chains, the country also remains significantly out of balance. Nigeria is currently producing 44.9 bcm/year of natural gas, exporting 26.7 bcm/year and flaring 8 bcm/year of gas (making Nigeria the sixth largest producer of flared gas).[59] This leaves 10.2 bcm/year of natural gas for domestic thermal power generation (approximately 20% of its total production and accounting for 12% of the country's primary energy consumption).[60] In addition, approximately 13% of Nigeria's off-grid power generation is fuelled by imported petrol and diesel and costs consumers between $6.7 billion and $10.47 billion per year, according to the World Bank.[61]

As referenced above, notwithstanding its abundant hydrocarbon reserves and production, the majority of Nigeria's population has no access to grid-based power, with an estimated 115 million people using biomass and waste to meet their domestic heating and cooking needs (accounting for 74% of Nigeria's primary energy consumption).[62] Nigeria's power generation deficit is acute. With 13,400 MW of installed power generation capacity, only 8,000 MW is mechanically available.[63] The

---

53 https://esa.un.org/unpd/wpp/Graphs/DemographicProfiles/.

54 www.bp.com/content/dam/bp/en/corporate/pdf/energy-economics/statistical-review-2017/bp-statistical-review-of-world-energy-2017-full-report.pdf.

55 Nigeria's number one import is oil products ($5.1 billion per year) www.worldstopexports.com/nigerias-top-10-imports/.

56 www.proshareng.com/news/Power/Nigerian-Power-Sector-Report—-Is-there-light-at-the-end-of-the-tunnel-/33896.

57 www.opec.org/opec_web/en/about_us/167.htm.

58 www.nigerianstat.gov.ng/pdfuploads/2016%20Petroleum%20Products%20Consumption%20(Jan-Sep)%20.pdf.

59 www.worldbank.org/en/news/press-release/2016/12/12/new-data-reveals-uptick-in-global-gas-flaring.

60 www.eia.gov/beta/international/analysis.cfm?iso=NGA.

61 www.nigeriaelectricityhub.com/2016/10/11/world-bank-nigerias-power-deficit-hits-94500-megawatts/.

62 www.eia.gov/beta/international/analysis.cfm?iso=NGA.

63 www.metering.com/magazine_articles/power-sector-reforms-nigeria/.

World Bank estimates that the country will require the installation of 95,000 MW to correct its existing power generation deficit.[64] Left unaddressed, this deficit will grow markedly as the country's population increases going forward.

Given the scale of Nigeria's hydrocarbon reserves and the speed with which the population is growing, the country urgently needs to add additional refining and power generation capacity. Fortunately, the domestic business community is stepping forward to offer and implement solutions. The Dangote Group is currently investing $18 billion to construct the world's second largest urea fertilizer plant, which will utilise approximately four bcm of natural gas feedstock and produce 3.85 million tonnes per year of products, together with the largest single train refinery in the world (650,000 bpd). In addition, the Dangote Group is constructing more than 2,000 kilometres of pipelines to transport gas from the wellhead to the urea fertilizer plant, thus reducing the amount of gas flared in Nigeria and putting those volumes to productive use.

While the Dangote Group investments are transformational to the downstream oil, gas and power sectors, a single business (however large) is unable to address the multiplicity of challenges facing Nigeria without the close cooperation of government (particularly with reference to master planning) and the participation of additional private sector investors. Nevertheless, the leadership demonstrated by the Dangote Group to address these challenges stands out for others in sub-Saharan Africa and the Middle East.

3. Key factors informing energy infrastructure policy considerations

There are a number of key factors that need to be considered when formulating policy decisions targeted to achieve a sustainable balance between government, business and community interests, and two of these will be considered here. The first factor requires an understanding of the relationship between infrastructure components and the overarching value chain, and the asymmetric incentives that inform stakeholder perspectives on this relationship. The second factor involves market perceptions of risk in the Middle East and sub-Saharan Africa. These intimately interrelated factors are briefly examined below.

3.1 Infrastructure components, value chains and asymmetric perceptions among stakeholders

The overarching commercial objective in implementing an energy infrastructure project is rarely complete upon project completion. Rather, all energy infrastructure is linked to a value chain that does not generate revenue until the entire chain of infrastructure components is complete and each component is, *inter alia,* either producing, transporting, separating, processing, cracking, liquefying or combusting energy. Consider the following simplified illustration of an LNG value chain:

Figure 1: Gas to LNG to Power Value Chain

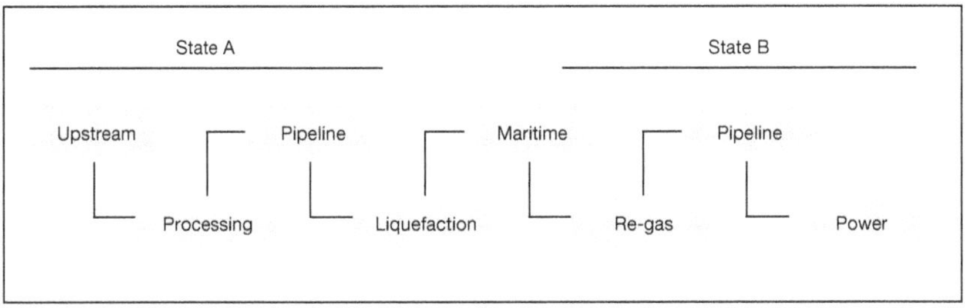

The above LNG diagram assumes that the value chain will straddle two sovereign states (A and B) and any such value chain will be constructed and operated across multiple communities.[65] In addition, it is extremely rare that an entire value chain would be owned by a single ultimate owner. Moreover, as the revenue generation models are rarely indexed to commodity price, there is frequently a misalignment of understanding between the owner/operator of the individual infrastructure components and the host governments and/or locally affected communities. The latter will sometimes assume that the infrastructure owner/operator will be generating large-scale revenues when in fact the revenue model for the component (eg, a processing facility, pipeline or liquefaction plant) may be limited to a service fee based on a 'tolling' model. As a consequence, misalignment of expectations will frequently arise.[66]

For local communities, the most direct and adverse impacts are caused when individual or communal land is expropriated to accommodate an energy infrastructure component project. Thereafter, communities can be adversely affected by the ongoing operations, whether by restrictions on usage of land, noise, traffic, pollution or otherwise. If the aggrieved community perceives that it has not been properly consulted or that the benefits enjoyed by the business are significantly asymmetric to those offered to the community, problems will invariably result.[67] However, at the very least, constant and appropriate engagement between the business and the locally affected communities is now being seen not only as a requirement, but as prudent.[68] Moreover, maximising local content, including local procurement of goods and services and training to enhance employment opportunities for local communities, is

64 www.worldbank.org/en/news/press-release/2017/04/22/world-bank-group-support-for-nigerias-power-sector-recovery-program.

65 In fact, LNG value chains can straddle multiple states and, as LNG is increasingly traded globally, the states and customers can frequently change.

66 Put simply, a community or state through which a gas transportation pipeline passes will naturally assume that the gas commodity is also owned and traded by the pipeline company. The revenue model for the pipeline company, however, will frequently be limited to receiving a per unit tariff for the shipment of gas. Aligning expectations between the state or community, on the one hand, and the pipeline company, on the other, can be challenging.

67 In certain circumstances, forms of community ownership can be offered more properly to align the interests of the infrastructure owner to those of the local community. This ownership structure is examined elsewhere in this book. See the "New risks, new opportunities: The growing role of indigenous peoples in project development" chapter by Mark Podlasly.

68 See the UN Guidelines on Business and Human Rights, www.ohchr.org/Documents/Publications/GuidingPrinciplesBusinessHR_EN.pdf.

also prudent. Finally, where governments have upstream oil and/or gas production, they will deliver greater societal benefits if upstream production can find its way back into domestic product refining and/or power generation rather than simply being exported. Thankfully, shifting demand growth forecasts will increasingly dictate this result as OECD Europe consumes fewer hydrocarbons, the United States becomes increasingly self-sufficient and the populations of the Middle East and sub-Saharan Africa not only grow in size but also in wealth.

3.2 Perceptions of risk to infrastructure investment in the Middle East and sub-Saharan Africa

According to a June 2016 study by the McKinsey Global Institute, $3.3 trillion will be required each year ($95 billion per year for sub-Saharan Africa) until 2030 to support current global growth rates.[69] Unfortunately, only a small fraction (approximately 5%) of total transactions involve infrastructure in the Middle East and Africa, with the overwhelming majority still concentrated in Europe, North America and Asia/Australia.[70] However, notwithstanding the fact that yields are falling in the developed world and private equity funds are now holding an estimated $1.5 trillion in 'dry powder'[71] solutions that unlock capital flows into infrastructure, investment in the Middle East and sub-Saharan Africa is urgently needed.

However, due to the perceptions of elevated risk prevailing across large parts of the Middle East and sub-Saharan Africa, financial investors have little appetite for greenfield infrastructure developments in these regions.[72] While local investors frequently have an intimate understanding of the dynamics of the local political and legal and regulatory environment, they lack the financial and often technical capacity to develop, finance, construct and operate large-scale local infrastructure projects.[73] With joint venture arrangements between private sector strategic investors and state-owned companies more common in the energy sector, infrastructure investments that do not include ownership in the underlying energy commodity are more rare in sub-Saharan Africa and the Middle East.[74]

Mobilising foreign capital investment into energy infrastructure will therefore require greater utilisation of PPP models[75] and a preparedness on the part of governments to offer investors, *inter alia,* feedstock, repayment, off-take and fiscal

---

69 McKinsey Global Institute, *Bridging Global Infrastructure Gaps*, June 2016.

70 www.pwc.com/gx/en/industries/assets/pwc-giia-global-infrastructure-investment-2017-web.pdf.

71 www.bain.com/about/press/press-releases/dry-powder-hits-new-record-high-as-private-equity-continues-to-outperform.aspx.

72 With the notable exception of smaller-scale renewable energy projects.

73 Industrial enterprises with the technical and financing capability of the Dangote Group are currently rare across sub-Saharan Africa. This situation will likely change markedly over time as the continent starts to train its young and growing populations and the capacity for innovation is unlocked.

74 This is very different in developed markets, where the steady state future funding requirements sought by pension funds find an ideal fit with the highly predictable cash-flows generated by infrastructure investments that are largely insulated from market risk.

75 PPP models enable an optimal alignment between private (foreign) capital and government and community requirements for energy infrastructure and are robustly supported by international institutions such as the World Bank. For example, see https://ppp.worldbank.org/public-private-partnership/library/model-request-proposal-ppp-projects-and-guidelines.

stabilisation guarantees to ensure financing can be repaid on a certain and predictable basis.[76] More recently, Chinese EPC and commercial/state banking interests have been shifting from commodity-driven financing in sub-Saharan Africa towards pure infrastructure investments – especially in the transport and power sectors. As noted above, this may in fact be part of a more comprehensive move to establish sub-Saharan Africa as a future manufacturing hub for the export of goods back to China pursuant to the 'One Belt, One Road' strategy. However, as with private sector western investors, the Chinese are now also requiring the same range of guarantees and increasingly teaming with western strategic and financial investors. Whether the recent shift in approach will unlock larger-scale capital commitments, improve quality and deliver greater levels of local content remains to be seen.

4. Conclusions

The Middle East and sub-Saharan Africa are regions facing unprecedented challenges across multiple dimensions, including geopolitical, macroeconomic, climatic, conflict and population growth. If properly managed, these challenges can also present tremendous opportunities for economic growth not seen since the emergence of the Asian Tiger economies from the 1980s to the early 2000s. Ensuring that challenges can be transformed into opportunities will require achieving a sustainable balance among government, business and community interests. In turn, this will require that governments increasingly shift their focus from raw commodity exports. Attracting inward investment, including investment into energy infrastructure projects that constitute oil to refining and gas to power value chains, will ignite growth in manufacturing, increase employment and enhance human development. With the expansion of the transportation linkages, inter-regional trade will enable greater flows of goods and services – an especially acute requirement for the land-locked countries of sub-Saharan Africa. Inviting greater participation from foreign strategic and financial investors – whether private sector or Chinese – to implement the requisite infrastructure projects through PPPs supported by appropriately stuctured government guarantees will help to unlock energy infrastructure across the Middle East and sub-Saharan Africa.

The author would like to thank Dr Helga Graham, Winifred Andersen, Richard Herbert, Ryan Dillan and Madeleine Dimitroff for reading through the text and offering important suggestions and edits.

---

76 These guarantees can often be provided by governments on an 'off-balance sheet' basis and are responsibly delivered provided that an adequate accounting is maintained to ensure that contingent liabilities can be accurately calculated and monitored.

New risks, new opportunities: The growing role of indigenous peoples in project development

Mark Podlasly
Nlaka'pamux Legacy Trust

1. Introduction

The ability of companies, governments and investors to dictate terms of projects developed in indigenous lands is changing. Indigenous populations – once relegated to minor or non-existent roles in project development in their traditional lands – have found new ways to impact and intervene in such projects. Pipelines, mines and transportation corridors once deemed essential to global growth are increasingly being opposed and delayed or blocked outright by indigenous peoples.[1]

From a Canadian indigenous perspective, this activism is the culmination of a long process that has evolved over decades. Assertions made by indigenous peoples demanding that their interests and rights in traditional territories no longer be ignored by distant governments and commercial companies have been increasingly successful. Canada, however, is not alone. Over the last 70 years, indigenous rights have gained prominence globally through indigenous rights court decisions, increasing availability of legal and technical resources, changing societal attitudes and, most importantly, the rise of internet-supported activism and knowledge sharing. These developments have given indigenous peoples new energy to press for changes on how projects are financed, constructed and operated in their lands.

Capitalising on these changes, there has been an incremental increase in indigenous influence and leadership on large capital and infrastructure projects through negotiated participation agreements with companies and governments. Viewed together, indigenous rights, technical developments and negotiated agreements point to where things are headed where major infrastructure projects are developed on indigenous lands or near indigenous communities.

Indigenous issues have usually been considered by many companies and governments as a corporate social responsibility (CSR) issue, where companies would narrowly address the social and environmental concerns of local indigenous populations as a sidecar issue separate from the commercial objectives of the

1 While the focus of this book is on energy infrastructure, this chapter will draw on examples of projects from sectors that include energy infrastructure, as well as mining and hydrocarbon production where valuable resources are extracted from traditional lands.

proposed project.[2] Indigenous issues were considered a minor part of a major capital project, and would rarely, if ever, be addressed by C-suite executives. In many cases, companies would delegate the responsibility of addressing local community concerns to mid-level or regional managers. Indigenous peoples – and their concerns, interests and aspirations – were seen as 'cosmetic' issues, inconsequential to the infrastructure plans of distant company executives and government officials.

In several cases in the Americas and Africa, indigenous peoples are moving beyond the mostly cosmetic CSR interpretation to new realities where indigenous communities are no longer passive hosts of infrastructure projects but share in resource development planning and benefit directly from the prosperity of the project. Community development needs – economic, as well as environmental and social – can be enabled by such projects. Remote corporate and federal or regional government decisions being foisted on indigenous communities are no longer acceptable.

From the Dakota Access oil pipeline in the United States,[3] to the Tía María copper and gold mine in Peru,[4] to Papua New Guinea's Exxon-Mobil Liquefied Natural Gas project,[5] to BC Hydro's Site C hydroelectric dam in Canada,[6] indigenous and local protests against large-scale projects are widespread and growing. These protests are no longer restricted to far-away project locations; mainstream media now regularly report on indigenous protests in overseas countries.

The reality of decades-long protests and ongoing community action is causing commercial investors to delay or defer investing in resource and infrastructure projects. The cost of project failure or substantive delay from indigenous community action is high. In a 2014 study, the National Academy of Sciences of the United States found that a community-led production delay at a major mine can result in losses of up to $20 million per week.[7]

The new reality is that investors, governments and project proponents must now address indigenous rights and concerns as a core element of their infrastructure and resource projects. Project proposals that enable and benefit the local community to meet shared development goals are more likely to proceed. Projects that do not, or are seen by increasingly vocal and activist communities as detrimental to community wellbeing, will not gain vital local support.

Many companies have been ill equipped to make this change in thinking. Going

---

2 'Corporate Social Responsibility' definition from UN Industrial Development Organisation www.unido.org/csr/o72054.html.

3 Levin, Sam, "Dakota Access Pipeline: The Who, What and Why of the Standing Rock Protests", *The Guardian*, 3 November 2016. Accessed 17 September 2017. www.theguardian.com/us-news/2016/nov/03/north-dakota-access-oil-pipeline-protests-explainer.

4 "From Conflict to Co-operation", *The Economist*, 6 February 2016. Accessed 17 September 2017. www.economist.com/news/americas/21690100-big-miners-have-better-record-their-critics-claim-it-up-governments-balance.

5 Tlozek, Eric, "Unpaid Royalties Prompt Protest at LNG Project near Port Moresby", *ABC News*, 20 February 2017. Accessed 17 September 2017. www.abc.net.au/news/2017-02-20/png-protesters-block-lng-project-near-port-moresby/8286894.

6 "3 Protesters Arrested at Site C Dam Project", *CBCnews*, 6 January 2016. Accessed 17 September 2017. www.cbc.ca/news/canada/british-columbia/site-c-protesters-arrested-1.3392884.

7 Franks, Daniel M, Rachel Davis, Anthony J Bebbington, Saleem H Ali, Deanna Kemp and Martin Scurrah. "Conflict translates environmental and social risk into business costs", *Proceedings of the National Academy of Sciences*. 19 March 2014. Accessed 17 September 2017. www.pnas.org/content/111/21/7576.short.

forward, companies that can make the turn to a new reality of partnership with indigenous peoples will succeed and see projects approved, constructed and put into operation. Companies – and governments – that cannot envision what is coming will see their projects stall or fail outright.

2. New realities

Indigenous activism upends the infrastructure and natural resource 'business as normal' model from a top-down decision-making function to one more akin to a commercial/community partnership between companies and indigenous peoples. While it is impossible to give a blanket summary of all indigenous opposition, patterns are starting to emerge that give context to the origin of the growing clout of indigenous communities in development and, more importantly, offer project proponents an indication of what is coming next.

2.1 Righting an imbalance

In the past, companies and governments enjoyed near-complete domination of all aspects of a project's development and operations. They held privileged access to land, capital, natural resources and information needed to develop projects. In short, project proponents enjoyed freedom to dictate how projects would be developed in indigenous homelands. Indigenous peoples and their interests were minimised or, in many cases, ignored by governments and companies.

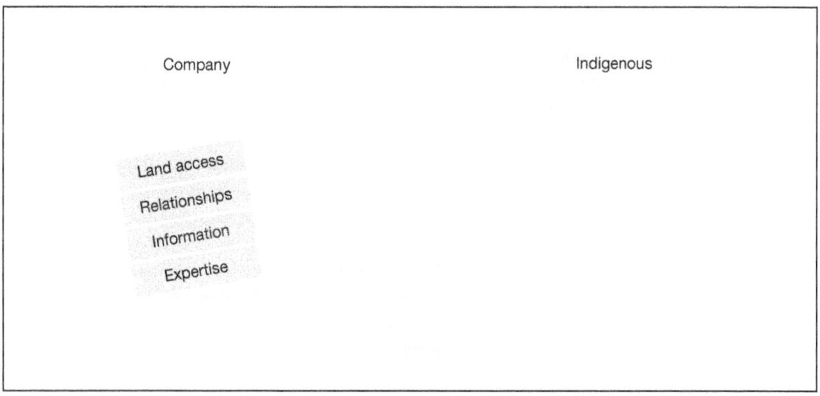

(a) Land access

Governments and companies (via concessions and other grants and allocations of land rights from governments) held near-complete free access to national lands and natural resources. In many cases, allocation of land and resources was determined by governments without regard for traditional indigenous rights, use or interests.

(b) Relationships

Access to government officials, capital/financial instruments, market access for end-user purchase agreements and, in many cases, national law courts and systems was limited to government and corporate parties.

(c) ***Information***

Information such as topography/mapping data, geological survey databases, resource planning professionals, information systems, etc was available only to companies and their agents.

(d) ***Expertise***

Access to technical skills professionals such as engineers, financial analysts and other trained technical resources were solely within the domain of companies and governments.

2.2 New balance

Starting in the 1950s, this imbalance between companies and governments began to shift. Indigenous peoples began accessing legal remedies, skills and communication technologies that started to equalise the company/government-led development model.

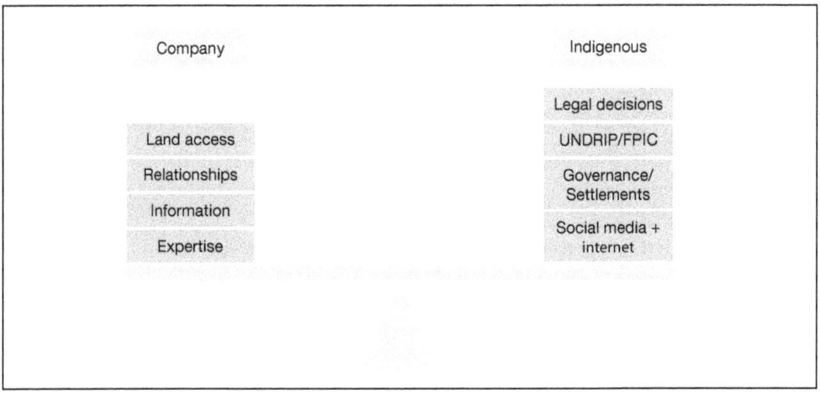

(a) ***Legal decisions***

Over the past 70+ years, numerous national courts have been recognising indigenous land rights in their respective jurisdictions. While not uniform in their decisions, there has been a trend towards recognising and reinforcing indigenous peoples' rights over lands that previously would have been administered exclusively by majority society governments.

It is beyond the scope of this chapter to summarise all indigenous legal decisions; however, when viewed from a global perspective, the trend towards indigenous influence over local land decisions is clear.

Malaysia: Starting in the 1950s, Malaysian court decisions ruled that customary indigenous lands were inalienable.[8] Subsequent Malaysian court decisions have declared indigenous rights to land to be property rights and as such protected by the Malaysian constitution.[9]

8 *Sumbang Anak Sekam v Engkarong Anak Ajah* [1958] SCR 95 (Malaysia).
9 *Selangor Pilot Association v Government of Malaysia* [1975] 2 MLJ 66 (Malaysia).

Canada: In 1973 the Supreme Court of Canada in the *Calder* decision acknowledged that indigenous title in Canada existed prior to European colonisation.[10] Subsequent court decisions (*Delgamuukw* in 1997) further advanced the concept of indigenous title by reaffirming the place of common law Aboriginal title in Canada.[11]

In 2014, the court issued the *Tsilhqot'in* decision, recognising an indigenous claim to 1,750 square kilometres of traditional lands. The court created a new land classification of Aboriginal Title which affirmed the right of indigenous peoples to decide how the land and its natural resources will be used, occupied and managed.[12]

New Zealand: In 1987, New Zealand courts via the *Lands* case recognised that existing indigenous rights in the 1840 Treaty of Waitangi continued to apply to the country.[13]

Australia: The 1992 *Mabo* case recognised Aboriginal and Torres Strait Islander peoples' rights. The court ruling led to Australia enacting the Native Title Act 1993, which recognised that Aboriginal people have rights to and interest in certain lands because of traditional laws and customs.[14]

Kenya: In 2010, the African Commission on Human and People's Rights condemned the eviction of the Endorois people from their traditional lands in Kenya. The commission ruled that the Endorois' expulsion from their traditional homeland for tourism development violated their human rights.[15]

(b) United Nations Declaration on the Rights of Indigenous Peoples and free prior informed consent

Adopted in 2007 by the UN General Assembly, the United Nations Declaration on the Rights of Indigenous Peoples (UNDRIP) is widely seen by indigenous peoples as a motivating document that not only recognises their rights to greater participation and decision-making in areas that affect their communities, but unites their aspirations with other indigenous groups around the world.

The declaration details the individual and collective rights of indigenous peoples in a wide range of areas including culture, identity, language, employment, health and education. The document:

> *emphasizes the rights of indigenous peoples to maintain and strengthen their own institutions, cultures and traditions, and to pursue their development in keeping with their own needs and aspirations*[16]

---

10 *Calder v Attorney-General of British Columbia* – SCC Cases (Lexum) 31 January 1973. Accessed 17 September 2017. https://scc-csc.lexum.com/scc-csc/scc-csc/en/item/5113/index.do.

11 *Delgamuukw v British Columbia* – SCC Cases (Lexum) 11 December 1997. Accessed 17 September 2017. https://scc-csc.lexum.com/scc-csc/scc-csc/en/item/1569/index.do.

12 *Tsilhqot'in Nation v British Columbia* – SCC Cases (Lexum) 26 June 2014. Accessed 17 September 2017. https://scc-csc.lexum.com/scc-csc/scc-csc/en/item/14246/index.do?r=AAAAAQA.

13 Burton, Mark, "The Significance of the Lands Case for Law and Society", *The Beehive*, 29 June 2007. Accessed 17 September 2017. www.beehive.govt.nz/speech/significance-lands-case-law-and-society.

14 "Mabo Case", *Australian Institute of Aboriginal and Torres Strait Islander Studies*, 11 September 2015. Accessed 17 September 2017. https://aiatsis.gov.au/explore/articles/mabo-case.

15 "Kenya: Landmark Ruling on Indigenous Land Rights", *Human Rights Watch*, 17 April 2015. Accessed 17 September 2017. www.hrw.org/news/2010/02/04/kenya-landmark-ruling-indigenous-land-rights.

16 United Nations Declaration on the Rights of Indigenous Peoples (2008).

and

promotes their full and effective participation in all matters that concern them and their right to remain distinct and to pursue their own visions of economic and social development.[17]

Of specific interest to project developers, article 19 of the document includes the concept of free, prior and informed consent (FPIC) as a core tenet of dealing with indigenous peoples:

States shall consult and cooperate in good faith with the Indigenous Peoples concerned through their own representative institutions in order to obtain their free, prior and informed consent before adopting and implementing legislative or administrative measures that may affect them.[18]

For many indigenous peoples, UNDRIP has had a profound effect on how they see development and their ability to impact decisions that are contrary to their interests. It has focused and energised indigenous understandings of rights and political organising around these rights locally and globally.

Ken Coates, a Canadian professor of public policy, notes that UNDRIP:

... has started to find deep traction with Aboriginal peoples. Hundreds of Indigenous groups see themselves, their history and their futures in UNDRIP. That their stories and dreams are shared by so many people around the world serves, in Indigenous communities, to provide both inspiration and hope that the global political system will right itself.[19]

(c) Governance

In parallel to the court decisions, national governments around the world have implemented self-government arrangements with indigenous populations that influence how they see themselves as self-determined peoples and how they can influence land and resource project plans.

Norway/Sweden/Finland – Saami Parliamentary Council: Comprised of Saami members from across Norway, Sweden and Finland, the council – created in 1956 – is a publicly elected parliament that represents the interests of the indigenous Saami population.[20]

Canada – Nunavut: Created in 1999 as part of an indigenous land claim settlement, the Nunavut Land Claims Agreement provides for broad self-government powers and jurisdiction for the majority indigenous population.[21]

Denmark – Greenland: In 2008, the 90% indigenous population of Greenland

---

17 United Nations Declaration on the Rights of Indigenous Peoples (2008).

18 Article 19, United Nations Declaration on the Rights of Indigenous Peoples (2008).

19 Coates, Ken, "From Aspiration to Inspiration: UNDRIP Finding Deep Traction in Indigenous Communities", *Centre for International Governance Innovation*, 18 September 2013. Accessed 17 September 2017. www.cigionline.org/articles/aspiration-inspiration-undrip-finding-deep-traction-indigenous-communities.

20 See Saami Council website, Sámiráđđi – Ruoktu. Accessed 17 September 2017. www.saamicouncil.net/en/.

21 See Nunavut Agreement. Accessed 17 September 2017. http://nlca.tunngavik.com/?lang=en.

endorsed a self-rule referendum that advances the Danish dependency towards eventual independence. Enacted in 2009, the agreement will eventually see the indigenous-led government assume full sovereignty over Greenland, including natural resources and revenues.[22]

(d) *Settlements*

For some indigenous communities, court decisions, land settlements and resource allocations have resulted in significant financial resources which – in certain cases – have allowed the creation of financial trusts and business and commercial opportunities.

United States – Alaska: The 1971 Alaska Native Settlement Act provided the indigenous population with 44 million acres (11% of Alaska) with both surface and subsurface rights and over $462 million.[23] Some of the resulting community corporations[24] set up under the act are now multi-million dollar operations employing residents – both indigenous and non-indigenous – across the state and beyond.

United States – Colorado: The Southern Ute Tribe, exercising its domestic sovereign rights, has directed profits from its on-reservation energy resources to an indigenous-controlled $4 billion private equity and investment fund with operations and assets in over 14 US states and the Gulf of Mexico.[25]

Canada – Quebec: The 1975 James Bay and Northern Québec Agreement provided the Cree and Inuit peoples with control over specified lands, education, health and economic development initiatives. The agreement allocated C$225 million to economic development corporations.[26]

New Zealand: In New Zealand, nearly NZ$12.5 billion is owned by indigenous Maori trusts, incorporations and other collectively owned enterprises, such as tribal organisations managing treaty settlement funds.[27]

(e) *Social media and the internet*

The largest impact on global indigenous movements has been the internet. The

---

22 Associated Press, "Greenland Voters Back Greater Autonomy from Denmark", *The Guardian*, 26 November 2008. Accessed 17 September 2017. www.theguardian.com/world/2008/nov/26/greenland-denmark-referendum.

23 "Alaska Native Claims Settlement Act", *Modern Alaska: Alaska History and Cultural Studies*. Accessed 17 September 2017. www.akhistorycourse.org/modern-alaska/alaska-native-claims-settlement-act.

24 "Alaska Native Corporation Links", *Alaskan Native Corporation Links*. Accessed 17 September 2017. http://fairbanks-alaska.com/alaska-native-corporations.htm.

25 Anderson, Terry L, *Unlocking the Wealth of Indian Nations*. Lanham, MD: Lexington Books, 2016.

26 Price, John A and Brian Craik. "James Bay and Northern Québec Agreement", *The Canadian Encyclopedia*. Accessed 17 September 2017. www.thecanadianencyclopedia.ca/en/article/james-bay-and-northern-quebec-agreement/.

27 Harvey, Helen, "$42 Billion Maori Economy about More than Just Treaty Settlements", *Stuff*, 3 February 2017. Accessed 17 September 2017. www.stuff.co.nz/business/88915435/maori-economy-about-more-than-just-treaty-settlements.

advent of computers and smartphones into previously remote communities, and accompanying social media platforms, has connected indigenous peoples across the planet to each other and to resources that were previously unavailable. Information databases, global media, group chat sites and direct person-to-person connections are now available in many parts of the indigenous world.

Combined with the previously noted court decisions, self-government agreements and growing pools of capital, the result has revolutionised indigenous aspirations about what is possible in their lands.

The internet has transformed indigenous political, community, business negotiation and individual organising.[28] While some indigenous communities lack basic infrastructure and are located in remote regions, many people have access to a computer or a smartphone and have an internet connection.[29] The result is that what happens to one indigenous community is often instantly transmitted to other indigenous communities worldwide. If an energy or mining company is behaving badly in a local mine or pipeline project in one part of the world, indigenous communities elsewhere will likely become aware very quickly. Furthermore, details of positive information – such as progressive public policy, business agreements and revenue sharing deals, or environmental protection concessions – in one part of the world will be shared with indigenous peoples in other regions. Precedents regarding indigenous political, social and business deals are being set and communicated around the world.

Mongolia: One of the most direct examples of the power of the internet to disrupt a resource project happened in 2005 around the Oyu Tolgoi mining project in Mongolia. Robert Friedland, then chief executive officer of Ivanhoe Mining, when attempting to raise capital for the mining project at a Tampa, Florida investment conference, boasted that mining in Mongolia was like "You're making T-shirts for five bucks and selling them for $100".[30] Mr Friedland's speech was posted on the internet and portions of the speech – especially the references to making 95% profit – were translated into Mongolian. According to media reports, "even in the most remote corners of the Gobi, it seems that every nomad can quote from the Tampa speech".[31] Mongolians, outraged, launched protests in the capital Ulan Bator, where Mr Friedland was burned in effigy.[32] The government of Mongolia was eventually forced to change the mining tax regime to eliminate windfall profits and, in time, Mr Friedland was forced to relinquish the project.

---

28 "The Indigenous Internet", ScienceDaily, 25 January 2016. Accessed 17 September 2017. www.sciencedaily.com/releases/2016/01/160125090810.htm.

29 Cisler, Steve, "Introduction: The Internet and Indigenous Groups", *Cultural Survival*, March 2000. Accessed 17 September 2017. www.culturalsurvival.org/publications/cultural-survival-quarterly/introduction-internet-and-indigenous-groups.

30 York, Geoffrey, "Desert Storm", *The Globe and Mail*, 28 March 2017. Accessed 17 September 2017. https://beta.theglobeandmail.com/report-on-business/rob-magazine/desert-storm/article18249363/?ref=http%3A%2F%2Fwww.theglobeandmail.com&page=all.

31 *Ibid.*

32 Kneen, Jamie, "Mining Mongolia: Ivanhoe, T-shirts, NGOs, and Wikileaks", *MiningWatch Canada*, 5 June 2011. Accessed 17 September 2017. https://miningwatch.ca/blog/2011/6/5/mining-mongolia-ivanhoe-t-shirts-ngos-and-wikileaks.

Canada: In 2014, the Supreme Court of Canada issued the earlier mentioned *Tsilhqot'in* judgment, a decision that established Aboriginal land title for the Tslihqot'in Nation. Within hours of the decision being announced by the Supreme Court, the Tsilhqot'in received phone calls from indigenous groups in Belize who had learned of the decision via the internet, seeking information about how the Canadian indigenous group had achieved their victory, and if there was a way that they could replicate the Tsilhqot'in example in their territories.[33]

3. Increased indigenous participation in projects

Indigenous peoples have begun to capitalise on legal, capital and internet-related changes through various forms of participation agreement. These are written agreements entered into between indigenous communities and companies that help to manage project impacts and ensure that environmental, employment and economic benefits accrue to local indigenous communities. They have become a common way for communities, governments and project proponents to advance mutual interests around projects. In Canada, the Gordon Foundation makes available a free agreement toolkit to assist indigenous communities with negotiating participation agreements.[34]

When viewed collectively, the agreements reveal that approximately every 10 years, indigenous peoples advance new concessions in increasingly complex agreements that address community and company objectives. As the agreements have developed, successive agreements build on the earlier successes, incrementally advancing indigenous interests in successive projects. When viewed in hindsight from the 1970s to today, these agreements provide a clear indication of what is coming next for indigenous peoples' engagement in projects.

Today

1970s>	1980s>	2000s>	2010s>	Future
Employment + Environment	Support businesses	Revenue	Equity	Owner/partner
• Joining workforce • Entry level jobs • Training opportunities • Environmental protections	• Support businesses (transport, repair, catering, environmental monitoring) • Joint ventures	• United revenues to indigenous communities • Community decides use for funds • Community and tribal nation building	• Minority ownership of projects • Equity grants and/or buy-in provisions	• Indigenous community leads project • Secures financing, develops and operates project

In the early 1970s, early versions of participation agreements started to include employment and environmental provisions that encouraged indigenous participation in entry-level jobs and training opportunities. At that time,

33 Interview with the Tslihqot'in Central Government.
34 See http://gordonfoundation.ca/resource/iba-community-toolkit/.

environmental protections for wildlife, food, water and air, as well as agreements on environmental monitoring and remediation protocols, became the new standard in agreements between indigenous communities and companies.

Around 1980, agreements that fostered the establishment of indigenous-owned support service businesses to service the projects began to appear. These agreements allowed indigenous peoples to establish employee transportation services, repair contractor agreements, and catering/cleaning service companies, etc. In some cases, joint ventures with the company or other parties were encouraged as a means of increasing the abilities of indigenous peoples to participate in the economic value of projects.

Revenue sharing	Equity	Owner/partnership
Nickel mine (Canada 2002)	**Iron ore mine (Australia 2011)**	**Royal Bafokeng Nation (South Africa)**
• Annual payment + % based on nickel price • Multi-million dollar signing bonus loaned back to company with a 10-year repayment • Segregated treasury established to manage income	• 5% equity grant • 7% purchase option at signing • 1.75% to 3% of gross revenue depending on production with annual minimum payments • A$8 million upfront payment	• Indigenous-controlled platinum mine • 196,000 oz/year platinum • 7,400 employees • Community first focus • Revenue to investments holding company – $2.2 billion net value

At the start of the 21st century, revenue sharing clauses from projects to indigenous peoples started to be included in agreements. The first agreements were restricted by companies who would decide how the revenues could be spent, but increasingly funds are now often unrestricted, allowing the communities to decide how best to invest for future prosperity.

In Canada, one indigenous group's participation agreement for a new nickel mine included provisions that saw the community receive a multi-million dollar signing bonus plus an annual payment, and a percentage of mine revenue based on annual mine production. In order to reduce the cash flow impact on the company in the early years of mine production, the indigenous community loaned their proceeds back to the company for 10 years at a guaranteed interest rate. The community subsequently established a segregated treasury to manage the income stream at arms-length from their political operations ensuring that the funds were invested in a non-political manner.[35]

In the past decade, some communities have negotiated minority equity stakes in projects via grants or buy-in provisions that saw indigenous ownership become a reality. The first equity holdings were small but the examples have been increasing

35 The identity of the indigenous community is withheld due to non-disclosure agreements signed between the company and the community. While the terms of the agreements are generally not available, indigenous peoples often share the details of the agreements with other communities who are negotiating participation in similar projects.

in percentage terms. For example, in 2011, an Australian iron ore mining operation reached an indigenous agreement that included a 5% equity grant with an additional 7% purchase option available at signing. In addition, the community received an A$8 million upfront payment (which they applied to the additional 7% equity purchase option) along with 1.75% to 3% of annual gross mine revenue scaled to production with annual minimum payments.[36]

Going forward, there are now examples of indigenous communities seeking greater decision-making powers over how projects will be developed on or near their lands. In South Africa, the Royal Bafokeng Nation holds a 52% majority controlling interest over a platinum mine, producing nearly 196,000 oz/year and employing 7,400 permanent employees and contractors.[37] While not exactly the result of a negotiated participation agreement, the Royal Bafokeng started with a minority interest in the mine and slowly increased its ownership over time. Revenue from the mine has been used to set up Royal Bafokeng Holdings (RBH), a community-based investment company focused on creating intergenerational wealth for its community members. With assets in mining, telecommunications, real estate, mining services and financial services, RBH's current net value is $2.2 billion.[38] RBH's commercial acumen and its focus on community improvement has become an inspiration for many indigenous communities.

These participation examples – seen collectively – are informing indigenous peoples around the world about what is possible for projects in their respective traditional territories. Each commercial, rights and community advancement is communicated in real time to increasingly globally aware indigenous communities who will not accept a model where projects benefit only distant companies, shareholders or government treasuries.

4. Conclusion

It is no longer 'business as usual' in the indigenous world. The desire of indigenous peoples to advance their home communities with environmental protections, employment, base infrastructure, education and income that projects can provide will continue to drive communities to pursue greater involvement in projects in their homelands.

Indigenous peoples are reaching out to other indigenous peoples – their own and others around the world – to access skills, talent, capital, media, political resources and comparative experiences to protect and enhance their lives and their community members.

Not all projects will be supported by indigenous peoples; nor will all indigenous peoples be able to replicate the company- and country-specific examples cited in this chapter. Yet, companies and projects that support indigenous peoples' rights,

---

36 The identity of the indigenous community is withheld due to non-disclosure agreements signed between the company and the community. While the terms of the agreements are generally not available, indigenous peoples often share the details of the agreements with other communities who are negotiating participation in similar projects.

37 *Royal Bafokeng Holdiings Integrated Review* 2016. Accessed 17 September 2017. www.bafokengholdings.com/index.html.

38 *Ibid.*

interests and values – and can tangibly demonstrate this via shared prosperity participation agreements – are likely to succeed.

For many companies, this shift in mindset from an arms-length developer to one of a collaborative and equal community partner will be difficult. It will mean reinventing the way projects have been done in the past and embracing people who have not traditionally been seen as full partners. It will take creativity, innovation – and at times courage – to find ways to identify, value and capture shared interests that lead to shared prosperity.

As stated earlier, not all indigenous peoples are opposed to development. If development addresses the rights, values and aspirations of the indigenous communities, and furthers the ability of the community and environment to thrive, it will stand a better chance of being accepted. Indigenous peoples – like all peoples – value a clean environment, safe ecosystems, sustainable communities, education options and economic fairness.

To succeed, companies will need to learn and understand what shared prosperity means to a host indigenous community. Company-driven CSR actions that narrowly focus on only social and environmental issues are no longer enough for many indigenous communities. Many communities now have access to more levers of influence over development decisions in their lands.

Companies that are open with information – and realise that precedence information on what is possible in environmental, employment and training, community infrastructure, revenue sharing and equity ownership is freely available – will be better positioned to engage indigenous peoples in an open and mutually respectful manner that leads to shared prosperity.

Macro risks a decade after the global financial crisis

Kevin Gardiner
Senior investment strategist

1. Introduction

Economists like to qualify their predictions with the stock phrase "these are especially uncertain times", and it is particularly tempting to resort to it when surveying the prospects for energy infrastructure now, in late 2017. Superimposed on some novel geopolitical and financial uncertainties, we face structural change in both the sourcing of carbon-based energy and in the use of alternative sources of energy.

In reality, however, most times are similarly uncertain: many of the things that can happen from here were probably always capable of happening, but we simply did not realise it. When the definitive histories are written, uncertainty and risk are unlikely to be seen as the defining characteristics of modern economic life, despite the numerous economic and market crises that have punctuated the post-1945 epoch. The growth and spread of prosperity across much of the world is likely to be a more dominant feature – whatever the source of our energy. Sheikh Yamani's comment that "The stone age did not end for lack of stone…" was both a far-sighted warning to the energy status quo and a reminder of human progress.

We know that risk registers are essential, even as we also know that they must always be incomplete. But making an awareness of risk the dominant consideration in trying to gauge our macroeconomic prospects would not, thus far, have been a useful guide to business and investing these last 70 years or so – or indeed, in the seven years since the first edition of this book.

We were writing then with the tumultuous events of the global financial crisis (GFC) that began in 2007, and peaked in the winter of 2008/2009, still fresh in our collective memory. We were concerned to point out the dangers of hubris, to remind ourselves of the collective complacency that can creep in after prolonged periods of stability such as 'the Great Moderation' that preceded the GFC. We concluded, however, that the mood in 2010 had perhaps become overly contrite, with talk of 'new normals', debt overhangs and sustainably lower investment returns, and we cautioned against confusing what might have been essentially a financial farce with an underlying change in the productive capacity of the global economy.

The intervening seven years have had their share of political, economic and financial drama. We have seen ongoing conflict and humanitarian trauma in the Middle East and North Africa, with associated mass migrations. There have been Russia/NATO tensions over Ukraine. The eurozone has been threatened by a sovereign debt crisis in its periphery. US government debt has been rated at less than triple-A for the first time. More recently, the British electorate has voted to leave the European Union, the US electorate has chosen an idiosyncratic new US president with explicitly protectionist (and in energy matters, reactionary) views, and waves of populism and nationalism have seemed to threaten the wider cohesiveness of the European Union.

Meanwhile, gross financial liabilities have remained large relative to incomes, and monetary policy settings have been held at emergency levels in the United States, Europe and Japan. Central bank balance sheets have ballooned as a result of the bonds bought in 'quantitative easing' (QE) programmes, and many interest rates and bond yields have turned negative, even before inflation is taken into account. Talk of commodity and emerging market 'supercycles' has been quietly shelved. China's economy in particular is no longer viewed as the next big thing, but instead is seen by many as an economic accident waiting to happen.

These developments have constituted a proverbial 'wall of worry' for economists and investors – and as so often happens, that wall has been climbed. Gardiner (2015) offers a more careful account of investors' concerns, and why they have not been insurmountable.[1] The global economy has expanded steadily, if rather sluggishly, and as we write is almost one-third bigger in real terms, and roughly one-eighth in real per capita terms, than at its highest point before the GFC. The US, UK and German economies are close to what these days might be thought of as full employment. Stock and bond markets have performed strongly (although bond performance at least has been flattered by those QE programmes – of which more below). Financial volatility, for much of the time, has again been subdued. However, that wall of worry (and contrition perhaps) has perhaps kept complacency and hubris at bay.

2. Uncertainty and risk as facts of life

The future is profoundly unknowable, and no risk analysis, no matter how diligent, can alter this inconvenient fact. From time to time however we persuade ourselves that perhaps it may not be – most recently, during the decade or so of remarkable economic stability that ended in 2007. Just as nemesis follows hubris, 'the Great Recession' duly followed hard on the heels of 'the Great Moderation': the crisis that erupted was a brutal reminder both that economic and market volatility has not been tamed, and that the events triggering it cannot easily be identified in advance. 'Unknown unknowns' and 'black swans' lie in wait for forecasters rash enough to reason by induction, but even if planners were lucky enough to live in a world in which they did not, and in which all possible events had been identified in advance – a world in which the future were merely probabilistically 'risky', in the way that the results of flipping a coin are risky, as opposed to genuinely 'uncertain' – the difficulties of gauging the scale and likelihood of those events would still be daunting. The distinction between probabilistic risk and more profound uncertainty dates back at least to Keynes and Knight in the early twentieth century, and is discussed more fully in Bernstein (1996)[2] and Taleb (2007).[3]

---

1 Gardiner, Kevin (2015), *Making Sense of Markets: An Investor's Guide to Profiting Amidst the Gloom*, Palgrave Macmillan.

The discussion here of the range and extent of macroeconomic and financial risk facing the planners of large-scale transnational energy supply projects is intended to help organise discussion, and carries no pretence to completeness or precision, even heuristically. It offers some practical advice nonetheless.

3. Steering by the rear-view mirror

In attempting to plan for the future, we usually start by looking at the past: we assume that history is known, and is relevant to what might happen in the future. In practice, outside the physical developments that can be traced with some confidence by the natural sciences, and the simple chronology of major events, our knowledge of the past is less soundly based than we like to think. The identification of much causality in history is unavoidably subjective, for one thing. And in the realm of economics and finance in particular, the further back we look, the less convincing are attempts at quantification. The older the data, the less credible it is – some heroic academic feats of estimation and collation notwithstanding (see, for example, Maddison (1998),[4] which offers quantitative analysis spanning a period of more than 1,000 years, or Homer (1963),[5] whose narrower focus allows him to present data from the Classical world and earlier).

Ambiguity arises because much data is simply not available. The concept of 'gross domestic product' or 'GDP', for example, dates from the work of Kuznets in the 1930s only, and was calculated first for the United States in the early 1940s. When it is, we cannot be sure that the things being measured are comparable. How similar were products traded in the medieval period to today's? What would an accountant today make of a set of corporate accounts that pre-dates the Great Depression and modern accounting standards? Natural scientists can often backfill their historical data series, but economic activities and rates of exchange can leave few traces.

We use the past as a guide to gauging future risk because outside our imagination, it is all that we have. A brief review of some relatively recent history has to be the starting point for considering future risk, then. We know that neither the scale nor the nature of that future risk is necessarily bounded by this historical experience, but some approximate awareness of what has gone before might at least foster the open-mindedness and nimbleness needed to gauge and respond to the macro risks facing planned projects today.

4. The road to 2017

In fact, the scale of social, economic and financial change seen within a recent single lifetime has been remarkable. It may have slowed in recent decades – Gordon (2016) argues that technological progress in particular slowed markedly after 1970.[6] But it has been remarkable nonetheless, and like most progress, was largely unpredicted.

---

2 Bernstein, Peter L (1996), *Against The Gods: The Remarkable Story of Risk*, New York: John Wiley & Sons.
3 Taleb, Nassim Nicholas (2007), *The Black Swan: The Impact of the Highly Improbable*, Allen Lane.
4 Maddison, Angus (1998), *Chinese Economic Performance in the Long Run*, OECD.
5 Homer, Sidney (1963), *A History of Interest Rates*, John Wiley & Sons.
6 Gordon, Robert (2016), *The Rise and Fall of American Growth: The U.S. Standard of Living since the Civil War*, Princeton.

The cataclysm of the Second World War illustrated just how quickly the fabric of civilised society could unravel. The post-war decades then contained their share of trauma, starting even as Europe and Japan were rebuilding. The outbreak of a third world war was narrowly avoided in Korea, Cuba and, arguably, Vietnam; tens of millions died in the mass famine that accompanied 'The Great Leap Forward'; the Cold War and the doctrine of 'Mutual Assured Destruction' cast a daunting shadow over the lives of many more; the industrial slaughter of the First World War was revived on the Iran/Iraq border; there were examples of genocide in Rwanda, Cambodia and Bosnia. Localised conflicts and civil wars have been plentiful, and in some cases have been long lasting and are ongoing, most visibly perhaps in and around the Middle East and North Africa. At the time of writing, chemical weapons have (again) been seen in Syria. This list ignores the numerous humanitarian and natural disasters that have punctuated the period.

Yet despite many and varied crises, the world has been less geopolitically volatile recently than it was half a century ago. The tensions of the Cold War subsided after much high-profile negotiation (initiated by another idiosyncratic US president) and the eventual collapse from within of the Soviet bloc. Widespread conflict between developed states has not erupted – partly no doubt because of the work of international bodies such as the United Nations, but partly also because the credibility and attractiveness of collectivism has been so visibly and widely undermined by its material failure (the latest illustration perhaps being in Venezuela), and liberal democracies tend to be less belligerent than authoritarian regimes. We may not have seen what Fukuyama (1993) labelled the "End of History",[7] but we have seen the possible causes of conflict tempered at least. Since the first edition of this book, Steven Pinker has published his masterly analysis of the historical decline of conflict and of violence generally, which carefully and objectively describes what we were only intuiting then.[8]

This does not mean, of course, that things will stay as relatively safe as they recently have been. The period immediately ahead of the First World War was marked by a widespread belief that conflict amongst advanced industrial nations was all but impossible (as Ahamed (2009) reminds us).[9] Nor does it mean that the destination arrived at was inevitable. It is easy to imagine how the outcome could have been very different had the protagonists at one of several global flashpoints acted differently. Sanity mostly prevailed, but it might not have.

As we write, the uncertainty surrounding the foreign policy of the new US administration seems especially intense, and is understandably unsettling many observers. There are some very visible potential flashpoints in the geopolitical laboratory. Dramatic political developments and humanitarian crises do not, however, always make themselves felt on the global economy, which is shaped by so many different moving parts, and capital markets in particular can be callous, focusing mainly on the narrow bottom lines of interest rates and corporate profitability.

7 Fukuyama, Francis (1993), *The End of History and the Last Man*, Penguin.
8 Pinker, Steven (2011), *The Better Angels of our Nature: Why Violence Has Declined*, Viking.
9 Ahamed, Liaquat (2009), *Lords of Finance: 1929, The Great Depression, and the Bankers who Broke the World*, Penguin.

There have been economic and capital market crises in the last 60 years. As in the geopolitical arena, however, the primary trend has nonetheless been a favourable one. Here too there is of course no guarantee that things will necessarily stay as they are.

The immediate aftermath of the Second World War was characterised by the challenges of economic rebuilding and its financing, and those posed by mass demobilisation. 'Keynesian' fiscal demand management was first used to try to suppress the potential inflation that might be unleashed as the suppressed consumer demand of the war years reverted to normal. The financial infrastructure designed at the 1944 negotiations at Bretton Woods fostered both reconstruction and financial stability, while avoiding the punitive reparations that had done so much to undermine the peace after 1918. Gradually, rationing ended, international transactions revived, currency convertibility was resumed and extended, and tariffs and other trade barriers were slowly but steadily dismantled. In Europe the long journey towards 'ever closer union' formally began with the Treaty of Rome in 1957, but the first moves in that direction had been made a decade earlier. Most fixed exchange rates – and links to gold – were eventually jettisoned in the 1970s. Capital markets became steadily more open, credit controls were reduced – completely in some cases – and financial instruments became more complex and contingent, culminating in the widespread deregulation that characterised the millennium.

The general increase in living standards has, as noted, been punctuated by business cycles, crises and diverse secular trends. Individual countries and regions have grown and inflated at markedly different rates; there have been many instances of industrial unrest and financial emergency – with the latest episode of the latter, the global financial crisis, counting arguably as the most pressing since the bank failures of the 1930s.

5. Macroeconomic risks

Starting with perhaps the most obvious macroeconomic risk to project planners, the business cycle, there have been many individual instances of recession since 1945. In the case of the United States, for example, the National Bureau of Economic Research identifies 11 distinct cycles since 1945 (the twelfth is still incomplete as we write), coincidentally matching the number of years when the level of real GDP registered an annual decline. The average length of the cycles they identify is 69 months. The declines in real annual GDP look modest – 2% is a large number in this context – but GDP is a 'net' or 'value-added' measure of activity, and the number of gross transactions taking place can be more volatile, and may matter more for individual project revenues. The United States, of course, is also a large, diverse economy, and in smaller countries the movements even in GDP can be marked.

Regional or global business cycles are more muted, reflecting the natural diversification imparted by a larger sample. It is highly unusual for the level of global GDP to fall, for example. That said, geographic proximity is still a very important determinant of trade, and a country experiencing a severe downturn will usually cast some economic shadow across its immediate borders.

Inflation and interest rates also fluctuated alongside economic activity in the United States and elsewhere. The business cycle is not tamed, as 2008/2009 reminded us, and project planners thus need to recognise that the level of demand, input costs, pricing power and capital charges are all likely to be subject to considerable cyclical variation.

As noted, the relatively short-term gyrations of the business cycle can coincide with evolving longer-term or secular trends. As a result, projections of the likely level of even economy-wide cashflow (let alone specific project revenues) several years or more into the future are surrounded by considerable margins of error. For example, if the rate of growth of the US economy over the 20 years to 1996 had been repeated in the following two decades, US nominal GDP would be nine-tenths bigger than it is, and real GDP would be one-fifth bigger.

Cross-country variations can be even more striking. In Japan, the level of nominal GDP in 2016 was little changed from its level 20 years earlier. In Italy, it has grown by more than half, but has broadly stagnated since 2008. In the United States it has more than doubled; in China, it is 10 times as large as it was.

Viewed in an even longer-term context, the available data suggests that the United States at least saw more dramatic and longer-lasting downturns before the Second World War. The brush with financial disaster in 2008, however, served notice that we cannot take even this apparent longer-term decline in volatility for granted: the drop in output in 2009 was the biggest since 1946, and at the low point commentators were drawing comparisons with the 1930s. If the fall in output had developed into something more dramatic, deflation similarly might have gathered more momentum than it did.

Planners need also to take into account the possibility of autonomous (or 'exogenous') volatility in some important macro variables such as interest and exchange rates, and the relative prices of factors of production such as labour, real estate and commodities (including, of course, energy). Such changes can be driven, for example, by trade imbalances, industrial relations and the operation of cartels (eg, OPEC); or by new technology (eg, the development of renewable energy, and shale extraction). A topical source of such risk is the United Kingdom's pending secession from the European Union, which seems likely to result in some increase in the cost of doing business in and with the United Kingdom. The increased friction may come from rebuilt tariffs, non-tariff barriers, reduced labour mobility and market access, or simply from the considerable uncertainty (which might not only affect UK–EU business) that seems likely to prevail during the multi-year period during which the details are worked out. In the subjective view of this author, these costs are unlikely to be critical – but the point, in the context of this book, is their objective unfathomability.

Governments and central banks often intervene to try to reduce the volatility of interest and exchange rates in particular, but in so doing sometimes introduce another degree of uncertainty in the shape of capital controls, particularly in the case of smaller economies whose markets are most likely to be affected by portfolio flows. As noted above, for the first quarter-century after the Second World War, under the prevalent Bretton Woods regime, pegged exchange rates and varying restrictions on capital flows were the norm rather than the exception, and many capital accounts in the emerging world are controlled – most visibly in the case of China. Controls were partially reintroduced in a number of countries in the wake of the Asian crises of the mid/late 1990s, and have been considered more recently by a number of other emerging economies concerned at the scale of inflows of funds.

Financial markets themselves can be another autonomous source of considerable macro uncertainty, although the 'objective' nature of the risk is perhaps questionable. The collective behaviour of investors and banks, in the context of largely deregulated but highly complex and interconnected markets, can foster extrapolative expectations and asset price bubbles. When those bubbles burst, the impact on balance sheets, discount rates and the financial system at large can be potent. Instances include: the Long-Term Capital Management crisis in late 1998; the 'technology' boom and bust in 2000; and most obviously, of course, the GFC in 2008/2009, when problems originating in the sub-prime US mortgage market escalated into a real world "liquidity trap" which saw central banks lose control over key lending rates, companies across the world lose access to working capital, and a major recession.

Reinhart and Rogoff (2009) identified 18 instances of bank-centred financial crises in advanced economies between 1945 and 2003, and 60 if emerging economies and the experiences of 2007/2008 are taken into account.[10] Most of them passed without major macroeconomic consequences, but the risk of systemic collapse is something of which planners should be aware – particularly if the project is coinciding with a local property boom. Banking failure and sudden illiquidity in capital markets does not need to go global to cause considerable local or regional distress – as we have seen since the first edition of this book in Greece, for example. Regulators have of course tightened vigilance and bolstered systems – the Greek crisis has accelerated overdue progress towards a unified eurozone approach to banking supervision – but free markets by definition will always face the risk of bandwagons and speculative excess.

6. Contextual risk

Geopolitical, macroeconomic and financial volatility is very visible: when it happens, we know about it. However, planners of long-term large-scale projects also face more subtle high-level risks that we might characterise loosely as 'contextual' in nature, but which might nonetheless be material.

Such risks might include: domestic and cross-border legal and regulatory risk of the sort discussed elsewhere in this book; altered monetary and fiscal policy frameworks; a change in the analytical toolkit used by the planners; macro measurement error and ambiguity; altered contagion and 'tail' risk; and the ever-present risk of a change in the crucial but invisible realm of consumer taste and confidence.

Differing policy frameworks can affect project risk because they might affect the way in which economies behave. For example, the chances of a recession turning into a more prolonged downturn may be influenced by whether the policymakers of

10 Reinhart, Carmen M and Rogoff, Kenneth S (2009), *This Time is Different: Eight Centuries of Financial Folly*, Princeton.

the day believe in using aggregate demand-management tools in a counter-cyclical fashion. The danger of a single large bank failure developing into a systemic threat to the global money supply can depend on whether key policymakers believe some institutions are 'too big to fail' or not. In these examples, whether the policies are fully effective or not, the evolution of short- and long-term discount rates, for example, could be very different to what might otherwise have happened.

There have indeed been many different macroeconomic policy regimes in operation within the market-led economies during the last 60 years or so, often alongside each other, and with some being pursued more zealously than others. A stylised chronology for the United Kingdom, for example, which has arguably seen more experimentation than most other large market economies over this period, would show an initial post-war framework of Keynesian demand-management policy using fiscal and increasingly monetary tools. This led, after some disenchantment with the resultant 'stop-go' results, to a half-hearted flirtation with industrial planning, and with prices and incomes controls. These led in turn to further disenchantment and – after several balance of payments and fixed and flexible exchange rate crises – an enforced adoption of some monetarist and eventually new classical ideas. A further experiment saw the temporary readoption of a pegged exchange rate; an enforced pragmatism; and most recently, the adoption of inflation targeting under the auspices of an operationally independent central bank – a regime that until the banking crisis of 2007–2009 was showing signs of some durability. Subsequently, the crisis-induced revival in more active demand-management has been showing signs of evolving into something longer lasting.

A new risk has arguably been introduced by a specific policy response to the GFC – namely, the policy of quantitative easing (QE), whereby central banks attempt to subdue long-term interest rates by buying substantial quantities of bonds in the market. This has boosted banking liquidity, although its effect on economic activity is more debatable. The lower bond yields than would otherwise have occurred are arguably a distortion in capital markets, and the risks to project planners are twofold. First, the novel nature of these policies (in modern times at least) means that collectively we do not know how easily reversible they will be: selling bonds back into the market could have disruptive repercussions if not handled sensitively. Second, while they persist, the distorted (or 'repressed', in current jargon) yields might lead to overly optimistic project valuations.

Alongside the persistence of QE, since the first edition of this book we have also seen the general level of interest rates fall further, and stay low, for longer than then seemed likely. As we write, the Federal Reserve has been slowly normalising its short-term policy rates, but rates elsewhere are still at or close to historic lows (in the case of the United Kingdom, the Bank of England cut rates to a new all-time nominal low after the EU referendum, and also restarted its QE). In many European cases, short-term policy rates and even some long-dated bond yields have turned negative. At one point in 2016, roughly one-quarter of all high-quality government bonds in issue had a negative yield.

As with the impact of QE, project planners need to recognise the possibility of distortion, and substitute more realistic – positive – real discount rates in their appraisals. In fact, while negative nominal interest rates are a new development, real (inflation-adjusted) interest rates have often been negative in the past. But deciding what 'normalised' real interest rate to use is not easy. There is a useful approximation between (for example) US and UK interest rates and the growth rate of the economy, and some theoretical reasons for thinking that there should be, but this relationship in practice has held only over the very long term, with considerable shorter-term divergences.

A further source of contextual risk for planners is the possibility of a wholesale change in the analytical toolkit used to evaluate projects. Details relating to the refinement of a specific methodology – whether to present results in terms of an internal rate of return or as a net present value, for example, when framing a discounted cashflow analysis – can hardly be termed a macro issue. But the decision to choose a particular methodology might be, and that decision is influenced by evolving views on what constitutes best practice.

Some proponents of 'value'-based stock market investing, for example, argue that any forward-looking approach to valuing assets is misplaced, and that a lengthy moving average of trailing (historic) earnings offers the least risky way of gauging underlying value. Others advocate a comparison of the replacement value of a company's assets with the value of those assets implied by its current stock price. Of course, neither approach is directly relevant to the assessment of a new project, where there is no past stream of earnings, or stock price, to analyse; but post-GFC scepticism about the validity of forward-looking cost-benefit analysis remains widespread, and might foster greater reliance on valuations derived from the value of comparable projects already in place, for example. As noted, when discount rates are unusually low, the result could be a big discrepancy between (higher) estimated values derived from projected discounted cashflows and those derived from projects already in place.

The basic principle underlying the dominant project valuation methodology today, the forward-looking discounted cashflow framework, has been around for a long time – indeed, for as long as interest rates have existed (Homer (1963) reminds us how long that is).[11] However, several important refinements are relatively recent. 'Modern Portfolio Theory', linking risk and return, dates from the early 1950s. The related 'Capital Asset Pricing Model', and the idea of diversifiable and non-diversifiable risk, dates from the early 1960s. More recent focus on 'economic value added' and the 'cashflow return on invested capital' compare net present values with the amount of capital used to generate them.

As noted, some analysts have always doubted the validity of such an approach. In the wake of the GFC and QE, however, these doubts have spread. The nature of the link between risk and return is being questioned after a prolonged period in which developed stock markets delivered worse returns than 'riskless' assets, and as it becomes more apparent that within the global stock and credit markets, some relatively less risky sectors and regions have been among the best long-term performers. The relative riskiness of a particular industry is clearly not always reflected by the historical correlation of its stock prices with wider market indices.

11 Homer, Sidney (1963), *A History of Interest Rates*, John Wiley & Sons.

Further, the 'riskless' interest rate, for example, a central component of discounted cashflow analysis, is not easy to identify. The most obvious candidate is the rate of interest paid on long-term government bonds. To return to the earlier point, these rates can vary hugely, even in normal times, and it is not easy to decide on the appropriate level to use in project appraisal. In the largest, most liquid long-term interest rate market in the world, namely that for US government bonds, nominal 10-year yields have fluctuated between 7% and 1% in the last two decades. Nominal yields less the current annual rate of inflation (a popularly used proxy for real yields) have fluctuated between 6% and -2%. When yields are as low as 1%, even small changes can have a material impact on net present values (even when yields are augmented to reflect the extra riskiness of the private sector cashflows).

Not all markets are as liquid as that for US Treasuries or UK gilts. In 2008/2009, the massive interbank loan and asset-backed securities markets in both the United States and Europe effectively froze for prolonged periods. In some emerging countries, money markets may not exist to begin with, and when they do, yield curves can be poorly defined. Such illiquidity is not always a result of local shortcomings: their governments may simply have little need to borrow (most visibly perhaps in the case of oil-rich states in the Middle East).

The difficulties encountered in selecting an appropriate long-term discount rate to use in a long-term cost-benefit analysis were illustrated prominently in the Stern Review on the Economics of Climate Change produced for the UK government in 2006. Stern used a real discount rate below most estimates of the likely growth in the economy's productive capacity, an assumption markedly at odds both with most market rates at the time and those used in forward-looking private analyses. The review's quantitative conclusions were largely shaped by this contentious assumption, which led some commentators to dismiss them.

One response to the ambiguities of conventional 'rational' cost-benefit analysis has been to turn to behavioural finance, which has grown in popularity as disenchantment with the conventional economic research programme has spread. On the subject of discount rates, the behavioural finance literature points to a marked discrepancy between individuals' revealed time preferences and those priced into conventional yield curves – specifically, studies reveal a very strong 'present bias': high discount rates over the immediate future, and then much lower 'forward' rates than those embodied in existing market yield curves. More generally, project planners are seen as likely to suffer from overconfidence and hubris in their ability to forecast, and in particular to be likely to underestimate costs and the likely time needed to deliver a project, and to overestimate the likely benefits attaching to it. A sudden shift towards a behaviourally informed analytical framework from a conventional project appraisal could feasibly make the difference between viability and non-viability – particularly at a time of low market discount rates.

A further source of contextual uncertainty is the way in which investor expectations can interact to create the possibility of systemic risk, the domino-like effect that can transform a localised problem into a bigger, system-wide failure. There is some overlap here with the financial risks noted above. Such an event requires certain objective conditions to be in place, including, for example, the 'scalability' noted by Taleb in his discussion of 'black swan' events,[12] but those conditions are not always fully visible and the catalyst for the event is often subjective in nature.

For example, systemic banking risk would be small if banks limited their lending strictly to a small portion of their deposit base, refrained from real estate lending and made only conventional, transparent loans. However, fractional reserve banking existed alongside substantial commercial and residential mortgage markets, with the latter often in securitised form, for several decades before the GFC. There were some new, complicating variables in the loan cycle that preceded the crisis, most notably the existence of complex credit derivatives and contingent liabilities that made it even more difficult than usual to value bank loan books, but the ultimate trigger for the crisis was a loss of confidence on the part of investors in property values and bank balance sheets. Similarly, the 2011–2012 sovereign debt crisis in the eurozone, and the systemic risk that it posed, was arguably not precipitated by new information about levels of debt, but by altered investor perceptions regarding countries' ability to repay it; with regard to the willingness of partner governments to offer support, the broad magnitude of their indebtedness had long been visible, and the flawed fiscal architecture of the single currency project had been known since its inception.

Another contextual risk for project planners to keep in mind is the ever-present possibility of an unexpected change in demand for the commodity, utility or service being provided, not because of a sudden change in any objective macro variable or resource price, but because of a shift in subjective consumer tastes or preferences. This is one of the sources of the structural changes facing the energy sector noted above. Many conventional energy supply projects face intensified environmental concerns, and some renewable energy sources are increasingly popular as a result (an exception being the perceived viability of nuclear energy projects, which has been further undermined by the 2011 Fukushima accident).

7. Main macro risks identified

Some of the most visible objective macro risks facing project planners are identified and shown in the table on the next page. They are grouped under two broad headings: those that are political or geophysical in nature, and those that are economic or financial. The table also illustrates some of what we have labelled as 'contextual' or more subjective risks. As we have noted, the distinction between objectivity and subjectivity in a market economy is (by definition) not always clear.

12 Taleb, Nassim Nicholas (2007), *The Black Swan: The Impact of the Highly Improbable*, Allen Lane.

Macro risks facing planners of large-scale cross-border projects

Political/geophysical	Economic/financial	Contextual
War between sovereign states	Growth, inflation and interest rates (cyclical and secular variations)	Policy regime
Civil war/revolution	Exchange rate volatility	Investment analytics
Terrorism	Housing/banking	Measurement error
Industrial unrest	Sovereign credit	Systemic risk
Asset seizure, punitive taxation	Competitiveness (including participation in arrangements such as the EU and NAFTA)	Customer tastes
Natural disasters	Demography/ participation	
Environmental/climate change	Natural resources	
	Technology change	

8. Conclusion

The future is unknowable, and the past can be only the loosest of guides to the potential macro risks facing planners of large-scale infrastructure projects. Nonetheless, this brief discussion has identified many sources of such risk, ranging from the objective threats posed by conflict and natural disasters, and by cyclical and secular economic volatility, to the more subjective or contextual risks arising from altered policy and analytical paradigms, and from changes in investor and consumer sentiment.

The range and scale of macro shocks seen in the last half-century has been dramatic, and there are doubtless new 'unknown unknowns' looming ahead. Genuine 'risk' is not the smoothly varying, statistically tractable quantity found in textbooks, but the more profound uncertainty that encompasses the possibility of wrenching dislocations, systemic collapses and worse. The best advice to planners is that they should stress test their calculations extensively, and do their best to keep an open mind and to stay nimble.

The somewhat one-sided nature of this conclusion is daunting, but likely realistic. Being human involves facing more potential bad stuff than good. But an awareness of risk does not mean that we are shackled by it. The bad stuff does not always happen, and prosaic day-to-day success can persist for years at a stretch.

The causes of long-term prosperity are our endowment with real resources – land, labour, capital – and our ability to innovate and to 'learn by doing'. The last decade has not changed that fact, nor those endowments, nor our capacity for invention and improvement. The remarkable economic and political gains of the last half-century do not have to be repeated – but they might be. I still think the late Julian Simon put it best:

> *This is my long-run forecast in brief. The material conditions of life will continue to get better for most people, in most countries, most of the time, indefinitely. Within a century or two, all nations and most of humanity will be at or above today's Western living standards. I also speculate, however, that many people will continue to think and say that the conditions of life are getting worse.*

Master planning energy infrastructure

Drew Slaton
Senior project manager

1. Introduction

In our increasingly interconnected world, the need for thoughtful and rigorous planning to meet energy demand is more critical than ever. Primary fuel supply and energy security are pieces of the master plan. The infrastructure required to process, transport and produce energy needs to be intricately interwoven within existing and planned transportation networks, housing, water and sewerage systems, and industry, as well as, importantly, being tied into our basic social fabric and culture. This chapter seeks to identify the interfaces and analysis necessary to master plan meaningfully activities in the energy infrastructure environment. It will cover both risks and opportunities as we explore several specific examples of how master planning can impact the ultimate success or failure of an energy infrastructure development.

The following perspectives are based on personal experiences and are intended to demonstrate how master planning, specifically in the energy infrastructure sector, is needed now more than ever. The chapter will first look at the primary risk factors that need to be considered when master planning infrastructure projects. Examples of countries that are either preparing for or are in the process of implementing projects will be examined to identify opportunities for appropriate master planning. The chapter will then go on to examine the roles of government and the private sector respectively, before concluding by identifying the main factors that define well-master-planned energy infrastructure projects.

2. Risks

According to the International Monetary Fund, 60% of the global gross domestic product (GDP) is within the developing and emerging economies.[1] The term 'developing and emerging markets' represents a group of 30 to 50 countries which are neither poor nor rich, but are in a rapid transition phase. These countries are uniquely positioned to leverage their anticipated growth to the benefit of their citizens or simply stagnate by maintaining the status quo and falling further behind the rest of the world.

There are several 'giant killer' risks that shape the 'why, what and how' thinking

1 Lagarde, Christine, (2016) 'The Role of Emerging Markets in a New Global Partnership for Growth by IMF Managing Director Christine Lagarde, International Monetary Fund', [Online] Retrieved from http://www.imf.org/en/News/Articles/2015/09/28/04/53/sp020416 on 15 February 2017.

process that goes into the master planning effort. It is quite easy to see the challenges faced, yet quite another to solve the issue. While some energy production efforts are stop-gap measures to alleviate tactical and localised issues, many major energy investments are part of larger, mega developments. These huge programmes attempt to address the holistic issues of future demand, urban planning and societal challenges simultaneously. They are subject to the risks of political turmoil (and sometimes political whim), geological anomalies, and even natural disasters.

A few of the key risks (and several risk responses) are referenced below, including:

- gaps;
- overlaps;
- political/geo-political;
- regulatory;
- technology obsolescence; and
- societal impact.

Each risk can be independent or interconnected as evidenced in the examples cited below.

2.1 Gaps

Gaps in infrastructure occur more frequently than one might imagine. For example, ports and airports that are developed with the best of intentions, but are lacking:

- adequate energy supply;
- onward connecting transportation systems; and
- worker accommodation (physical housing as well as basic services such as water, sewage, medical care, etc).

When these gaps materialise, the project fails to meet expectations and reach its full potential.

Well-thought-out energy infrastructure is at the heart of mitigating this risk. Baseload energy must be available in synchronisation and typically ahead of the other key components since power supply is critical to its success (eg, water treatment facilities). Additionally, the energy needs must be planned in such a manner as to meet anticipated expansion at a measured and practical pace. This may include 'energy islands' that operate from a hub and spoke configuration or simply appropriate expansion space and capacity in a centralised energy zone. A mix of energy sources can provide protection against single points of failure, help to meet energy demand 'spikes', optimise load capacity for domestic and industrial use, provide greater energy security, and diversify economic opportunities.

2.2 Overlaps

Overlaps occur when excess or conflicting capacity is installed. Staying with a port scenario, a major expressway is planned with tolls from passenger traffic and heavy trucking provided to a concessionaire in exchange for the initial construction and ongoing maintenance of the road. The economics behind the road development hinge on specific rate of return on investment (ROI) financial models which are based on anticipated volume of traffic, types of traffic and ancillary infrastructure (eg, fuelling stations, motels and dining facilities, and adjacent manufacturing and distribution facilities, etc).

If a new railway development is subsequently approved outside the approved master plan, then:

- the road, rail and port projects may fail to meet financial expectations;
- local and regional communities may suffer the consequences of poorly planned implementations as redundant work disrupts traffic and increases demand on limited resources; and
- there may be greater adverse environmental impact as the projects leave a larger imprint.

Realistic short-, medium- and long-term forecasting are critical to mitigate this risk. Again, the associated energy requirements must be considered in conjunction with the overall master plan to ensure each complementary component's needs are met and, critically, at the right time.

2.3 Political and geo-political

These are perhaps some of the most challenging risks to address in our increasingly globalised world. Conflicting internal demands within a country or sub-region can easily result in overlaps as described above when multiple parties pursue the same goal but with different strategies. These conflicts can erupt along one or more fault lines:

- party affiliation (as one group seeks to strengthen its grip on power at the expense of others);
- racial or religious discrimination;
- disparity in the distribution of natural resources/national wealth;
- ideological differences; and
- tribal or cultural affiliation.

These are just a few of the sources for internal conflict which vary widely by country or region.

In the broader political spectrum, well-established trade arrangements such as the Eurozone and NAFTA can find themselves at risk with changing political policy and strategy, as shown in recent developments. Trade sanctions can disrupt supply chains and the basic underpinning of major projects. In this scenario, the best master-planning efforts may be simply abandoned due to completely unrelated issues.

2.4 Regulatory

This term is used in the broadest possible context to address an array of related issues, such as:

- environmental policy;
- energy policy;
- indigenous citizen rights;

- permitting and zoning; and (ironically)
- de-regulation (which can spur excess or uncontrolled growth).

Each of these areas can derail major energy and other infrastructure plans. There is also potential risk with cross-country or regional arrangements where energy security or distribution channels are involved (eg, pipelines crossing multiple jurisdictions from source to port). Uncontained, rapid buildout of energy infrastructure can be almost as destructive as the lack of infrastructure, as overlaps turn cost-effective and positive efforts into marginal investments (or worse).

In a related manner, archaic legislation or political ('pork barrel') favouritism which supports one technology or geographical area over another creates inefficient resource allocation. In turn, this creates both direct (eg, physical supply and distribution) and indirect (eg, pricing, economic growth potential, etc) energy disparity.

2.5 Technology obsolescence

Technology obsolescence is a very real threat to major energy infrastructure investments. Most investments need 20 to 30 years to achieve full ROI. One has only to look at recent history to see the massive impact that that the US shale industry has caused in oil and gas markets. Existing transportation and distribution networks were ill-equipped to handle this relative newcomer to the energy mix, thus requiring even more investment to mature the industry segment.

And the million (trillion?) dollar question is: 'How long will it be before another technology such as 'mega-storage battery capacity' will completely disrupt the current market and underpinning infrastructure?' We like to think of 'black swan' events as being exceedingly rare; however, with our exponentially escalating volume of knowledge, these disruptive technology cycles are appearing more frequently and on tighter cycles.

2.6 Societal impact

Major infrastructure projects almost inevitably carry the 'boom/bust' risk. As 'hot' money floods into an area in the form of wages, materials and equipment procurement:

- demand for housing and other services rapidly increases;
- increased employment (while generally welcomed) often drains other local businesses and organisations of their key staff; and
- in turn, this large influx of workers often results in other related and compounding challenges as workers move their entire families to the area (eg, increasing demand on education institutions, creating hyper-inflation for goods and services, road congestion, etc).

Unfortunately, large projects also frequently bring social ills with them. Ranging from drug and alcohol abuse, to prostitution, to rising crime rates to name a few, the benefits during the development phase do not come without cost. Energy infrastructure projects are no exception. The large workforce needed to build a thermal plant, a refinery or a pipeline rapidly diminishes as the project reaches completion. This can result in:

- large unemployment rates;
- rapid deflation;
- family displacement; and
- a painful economic readjustment for all stakeholders (eg, governments' tax revenues often suffer significant losses).

For those who choose to remain in the area, there is a major adjustment to the new reality.

Equally important is the factor of public acceptance. Referencing the 'shale revolution' again, it did not come without a cost. While the public welcomed the lower energy prices for their homes and cars, they were less than enthusiastic when environmental and societal concerns started being raised, including water table pollution, economic boom/bust cycles, and even seismic events potentially related to the fracking and extraction process. Other examples include entire communities being uprooted to make way for energy-related projects (eg, Three Gorges Dam in China) and pipelines crossing sensitive cultural and environmentally protected lands (eg, in Canada, Nigeria and the United States). We all want 'the lights to stay on', but not if it is at our personal, cultural or environmental expense.

However, all is not gloom and doom. With appropriate master planning, effective regulation, consistent political direction, and genuine commitment to bettering the world for future generations, it is possible to meet the 'needs of the many' while reducing the negative impact on all stakeholders. Master planning not only addresses the current needs, but also anticipates the challenges of the future.

3. Opportunities abound

As noted in the introduction, there are many risks associated with energy infrastructure development, but equally there are many opportunities as well. Around the world there is tremendous potential for structured master planning and subsequent benefits for people, the environment, industry and the respective governments.

I will start with a few examples from emerging markets which present the greatest potential and reap the most from well-structured master planning. Then I will examine some other examples which are in process and look at what is going right and what could be improved. Finally, I will look at some excellent examples of how a strategic master plan that is carefully executed can yield tremendous benefits.

3.1 Potential for undeveloped, under-developed and emerging markets

(a) Rwanda

Rwanda represents one of the brightest opportunities in Africa despite the number of challenges it faces. Small in size, landlocked and poor in natural resources, Rwanda has one outstanding asset: location. By the very virtue of its near-perfect centrality within sub-Saharan Africa, Rwanda has several parallels with another country with a well-known success story: Singapore. Both countries faced similar challenges yet Singapore has been able to leverage its location to become an economic powerhouse. It was able to achieve this through careful master planning, controlled growth and strategic economic guidance. Rwanda sits at the axis of air travel across one of the most populous regions of the world (versus Singapore's strategic ocean route) and represents one of the most stable security and business environments in Africa. Yet its lack of master planning, specifically in the energy sector, has restrained its ability to make real economic progress.

Rwanda has diversified its energy mix to include traditional, emerging and innovative energy sources. Hydroelectric (including mini- and micro-hydro plants in remote areas), purchasing power from neighbouring countries, diesel generators, solar, peat thermal plants, and even harvesting methane from Lake Kivu all contribute to the energy mix. However, there are two major flaws in the approach. First, there is a lack of standardisation which prevents Rwanda from leveraging its diverse energy sources. With hydroelectric plants from countless suppliers, and no attendant master parts inventory and consistent maintenance and operations regime, it is unable to maintain consistent and reliable levels of electrical supply across the country. Even the capital Kigali is subject to frequent blackouts as unpredictable load shedding occurs. In turn, this prevents many potential companies from establishing light manufacturing or service industries which rely on steady state power supply.

Secondly, the lack of basic infrastructure, including redundant transmission lines/power routing and well-designed and properly maintained sub-stations, and the lack of a reliable supervisory control and data acquisition (SCADA) system means that producing more electricity will not necessarily result in greater reliability or availability to end consumers. Underpinning these physical infrastructure issues is the lack of qualified, well-trained staff with appropriate levels of parts inventory to maintain the system.

Rwanda is a classic textbook example of where the lack of an energy master plan has led to chaos and a very significant amount of domestic and international investment has been wasted. However, with appropriate effort and government support, Rwanda could implement a multi-year investment into master planning and follow-on implementation, leading to a very bright future.

(b) Afghanistan

Needless to say, Afghanistan is a country in a state of perpetual flux. War-ravaged, isolated and torn by internal conflict, it is difficult to see a clear path forward for this country. Compounding these significant challenges is the heavily negative perspective of outsiders, which further reduces any investment interest. However, Afghanistan is, if nothing else, resilient, and the country has, by any reasonable standard, a broad and attractive natural resource base. Contrary to general perceptions, Afghanistan has significant mineral and other extractable resources. It also has very good potential energy generation capacity in multiple forms, including thermal, hydroelectric, solar and wind power.

The combination of security instability, negative perception and the lack of an effective master plan to exploit the natural resources and develop opportunities for the population will continue to block growth for the foreseeable future. The development of a practical and paced master plan is critical to addressing the instability and negative perception. This is not a naïve, politically correct opinion by the '8000-mile screwdriver'; it is reality. The world has seen many equally challenging situations which have shown remarkable progress. For example, the Balkan region has suffered incredibly in the past, yet has been able to create a more stable and vibrant group of economies than ever before. With energy production increasing and availability growing, the economies and welfare of the respective populations in this region are rapidly improving.

(c) Nigeria

By all accounts Nigeria has the basic ingredients for self-sustaining power and energy security. With a massive population, well-educated workforce, large physical land and natural resources, regional influence and a large, growing GDP, Nigeria should be an energy powerhouse for west and central Africa. However, the lack of a clear strategy and energy master plan has seen the country living in crisis for decades. In addition to endemic corruption, the lack of basic energy infrastructure means the country's true potential is crippled. While aggressive steps are being taken to address the corruption issues, the lack of a socially responsible plan to share the country's oil, gas and hydroelectric resources results in the country being torn apart by internal conflicting interests.

The lack of national refining capacity means raw crude is exported, refined offshore, imported (at a premium), and then cost-subsidised to allow ordinary Nigerians to afford fuel products. Dilapidated power plants, sub-stations and distribution networks, and no functioning SCADA results in unreliable electrical power for individual and business consumers alike. In turn, this results in a growing market for diesel, needed to power local generators, with the fuel sourced from the illegal, offline markets, thus propagating the corruption that is bleeding the country dry.

First and foremost, Nigeria must confront the corruption plague which drives so many of its other social issues, such as crime, militancy, terrorism and a swamp of poverty that traps generations of Nigerians and results in many of Nigeria's most talented people electing to move abroad. In parallel, an effective and practical master plan can chart the path which will lead to all Nigerians' best interests.

3.2 Efforts underway: The jury is still out on these developed markets

Many other developed and developing countries understand the importance of controlled, well-planned and well-executed master planning. Yet after preparing elaborate five-year, 10-year and even longer strategies, we see them gutted by advances in technology, public backlash and geo-political upheaval. Liquefied natural gas (LNG) was the darling of the energy industry, growing in influence over the past several decades. Many of the 'Asian Tiger' (eg, Singapore, South Korea) economies grew through heavy dependence on this imported resource. Globally, the countries with the gas, technology and infrastructure exploded in a massive buildout of processing and export capacity. Governments saw the potential economic benefits and pushed through legislation to make the projects a reality.

Then the shale oil and gas revolution shook the world. Suddenly, net importers of LNG such as the United States started looking at becoming net exporters as advances in fracking began to flood the market. In parallel, massive pipeline projects complementary to the effort were approved and a major sector of world economics was suddenly turned on its head. Russian threats to cut off natural gas to Europe lost much of their bite. Middle East economies saw their GDPs and aggressive diversification plans suddenly starving when prices dove to levels not seen in decades. Efforts by OPEC have largely been ineffectual to date, as more countries such as Iran come out from under economic sanctions and desperately need hard cash despite historically low prices. And even with international cooperation, the United States and other countries with spare capacity and improving technology simply 'turn up the spigot', thus negating any production cuts designed to prop up pricing.

Will the massive infrastructure projects realise their full potential? Or will another technology (possibly the 'mother of all batteries' being developed by some college student in their 'internet garage') simply make these long-term investments obsolete? Let us begin by looking at two examples of major energy infrastructure initiatives in Australia and Canada.

(a) ***Australia***

Australia has embarked on an LNG buildout of near epic proportions. In 2015–2016, Australia exported 37 million tonnes of LNG with a value of $16.55 billion and its production was 48% higher than in 2014–2015. Australia is now the world's second-largest LNG exporter. It is projected to become the world's largest LNG exporter by 2020.[2]

Three massive processing and export facilities were approved to be built on Gladstone Island on the east coast of Australia. The US-based engineering, construction and project management giant Bechtel Corporation simultaneously developed and commissioned the plants in an amazing feat of coordination and cooperation with stakeholders, including major industry partners, global suppliers, local and regional workers, and government entities. In addition, another massive LNG project was started on the west coast of Australia. This injection of LNG capacity came at a time when major importers began re-examining their energy needs, energy security and potential for energy self-sufficiency.

And as is always the case with massive infrastructure investments, Australia will now need to manage carefully the historic 'boom/bust' cycle that occurs so often following the completion of major projects. Large-scale training efforts and the years of experience gained by the Australian workforce while completing the projects are invaluable, but is the Australian economy prepared to absorb the direct and indirect reduction in 'hot money' that has been pumped into the system?

2 Australian Petroleum Production & Exploration Association (APPEA). Retrieved from www.appea.com.au/oil-gas-explained/benefits/benefits-of-lng/export-revenue on 2 August 2017.

(b) Canada

In a similar approach, Canada pushed an aggressive LNG processing and export agenda, coupled with several major pipeline projects (some of which overlapped into the United States).[3] However, the works were not without controversy. Local populations demonstrated against what they felt was an invasion of their values and way of life. Environmentalist advocacy groups aggressively protested against the projects on the grounds of potential dangers to the environment and in light of growing climate change evidence. Further, was the sheer volume of projects (processing plants and pipelines) appropriate and necessary?

Ultimately, time will tell whether the economic growth and sustainment benefits will be sufficient to address adequately the social and environmental impacts. In some instances, there will be compromises that allow all stakeholders to feel their needs were appropriately met. In other cases, conflicting values simply cannot be aligned and the state of a zero-sum game will continue to exist.

In the Australian and Canadian examples, the countries conducted extensive studies, engaged local stakeholders and employed the world's best companies to execute the projects. However, the jury remains out to see whether these projects will bring the economic benefits for the 'greater good' or whether they will in turn become obsolete before their ROI is realised.

As a closing thought, not all variables are purely economic, technological or social. For example, the warming of the world's oceans has opened the Northern Passage which is creating a new reality and opportunity for countries such as Norway and Russia that are yet to be realised. The 2011 tsunami that severely damaged Japan's Fukushima nuclear power plant has had a very chilling effect on the anticipated 'nuclear renaissance'. Where will this (and other black swan events) lead us?

4. Successes (and continuing challenges)

As an observer, it is easy to examine upcoming initiatives and to comment on ongoing efforts. It is quite another to state accurately whether a given project will be ultimately successful or not (or will continue to be so in the future). However, there are examples where master planning has made a positive impact and has the potential to improve the lives and livelihoods of everyday people.

4.1 Kenya

Kenya represents one of the most enlightened countries on the African continent and has realised the necessity of master planning its future. With a growing economy and rising per capita income, Kenyans in general are reaping the benefits of the coordinated efforts of industry and government. However, while it has strongly diversified its energy mix, Kenya has yet to follow through with the other infrastructure needed to capitalise fully on its investment.

Energy infrastructure is so intrinsically interrelated that it is often difficult to understand where it starts and stops. Kenya has made tremendous strides in energy

3 British Columbia Oil and Gas Association. Retrieved from www.bcogc.ca/node/11415/download on 28 July 2017.

production, specifically its large investment in geothermal power. Lacking, however, is the means to utilise this energy effectively. More and better roads, ports, airports, pipelines, rail, distribution systems and information technology are badly needed. It is evident that Kenya has devoted a significant amount of thought to energy production; now it must apply an equal amount of effort into how it intends to utilise that energy.

One such initiative is a series of massive economic corridors which will open markets and access to neighbouring and nearby countries such as Ethiopia, Somalia, Uganda, South Sudan and Rwanda. One of these corridors is the Lamu Port-South Sudan-Ethiopia-Transport (LAPSSET) Corridor project.[4] Advancing this multi-pronged initiative will greatly enhance Kenya's economic and geo-political power. However, the project has struggled to gain momentum, with regional and self-interest conflicts stymying progress. The master planning for this massive investment started years ago, but has undergone so many changes that the path forward remains elusive even though it is in all stakeholders' best interests.

4.2 Saudi Arabia

Major programme management companies have adjusted their operating models to deliver more holistic solutions with greater value. Rather than simply providing a new thermal power plant, for example, companies such as Bechtel, CH2M, Hyundai and others provide customers with broader-reaching energy solutions, including tightly linked transportation systems (rail, ports), supply and mid-stream solutions (mines, pipelines), energy production and distribution systems (electrical generation plants, transmission lines), and communities to support direct and indirect labour forces along with their requisite needs (housing, water, sewerage, communications, etc). These holistic master-planned programmes carefully look at anticipated growth projections and associated changes such as societal and environmental impacts.

A prime example of this broader approach is the mega-industrial city of Jubail, which represents master planning on an enormous scale. US engineering, construction and project management giant Bechtel has been engaged in the scalable and carefully controlled development of this massive industrial city since the mid-1970s.[5] This type of carefully planned and executed master planning effort requires highly specialised expertise as well as strong government backing to achieve.

The evidence indicates Jubail has been a tremendous success and a major step towards economic diversification for the Saudi kingdom. This is a great example of how master planning, and specifically including the energy sector, has broader value and linkages which go beyond the core effort.

5. Energy initiatives by government and private sector

Government-led organisations and communities have been proactive in developing

4 LAPSSET Corridor Development Authority was established through Presidential Order in Kenya in 2013 to plan, coordinate and manage the implementation of the Lamu Port-South Sudan-Ethiopia Transport Corridor. Retrieved from www.lapsset.go.ke on 29 July 2017.

5 Bechtel Corporation. Retrieved from http://www.bechtel.com/projects/jubail-industrial-city on 1 July 2017.

energy-related programmes to provide greater access to energy. One such development in this area is the international donor community which has been making a focused investment towards energy-related development initiatives worldwide. In a similar effort, the United Nations declared 2012 as the 'International Year of Sustainable Energy For All'[6] in order to alleviate energy-related poverty. These organisations understand that energy availability improves health and wellbeing, thereby improving the living standards, economic activity and self-sufficiency of local populations.

In order to improve energy access for common households, private sector enterprises are also involved in a number of partnership programmes with respective government-led organisations across global, regional and bilateral levels in order to support energy-related infrastructure development and projects.

Among the many notable public and private partnerships is the Global Sustainable Electricity Partnership,[7] a not-for-profit international organisation focused on the growing energy crisis. This partnership is designed to address global electricity demand, while promoting sustainable energy projects and bringing electricity to emerging and developing nations. Many of the efforts are often smaller-scale, grassroots movements such as the public-private initiative 'Global Alliance for Clean Cook Stoves',[8] which was launched by the United Nations Development Programme and supported by the US government, with the objective of improving quality of living, saving lives, empowering women and combating climate change through clean, green, safe and efficient cooking solutions for every household.[9]

These efforts are certainly commendable and much needed. However, there is still much more to be done. Along with significant new investment in energy infrastructure, as noted in the UN/Bloomberg study, an additional $130 billion was spent on increasing energy efficiency in 2015. Taken together with projected population growth, these figures demonstrate that much more investment is necessary in order to meet the growing energy needs across the globe. However, the International Energy Agency[10] forecasts that even with significant new investment across all current energy sources, there is still a requirement to increase energy efficiency measures by $550 billion annually – evidence that we cannot simply spend our way out of the energy crisis. Instead, there must be a mix of more net energy produced, coupled with much greater efficiencies.

PriceWaterhouseCoopers reports that by 2030 70% of the world population will reside in cities, which will compel urban planners to make infrastructure, specifically energy infrastructure, investment a top priority.[11] Much of the global infrastructure investment will be spent to meet the growing and continued urbanisation. As much as $78 trillion is expected to be spent on infrastructure globally between 2014 and

---

6 United Nations. Retrieved from www.un.org/en/events/sustainableenergyforall on 11 May 2017.
7 Global Sustainable Electricity Partnership. Retrieved from www.globalelectricity.org/en on 1 April 2017.
8 Global Alliance for Clean Cook Stoves. Retrieved from http://cleancookstoves.org on 10 April 2017.
9 For more information on the level of activity by governments and corporate entities broken down by energy source see *Government and Corporate Investment in Renewable R&D, 2015*, United Nations Environmental Programme/Bloomberg New Energy Finance http://fs-unep-centre.org/sites/default/files/publications/globaltrendsinrenewableenergyinvestment2016lowres_0.pdf.
10 International Energy Agency. Retrieved from www.eia.gov/outlooks/ieo/ on 2 August 2017.
11 PriceWaterhouseCoopers. Retrieved from www.pwc.com/gx/en/government-public-services/assets/from-urbanization-to-aging-society.pdf on 2 August 2017.

2025, with Asian countries accounting for over $8 trillion in infrastructure spending (as per estimates by the Asian Development Bank).[12] More and more people continue to migrate to urban centres in search of jobs, opportunities, health and hygiene, electricity and better quality of life. India is a good example in terms of its pace of urbanisation, where it is estimated that in the coming decade nearly 500 million people will move to cities in search of better living conditions.

The energy infrastructure dilemma is certainly not limited to developing markets. The United States needs major investment and re-investment for the future.[13] A driving factor behind this investment requirement is the ageing infrastructure developed across the country which was built and developed 40 to 60 years ago. Crumbling infrastructure, technology obsolescence and growing demand require a major investment of approximately $3.6 trillion according to the ASCE report.

6. Conclusion

Energy infrastructure master planning is a complex and risky venture. This challenge is not limited to poor nations or developing countries. Highly developed countries can (and have) got it wrong as well. No country, region or organisation is immune to 'missing the mark' when addressing the complexities involved in meeting all stakeholders' expectations.

As investors, policy makers, local communities and other stakeholders look at master planning efforts before, during and after implementation, it is important that the key attributes of a successful master plan are identified and whether they meet expectations. While every implementation is different, four common attributes to consider are as follows:

Attribute	Positive	Neutral	Negative	Remarks
Return on investment	Meets or exceeds financial models. Creates additional value beyond original plan.	Meets financial expectation but fails to exploit additional opportunities.	Fails to achieve target financial goals (or other measures).	Projects may have widely variable measures for ROI depending on whether the effort is government, private or jointly driven.

continued on next page

12 Asian Development Bank. Retrieved from www.adb.org/publications/reports on 30 April 2017.
13 American Society of Civil Engineers. Retrieved from www.americanbar.org/content/dam/aba/administrative/litigation/materials/2016_joint_cle/1_2013_american_society_of_civil_engineers_report_card_for_americas_infrastructure.authcheckdam.pdf on 12 May 2017.

Attribute	Positive	Neutral	Negative	Remarks
Scalability	The master plan can be incrementally expanded or contracted, depending on changing needs.	The plan meets the original capacity targets within the stated timeframe.	The plan fails to address near-, medium- and/or long-term needs. Stop-gap (eg, unplanned supplemental resources) or radical measures (eg, load shedding) are required.	A good master plan needs to be able to accommodate the inevitable change which will occur.
Stakeholder acceptance	All parties implicitly or explicitly accept the plan and reap the anticipated benefit. Added-value opportunities are realised.	Each stakeholder acknowledges the master plan's importance. There is no overt or overwhelming resistance to the plan.	One or more stakeholders actively fight the master plan. One or more stakeholders are negatively impacted by the plan.	The concept of 'informed consent' may have to be benchmark for success. If all parties acknowledge the master plan, even without achieving full consensus, they at least know their concerns were evaluated.
Adaptability	The master plan is capable of absorbing new technologies readily, without major overhauls of investment. Opportunities are seized rather than avoided.	The master plan remains intact but may require substantial upgrades to infrastructure or have to co-exist rather than evolve.	The introduction of a new technology wreaks havoc on financial and physical investments already in place.	A master plan that cannot evolve will fail to achieve expectations on multiple fronts.

Master planning forms part of a much broader socio-economic planning effort that inevitably benefits some stakeholders while harming others. The trade-offs are challenging to balance and the economic 'sense' requires much more effort to analyse than ever before. The risk of public rejection or technical obsolescence looms over potential investors. What are some steps that can be taken to reduce the risk?

First, early and honest collaboration is needed between governments, corporations and the impacted communities. The 'good and the bad' need to be equally discussed at the onset so that all parties understand what is at risk for both sides. Collectively, the world has failed in this respect and the fall-out is evident. We must do better at educating each other on what is at stake, why it is important and how we can reach compromise.

Second, investors need to understand the impact of our rapidly expanding knowledge in all areas of human capability. For example, the old economic models do not work effectively in a world where new models and versions of smart phones are announced every month it seems. Technology cycles are tightening in frequency and expanding in impact. Greater analysis is needed to see how emerging technologies can meld with and complement existing infrastructure rather than radically disrupting it.

Finally, governments need to collaborate more closely with private industry to incubate and develop better, more efficient solutions. As noted, we cannot simply spend our way out of this growing energy crisis. More needs to be done on the supply side (eg, renewable energy) but, equally important, much more needs to be done on the demand side (eg, 'smart appliances').

One way of working towards this goal is to expand and further implement government-backed development funds along the lines of public-private partnerships. Unilateral, bilateral and collective guarantees by major development organisations help to bridge the gap between industry's capacity to deliver solutions, end consumers' needs, and respective governments' obligations to meet the needs of their people. Together, we can work to close the gap and meet the energy needs of the world.

Risks in the oil industry throughout the value chain*

Douglas Nordlinger

1. Introduction

The oil and gas business is a large industry, and there are many major integrated oil and gas companies, such as Exxon Mobil, BP, Shell and Chevron, that carry out exploration, production, transportation, treating, refining and, in some cases, marketing. For those companies, senior executives face almost all of the risks in the industry, and those risks can occur at any point along the value chain. For those kinds of company, the importance and magnitude of the risk can depend on the significance of the point in the integrated value chain where that risk crystalises.

For example, one company's pipelines for transportation of crude oil might comprise a relatively small portion of the assets of its entire business, so an outage at that company might not have as material an impact as a blowout of a well or an explosion at a refinery, where either an injury to persons or a destruction of assets of a much higher value might occur and have a more material effect. Another company may rank the same type of outage as a much larger risk. It is up to the company's senior executives to have a nuanced understanding of the overview of risks and how those risks will affect their company in particular.

These calculations are not, however, made in a static environment. Senior executives at major integrated oil and gas companies are also expected to weigh risks in a competitive landscape, which is fluid. The oil industry currently faces tremendous competition – not only from current players within the industry, but also from alternative and renewable energy sources and evolving technologies that are altering the landscape as we know it.

The following sections contain an illustration of the types of risk a major integrated oil and gas company may face at each point along the value chain.

2. Exploration, production and development

There are numerous components to oil exploration, ranging from geopolitical and geological considerations to business matters, including the negotiation of contracts and other legally binding instruments – and in many countries, the right to explore is put out to bid, creating an additional auction component. There are statutory and regulatory frameworks, but each one of these components entails risks.

* Douglas Nordlinger sadly passed away during the production of this edition. The publishers and consulting editors would like to extend their sincerest condolences to Douglas's family, friends and colleagues. Prior to his retirement, Douglas served as the head of Skadden's Energy and Infrastructure Projects Group and played an important role in its development as a leading practice.

2.1 Location risk

When a major integrated oil company is in the exploration phase, it searches first for a location that will allow it to transport its oil through the production chain with a certain level of ease. An inability to drill or to obtain permits to transport oil to a place where there is a market or an export route can be damaging – and the process of obtaining these kinds of permit can be a challenge. This is especially true if the oil needs to cross an international border, requiring the company to obtain approvals from more than one country.

In addition to the standard challenges of doing business and gaining approvals for new projects, major integrated oil and gas companies can face further tests. Because these companies need to go to places that contain oil resources, they can find themselves conducting business anywhere in the world, including in places that are prone to corruption in business and in government. This necessitates their instilling a culture of compliance within their companies to reduce as much as possible the risk of corruption or bribery, both at home and in far-flung places.

Here is an illustration of just some of the considerations that could arise during the exploration phase: the Great Lakes area of Africa is a current location of interest for major oil development, particularly around lakes Albert and Victoria. So, a number of countries, primarily Uganda and Kenya, are developing refineries and a network of pipelines to extract the oil from the lake Albert and Victoria regions to export routes on the Indian Ocean.[1] Because Uganda is landlocked, any oil extracted there will have to go through the ports to reach larger international markets. There is a port in Kenya at Mombasa, and that port is overwhelmed and creating bottlenecks, both for oil exports and imported supplies – so it would have to be expanded for any major increases in oil transport.[2] The Kenyans want to develop a port at Lamu,[3] but environmental and security factors may delay or even impede development of important infrastructure and projects, especially if they are financed by third-party or multilateral lenders, as they will generally require an environmental impact statement, which may contain a list of environmental mitigation measures.[4] In the alternative, Tanzania is seeking to develop a port at Tanga, also on the Indian Ocean, and it now appears that this will be the preferred route for Ugandan oil. If Uganda and Tanzania develop a pipeline, they will likely develop a ground transportation network around them, to the benefit of the region.

However, when a company crosses international borders with a pipeline, such as Uganda crossing over Tanzania to reach Tanga, the transporters have to pay a tariff on the pipeline, and they will likely be required to pay a transit fee, which is in the nature of a tax that Tanzania would impose for allowing them to ship goods over its

1 "Will Kenya or Uganda be east Africa's first oil producer?", *The Guardian*, 2 May 2014, www.theguardian.com/global-development/poverty-matters/2014/may/12/kenya-uganda-east-africa-first-oil-producer.

2 "Africa's ports: The bottleneck", *The Economist*, 19 March 2016, www.economist.com/news/middle-east-and-africa/21695054-new-investment-alone-will-not-fix-africas-ports-governments-need-deal.

3 "The race to become East Africa's biggest port", *BBC*, 7 June 2016, www.bbc.com/news/world-africa-36458946

4 "Disquiet over Lamu port project", *IRIN*, 31 October 2012, www.irinnews.org/report/96675/kenya-disquiet-over-lamu-port-project.

territory. There may also be port charges on top of that. Plus, the tariff could be subject to regulation, and the transit fee could be whatever the government wants to charge. So, an oil company may think it knows what it is going to cost to transport its oil, and then it could find out five years down the line that much of that has changed, depending on the legal requirements of its contracts.

If the company wants to go upstream, it first needs to conduct seismic studies, and to conduct those studies it needs a licence, usually from the government. If it wants to drill an exploration well, that may not be included in the survey permit, so an additional permit may be required. If it wants to drill on dry ground, that may not be difficult to arrange, but if it is planning on drilling in water, that can become expensive, especially offshore. The company may have to build out infrastructure to make that happen. Then, it has the risk that it drills an expensive well and nothing comes of it – and even if something does come of it, that is only useful if it is a commercial discovery, meaning there is enough oil there to make it worth all the other investments to move forward with production.

After taking into account all of these considerations, if a company decides to develop oil in a country in Africa such as Uganda, the first thing it will have to do is put together an agreement with the government. These are typically called production sharing agreements. In some places, instead of a production sharing agreement, companies can obtain a licence, but in Third World countries, production sharing agreements where the government shares in a portion of the oil that is produced are standard. Oil companies are used to these agreements since they have been around since 1966,[5] and they are typically amenable to using them so long as they think they can get a good return out of the venture – especially because most production sharing agreements leave the drilling and operations to the production companies, which is what the companies want. They do not want to cede production to the host state.

So, at the exploration stage, once a company has picked a location, it has contracting risk, business negotiations, and the commercial risks associated with those negotiations. Then, at the development and production stage, it has petroleum engineering risks. It will want to determine that the oil is, in fact, there, and once it has determined that it is, there are additional concerns, such as whether the company can extract the oil, how deep it will need to drill (especially if it is drilling offshore), the level of density of the sandstone where the oil-bearing reservoirs are located, and whether it is possible to build up the pressure required to produce the oil. Then, once the oil comes out, there is a question of quality. It could be high-quality or low-quality oil. The following section on geologic and product quality risks outlines the approach a senior oil and gas executive might take to resolve those questions.

---

5 Bindemann, Kirsten, *Production-Sharing Agreements: An Economic Analysis*, Oxford Institute for Energy Studies WPM 25, October 1999, p 1, www.oxfordenergy.org/wpcms/wp-content/uploads/2010/11/WPM25-ProductionSharingAgreementsAnEconomicAnalysis-KBindemann-1999.pdf.

2.2 Geologic and product quality risks

In the 1960s, several natural gas producers in the United States signed very long-term, low-priced gas sales contracts.[6] One company, Gulf Oil, which later endured a forced merger with Standard Oil of California and rebranded as Chevron,[7] thought that it had sufficient reserves to satisfy its obligations under its sales contracts with both Texas Eastern Transmission Company and Tennessee Gas Pipeline Company. It had had geological surveys conducted where it planned to drill wildcat wells, and it turned out that a large portion of the sandstone that it had identified in the area was not actually gas producing. It was, in fact, brine producing, and because of that, Gulf Oil did not have sufficient natural gas to satisfy its contracts. This resulted in a series of legal proceedings as Gulf Oil attempted and failed to amend the terms of those contracts.[8, 9] It was a damaging error to Gulf Oil Corporation, which no longer exists as an independent company.

Associated with this, there is also reservoir performance risk. In the North Sea, BP and other producers were successful at finding a significant amount of oil, so the United Kingdom was self-sufficient for at least a decade in finding oil and gas. However, the reservoirs in the North Sea have declined at a much more rapid rate than was predicted, so there is significantly less oil and gas left now than was projected in the 1990s.[10, 11]

Finally, not all oil is the same, so there is risk in the type of oil a company finds. If it finds a low-gravity, high-sulphur crude, that crude has a lower value than a high-gravity, low-sulphur crude, which is more liquid and easier to treat and refine into high-end products such as jet fuel, naphtha, gas oil or gasoline.

The science of petroleum engineering has moved forward since the 1990s and certainly since the 1960s, but even with more advanced technologies, a senior oil executive must always consider the possibility for geologic risk in oil and gas exploration. Expertise in correctly identifying reserves is a valuable skill for company management, as companies that have a history of success at finding and evaluating resources can make themselves stand out.

2.3 Infrastructure risk

Once an oil company starts production, there is risk in the type of infrastructure it has designed and constructed to produce its product. Refineries are designed to crack certain kinds of crude into certain kinds of product. Some refineries are flexible and can switch crude mix and product mix, but if, for example, an oil company's refinery is designed to take low-quality, high-sulphur crude from Russia, there is only so

---

6 J Michael Medina *et al*, "Take or Litigate: Enforcing the Plain Meaning of the Takeor-Pay Clause in Natural Gas Contracts", 40 *Arkansas Law Review* 185, 1986, p 187, http://fdlaw.com/articles/Take or Litigate.pdf.

7 "F.T.C. Approves Chevron-Gulf Deal", *The New York Times*, 25 October 1984, www.nytimes.com/1984/10/25/business/ftc-approves-chevron-gulf-deal.html.

8 *Gulf Oil Corp v FPC*, 563 F 2d 588, (3d Cir 1977), https://casetext.com/case/gulf-oil-corp-v-f-p-c.

9 *Gulf Oil Corp v Federal Energy Reg Com'n*, 575 F 2d 67 (3d Cir 1978), https://casetext.com/case/gulf-oil-corp-v-federal-energy-reg-comn.

10 "North Sea Oil and Gas Drilling Activity Plunges to All-Time Low," *Bloomberg*, 7 October 2016, www.bloomberg.com/news/articles/2016-10-07/north-sea-oil-and-gas-drilling-activity-plunges-to-all-time-low

11 "BBC News – North Sea oil: Falling off the cycle?", *BBC*, 27 September 2016, www.bbc.com/news/uk-scotland-37475381.

much it may be able to do with that crude. The market may be seeking jet fuel or gasoline, and that refinery may only be good for number 6 industrial fuel, which may not be in demand given the Paris Agreement and given the European emissions allowance scheme.[12] So, the company may only be able to sell that kind of crude to big cargo ships or to independently owned refineries.

Historically, the European market has had more demand for diesel than for gasoline for cars, and the North American market is more gasoline-oriented than diesel-oriented. So, if a company has a refinery sitting in north western Europe that can flip runs between diesel and gasoline, it could have a valuable asset. Every week or every month, it could compare the refinery margins and plan its runs based on where the margins are. But the refinery business is a volatile business, so many of the major integrated oil and gas companies are selling off their smaller refineries.[13]

2.4 Business and financial risk

There are a variety of business and financial risks associated with the oil industry. Although a senior oil executive considers these risks at each stage of the value chain, he or she will weigh their advance possibility from the very beginning.

One such risk involves the potential for large tax bills. Because the oil industry is viewed as a golden goose throughout the world, a company that is drawing up agreements with a host government will want to analyse thoroughly the types of taxes that government might impose. Chad, for example, has served a multi-billion-dollar fine for underpaying royalties to Exxon Mobile Corp.[14]

There are also risks surrounding oil prices. 2008 and 2014 proved how volatile oil prices can be, and the market saw similar price drops in the 1980s and 1990s. However, the examples in 2008 and 2014 differed slightly from the ones in the 1980s and the 1990s. In the 1980s, prices cratered because there was a recession, and demand fell off. In the 1990s, they declined after the Gulf War. In 2008 and 2014, prices plummeted partially because of a decrease in demand due to the Great Recession and partially because of a glut in supply.[15] Saudi Arabia announced in 2014 that it would not reduce its production, and oil prices fell from between $100 and $110 per barrel in the first quarter of 2014 to between $40 and $50 per barrel in the first quarter of 2015.[16, 17] For oil producers, this was a shock, and it was also a shock to the share price because much of the share price is based on commodity prices. It is good for consumers who get, in effect, a tax break. It is bad for oil and gas company employees, who face the risk of losing their jobs.

12 United Nations Framework Convention on Climate Change, "Summary of the Paris Agreement", http://bigpicture.unfccc.int/%20-%20content-the-paris-agreement.

13 "Global oil majors look to shed refineries as crude prices rebound", *Reuters*, 17 June 2016, www.reuters.com/article/us-oil-refineries-sales-idUSKCN0Z30ET.

14 "Exxon Is Hit With Fine From Chad Five Times Country's GDP," *Bloomberg*, 6 October 2016, www.bloomberg.com/news/articles/2016-10-06/exxon-mobil-disagrees-with-chadian-court-royalties-ruling-itydgz6c.

15 "Why Oil Prices Went Down So Far So Fast", *Bloomberg*, 29 October 2014, www.bloomberg.com/news/articles/2014-10-29/why-oil-prices-went-down-so-far-so-fast.

16 "Saudi Arabia: We'll never cut oil production", CNN, 22 December 2014, http://money.cnn.com/2014/12/22/news/economy/saudi-arabia-oil-production/.

17 "Crude oil prices started 2015 relatively low, ended the year lower", US Energy Information Administration, 6 January 2016, www.eia.gov/todayinenergy/detail.php?id=24432.

Another consideration for senior oil executives is the cost of capital. Because oil production is risky, many oil companies have had capitalisations that are lower leveraged than other types of industry, with more equity compared to debt – but there is debt. Oil companies in the North Sea that took on debt based on proved reserves and the valuation of proved reserves are currently struggling as the region's oil reserves perform below expectations,[18] and the US Securities Exchange Commission recently pressured Exxon to slash the value of its proved reserves because of the value in crude oil prices.[19]

Finally, a senior oil executive will want to weigh the potential actions of activist shareholders. When oil prices went down from $110 per barrel to below $50 per barrel, the stocks were hit. The value of oil company stocks is partially driven by commodity prices, partially driven by size, and partially driven by quality of management. Activist shareholders will often come in and seek to require a sell-off of assets if they view those assets as non-essential so the company will make a special distribution to its shareholders. When oil prices dropped, activist shareholders at many companies likely began to consider their strategy for forcing a dividend or a stock buyback or a selloff.[20, 21] Even major integrated oil and gas companies are not immune to those kinds of pressure.

2.5 Political risk

At the start of any new venture, a major integrated oil and gas company will want to consider the variety of potential political risks associated with the endeavour. For example, a company could be in a productive field in a foreign country and everything could be going as planned, and then the country could face a political consequence such as falling under US sanctions.

There is a gas field in the North Sea called the Rhum Field, which was 50% owned and operated by BP and 50% owned and operated by the National Iranian Oil Company. When the European Union and the United States placed sanctions on Iran, BP ended up having to shut the field, and it was a substantial supply of gas for the United Kingdom.[22] Then, when they decided later to reopen the field, BP had to obtain a special derogation from the UK Government and from the US Treasury.[23, 24] So, in any oil venture, it is important for a company to consider its partners and any consequences to its partnerships, and that could change over time.

Another consideration is royalties. The United States has seen a shale revolution

18 "North Sea oil companies in danger amid debt spillage", *Financial Times*, 5 February 2016, www.ft.com/content/e67e4dac-ca76-11e5-a8ef-ea66e967dd44.

19 "S.E.C. Is Latest to Look Into Exxon Mobil's Workings", *The New York Times*, 20 September 2016, www.nytimes.com/2016/09/21/business/energy-environment/exxon-climate-change.html?_r=0.

20 "Oil, Gas Investors Sharpening Activist Knives", *Law360*, 8 May 2015, www.law360.com/articles/653867/oil-gas-investors-sharpening-activist-knives.

21 "Activist investors dig deep in energy company bets", *Reuters*, 19 February 2015, www.reuters.com/article/energy-activists-idUSL1N0VR2JG20150219.

22 "BP to restart North Sea gas field half-owned by Iran", *Reuters*, 17 October 2014, www.reuters.com/article/bp-gas-iran-idUSL6N0SC3Z120141017.

23 "Rhum North Sea gas field to restart production", Department of Energy and Climate Change, 22 October 2013, www.gov.uk/government/news/rhum-north-sea-gas-field-to-restart-production.

24 Total SA, Form 20-F for the year ended 31 December 2015, p 71 www.sec.gov/Archives/edgar/data/879764/000119312516506029/d83747d20f.htm.

in recent years.[25] Why has it happened in the United States and not as much elsewhere? Part of the reason is that in the United States, most of the land where the oil is produced is privately owned. In most places in the world, the oil resources are owned by the state, even if the land is owned by private landowners. In the United Kingdom, mineral rights belong to the Queen. There is much less incentive for oil companies to pursue shale oil elsewhere – in fact, it is just the opposite. Landowners are likely to protest companies' drilling on their private property for minerals if they cannot benefit from the drilling. In the United States, the landowners want companies to buy their mineral rights.

Of course, in a situation where an oil company is working with large numbers of individual private owners, the chance for legal disputes increases. In the United States, royalty holders have brought many lawsuits against the oil companies for more money. For example, in the state of Alaska in Prudhoe Bay, royalty holders sued the producers over and over again for more money.[26] That type of political consideration would be an ordinary course-of-business risk for oil companies.

Some of these political risks can be mitigated through investment treaties and contracts, and the major provision of such a contract is called a stabilisation clause. With a stabilisation clause, the oil company is making the case that it is signing an agreement into the legal world in its current state – the tax regime as it currently exists, the environmental regime as it currently exists, and the consent regime as it currently exists. If, during the term of the agreement, the government changes the regime in a way that is adverse to the company – and what is adverse is usually highly negotiated – then the government will compensate the company accordingly.

Stabilisation clauses are highly controversial because they lock in governments, and they are often criticised for their environmental provisions. A study conducted for the International Finance Corporation and the United Nations Special Representative of the Secretary-General on Business and Human Rights that examined stabilisation clauses around the world found that many stabilisation clauses are drafted in a way that can serve to exempt investors from complying with new laws created to protect environmental and human rights.[27]

When working with stabilisation clauses, it is important for a senior oil executive to be able to strike the right balance between safeguarding the company and respecting the host country's ability to enact environmental and social protections.

3. Transportation

Once an oil company has a product set for transport, it has to consider all of the potential risks in transporting that product. Typically, the company will need to treat the oil first. Usually there are oilfield pipes that will go from the well to a central

25 "The US shale revolution", *Financial Times*, 24 April 2015, www.ft.com/content/2ded7416-e930-11e4-a71a-00144feab7de.

26 "$43M Deal Ok'd In Securities Suit Over BP Spill", *Law360*, 9 April 2009, www.law360.com/articles/96237/43m-deal-ok-d-in-securities-suit-over-bp-spill.

27 Shemberg, Andrea, *Stabilization Clauses and Human Rights: a research project conducted for IFC and the United Nations Special Representative of the Secretary-General on Business and Humans Rights*. May 2009, p 37. http://www.ifc.org/wps/wcm/connect/9feb5b00488555eab8c4fa6a6515bb18/Stabilization+Paper.pdf?MOD=AJPERES.

treating station and then to a pipeline that takes the oil to a point closer to market, so those costs need to be accounted for. Many of these types of risk can be managed through contracts and money; yet a company can spend a significant amount on trying to mitigate risk, only to find that something still falls apart.

3.1 Shocks and disasters

It is not only the risks of the business that keep a senior oil executive up at night, it is the shocks – those things that happen unexpectedly. One such shock could be an environmental spill or some other kind of disaster, such as the Deepwater Horizon disaster or the Exxon Valdez oil spill – the type of calamity that will end up costing billions of dollars to remedy and will affect the perception of the brand globally. These types of catastrophe also tend to involve a variety of safety risks, including risks to company employees. The Deepwater Horizon explosions, for example, killed 11 people.[28]

Associated with all of this are legal violations. There are numerous regulations and laws – the Clean Water Act, the Clean Air Act, Environmental Protection Agency regulations – that have guidelines on every aspect of drilling and production, and if a company violates them, then that company can face major penalties. Even if it does not, it could still lose its licence or its lease to drill.

3.2 Location risk

The location of oil reserves is a major consideration for oil exploration, and it can also make a difference when it comes to transportation. When Kazakhstan came out of the Soviet orbit, it had limited access to pipelines, and companies had to use rail transport to move the oil, which was expensive. Even today, oil companies in Kazakhstan transport much of their oil via rail,[29] and oil companies are currently facing similar issues in North Dakota.[30] Pipelines are limited, so companies have relied on trucks and rail for transport, and there have been some accidents as a result.[31]

Another example where location could affect oil transport: to build an international pipeline from the oil fields of Chad to a port in Cameroon, an oil company would need to have an international agreement between Chad and Cameroon. Then, each government would need an agreement with the shippers, and the pipeline would also need an agreement with the shippers. These government agreements could prove challenging to negotiate, making it difficult for the company to move its product.

Then, there is competition. A company that is considering building pipelines from Uganda to ports through Tanzania may eventually decide that that route is ideal, but before it starts building, it will weigh the risks and benefits of its

---

28 "Deepwater Horizon's Final Hours", The New York Times, 25 December 2010, www.nytimes.com/2010/12/26/us/26spill.html?pagewanted=all.

29 "Moving crude by rail in Kazakhstan", Chevron, 23 February 2015, www.chevron.com/stories/moving-crude-by-rail-in-kazakhstan.

30 "North Dakota Oil Pipeline Battle: Who's Fighting and Why", *The New York Times*, 26 August 2016, www.nytimes.com/2016/11/02/us/north-dakota-oil-pipeline-battle-whos-fighting-and-why.html.

31 "Heimdal, North Dakota, Evacuated After Fiery Oil Train Crash", *NBC News*, 6 May 2015, www.nbcnews.com/news/us-news/heimdal-north-dakota-evacuated-after-fiery-oil-train-crash-n354686.

alternatives. Kenya could provide a more viable alternative. Mombasa is closer than Tanga, but it is not that much closer. The company could also have considered building routes through Ethiopia or Djibouti. Ethiopia is mountainous, which could make the project more difficult, but it is possible that those routes could prove to be commercially viable. There may also be diplomatic reasons for some companies to want to strike up a good relationship with one of these countries, and an international pipeline and transportation corridor would be a good way to do that. A multitude of considerations can go into building an international pipeline, especially when it serves to break down the barrier of being an isolated country in East Africa that is cut off from the sea.

Of course, once a company's oil reaches the sea, if it is headed there, there are additional transportation risks to consider. The Exxon Valdez disaster has illustrated that ships can be a problem, but aside from any concerns about catastrophes, there are financial considerations. Ship charter rates are volatile, although a company can use derivatives to hedge them. Major integrated oil and gas companies may also consider shipping as an alternative form of transport for gas. Typically, when a company produces natural gas, the gas goes into pipelines because pipelines are the cheapest and safest ways of transporting natural gas – but more and more liquefied natural gas (LNG) can be transported on cargo ships that take it to gasification facilities at ports. Many of the decisions surrounding natural gas transportation and storage rely on a company's ability to find a balance between demand, price and environmental concerns.

4. Marketing

Most of the major integrated oil and gas companies have trading operations to market their crude, and they may do it under contracts. Alternatively, they may use their own refineries to refine the crude into a product such as gasoline to sell to their own petrol stations or at ports or airports, making them subject to market price risk. In that case, they would have market price risk on the crude oil and on the refined product end, and that is a normal business risk. However, companies that take on too much risk may find it challenging to satisfy the requirements of third-party lenders.[32]

Finding oil requires massive investments. Usually, when companies put together financial agreements with third-party lenders, the lenders want to see monthly or six-monthly operating projects, and they will put together quarterly life-of-loan and debt coverage ratios. Then, when the ratios are calculated, if the company does not meet them, it is an event of default.

The bill Chad recently issued to Exxon could be an example of a political risk that could hurt a company's lender relationships. Historically, oil companies have used deep equity cushions, but much of Exxon's Chad–Cameroon Pipeline project was financed on a non-recourse debt basis,[33] which is unusual for an upstream

32 *Oil and Gas Exploration and Production Lending*, Office of the Comptroller of the Currency, March 2016, www.occ.gov/publications/publications-by-type/comptrollers-handbook/pub-ch-og.pdf.

33 "IFC Signs Loan for Chad-Cameroon Pipeline Project," International Finance Corporation, 21 June 2001, http://ifcext.ifc.org/ifcext/pressroom/ifcpressroom.nsf/1f70cd9a07d692d685256ee1001cdd37/69d3e7e2c40eae6185256a72007085d2?OpenDocument.

project, although it is not unusual for a pipeline. Chad is a country that is aligned with the United States and Nigeria in fighting Boko Haram, and many of Boko Haram's kidnapping victims have been abducted to Cameroon.[34, 35] It is possible that this tax is Chad's way of insisting on more help from the US Government. With a large bill to pay and a project financed with debt, Exxon's executives will need to find a way to manage the company's credit agreements and financial ratios while also keeping an eye out for any future political risks that Chad may impose.

In addition, a political situation such as Chad's can provide safety risks to an oil company's employees. Although it is necessary for oil companies to go where the resources are, those companies' senior executives should weigh the risks of putting employees or contractors in regions where they could be injured or worse.

5. Point of consumption

Once an oil company has taken its product all the way through the value chain to the point of consumption, it must consider the larger global market and how it affects its product sales strategy.

Oil can be stored, but natural gas can only be stored in more limited locations such as depleted reservoirs or salt domes and associated gas is often simply flared or vented as a consequence. Unless battery technology improves dramatically, electricity has not been able to be stored at all. That makes those three fuel industries quite different. For oil, if the spot market goes into what is called a contango – where forward prices are higher than current prices – traders store the oil, waiting for higher prices to come, and anyone with storage capacity is in the catbird seat, flying high. Oil can be stored in tank farms and also in oil cargo ships. With the current global oversupply of oil, it is in oil traders' best interest to fill cargo ships and put them in international waters while they wait for oil prices to rise, as that is one way of hedging oil price risk.

The oil and gas business has become very big because of the availability of oil and natural gas resources, which, starting in the 1970s, have been held mostly by national oil companies as opposed to the independent companies, such as Chevron and Exxon.[36] Nation states such as Ghana and Indonesia have basically held those resources for their own national oil companies to develop. For an independent company to enter the game, it must consider what it can bring to the table to entice a host country to let it have access to the resource. One thing an independent company usually has going for it is strong management capability and experience managing really large projects. Some of that management includes overseeing whole resource development programmes like in Chad, and some of it is LNG management.

Once a company takes over an LNG project, it needs to make a number of strategic decisions. It will consider, for example, where the gasification facilities are

34 "Boko Haram: State of emergency declared around Lake Chad", BBC, 9 November 2015, www.bbc.com/news/world-africa-34771128.

35 "Boko Haram attacks Cameroon with kidnapped girls", *Al Jazeera*, 1 April 2016, www.aljazeera.com/news/2016/03/weakened-boko-haram-sends-girl-bombers-cameroon-160331175822717.html.

36 "National oil companies: Really Big Oil", *The Economist*, 10 August 2006, www.economist.com/node/7276986.

located and where they can sell. Take Atlantic LNG, for example. It was built to be a major exporter of LNG – gas – to the United States, but in 2016 very few of its cargoes went to the United States; most went to Europe and South America.[37] The price for natural gas in Buenos Aires is much higher than the price in Boston because of the availability of shale gas in the United States. The price of natural gas in Spain and France is higher than in the United States. So, the owners of Atlantic LNG are diverting their cargoes to the higher-value markets, which was not the original purpose of the project. This just shows how the global market can change quickly. A company must be resilient and able to adapt to keep its profits afloat.

6. Technology-driven market changes

As technology advances, there is the potential for a significant number of major changes in the oil market, and many of those changes may work to reduce the price of oil. Oil exploration and development have become high-tech, so companies will be using technology to reduce risk and increase efficiency. The shale revolution in the United States occurred because of advances in technology,[38] and companies are seeing greater and greater capacity for deep-water drilling.[39] Alternative and renewable energy sources such as windmills and solar power are only becoming more competitive. Every year, voltaic cells are lighter, cheaper and more efficient, which is why megawatts produced by solar has increased so dramatically over the last decade.[40]

The electric car could hurt the oil companies unless they are supplying coal or gas to power plants that are producing much more electricity to support them. The car companies are also putting large amounts of money into self-driving cars,[41] and those cars may soon reach a tipping point when they take over the market.[42]

To stay competitive, major integrated oil and gas company senior executives will want to consider who their customers are, how those customers are currently using their products, and how they can pivot their business initiatives to enable those customers to continue to use their products as technology allows for more possibilities. One example: current natural gas customers are using it primarily for oil fuels, but they are also using it more and more for electric generation, which oil and gas companies can tie to electric cars as they become more popular.

7. Black swans

To prepare for future surprises, oil and gas senior executives consider a range of low-

---

37 "Atlantic CEO: Gas deficit getting worse", *The Trinidad Guardian Newspaper*, 10 November 2016, www.guardian.co.tt/business/2016-11-10/atlantic-ceo-gas-deficit-getting-worse.

38 Brown, Stephen PA, and Mine Yucel, "The Shale Gas and Tight Oil Boom: U.S. States' Economic Gains and Vulnerabilities", October 2013, Council on Foreign Relations, November 2016. www.cfr.org/united-states/shale-gas-tight-oil-boom-us-states-economic-gains-vulnerabilities/p31568.

39 "Deepwater technology," Exxon Mobil, http://corporate.exxonmobil.com/en/technology/deepwater-drilling/technology/overview.

40 "A Cheap Material Boosts Solar Cells by 50 Percent", *MIT Technology Review*, 30 January 2015, www.technologyreview.com/s/534511/a-cheap-material-boosts-solar-cells-by-50-percent/.

41 "Self-driving cars: from 2020 you will become a permanent backseat driver," *The Guardian*, 13 September 2015, www.theguardian.com/technology/2015/sep/13/self-driving-cars-bmw-google-2020-driving.

42 "Self-Driving Cars Will Take Over By 2040", *Forbes*, 25 September 2012, www.forbes.com/sites/economics/2012/09/25/self-driving-cars-will-take-over-by-2040/-2b2f8adb21f2.

probability, high-impact scenarios that could occur over the next 12 months. As of now, one such scenario could be a China collapse. Another could be an ISIS takeover of Saudi Arabia. If Vladimir Putin invades a country such as Estonia that triggers a NATO response, there could be war in Europe. There could be war in the South China Sea. There could be consequences to a Trump presidency and the partisan politics in the United States. In all of these scenarios, there will be conflict of interest issues and people ready to take advantage of them, and the oil and gas companies will want to be prepared for what might happen if they do.

A message from Thomas Dimitroff, consulting editor to this edition:
I first met Douglas Nordlinger in April 2011. Our respective firms were retained to support the Government of South Sudan to rationalise its petroleum sector in anticipation of and following the country's formal secession from the Republic of Sudan. We travelled together to Juba via Nairobi on multiple occasions between 2011 and 2013. I was continuously struck with Douglas's clarity of thought, his excellent judgement and drafting skills and learned much from him. But it was his qualities of integrity and compassion as a human being, demonstrated through his pragmatic and sensitive engagement with our client representatives and colleagues, that stand out in my memory. We connected again by telephone in November 2016, after I learned that he had been battling an illness. Anxious to be productive again, he enthusiastically embraced my suggestion that he write a chapter in this volume. The tenacity with which he produced the draft – within weeks of our conversation – and its quality were seamless with the person and work product that I knew during the time I was privileged to work together with Douglas. It was with tremendous sadness that I learned of his death through a mutual colleague in May 2017.

Risk in the gas value chain

David Baker
White & Case
Paul Griffin
White & Case, University of Dundee

1. Introduction

This chapter seeks to assess some of the main risks that arise when the several separate contracts which together constitute the relevant value chain butt against each other. For some, this is a study of 'contract to contract' risk. This chapter makes this assessment by reference to an example of a gas to power value chain (the energy chain) and by following the molecules from the point of production of hydrocarbons to the point of consumption of power. The example comprises diverse parties and several agreements in relation to the following matters:

- the transportation of gas by pipeline from a producing field to a liquefaction plant, made between the producers/owners of that gas and the owners of that pipeline (Gas Transportation Agreement);
- the receipt of gas at a liquefaction plant, its conversion to liquefied natural gas (LNG) and the delivery of LNG for tanker loading, made between the owners of the liquefaction plant and the producers/owners of that gas and, subsequently, LNG (Gas Tolling Agreement);
- the receipt of LNG onto a tanker, the transportation of that LNG by sea from the state of production to the state of regasification and the making of that LNG available for delivery to a regasification terminal, made between the owner of that LNG tanker and the producers/owners of that LNG (LNG Shipping Agreement);
- the sale of LNG by its producers/owners to a purchaser of that LNG at the point of unloading from the LNG tanker (LNG Sale Agreement);
- the receipt of LNG at a regasification terminal, its conversion to gas and the delivery of gas for transportation away from that regasification terminal, made between the owner of the regasification terminal and the purchaser/owner of that LNG and, subsequently, gas (Regasification Agreement);
- the transportation of gas by pipeline from the regasification terminal to a power station, made between the purchaser/owner of that gas to the owner of that pipeline (Gas Distribution Agreement);
- the sale of gas by its purchaser/owner at the point of entry to the power station, made between the purchaser/owner of that gas and the owner of the power station (Gas Sale Agreement); and
- the consumption of gas by the owner of the power station for the purposes of generating electricity and the supply of electricity through wires to the consumers of that power under regulated arrangements (Power Supply Agreement).

This example has little integration of infrastructure and little integration of contractual interest. It constitutes a chain of linked and complementary contractual arrangements providing for transportation by pipeline and maritime vessel, conversion of gas and LNG, and sale and purchase of several commodities. These commodities are, in turn, petroleum at the point of production, processed gas, LNG, gas again, then power. It also contemplates very long distances from the point of petroleum production to the point of power consumption, with many relevant jurisdictions, not least separate states of production of petroleum and consumption of electricity.

This chapter is written with reference primarily to English law, often the choice of governing law for contracting parties where there is a choice to be made in respect of the contracts of the energy chain. Also, this chapter assumes that these arrangements are made at the same time in relation to new developments on the basis of molecules moving from the point of petroleum production to the point of electricity consumption.

There are several separate projects which appear in the energy chain (liquefaction facilities, regasification facilities, pipelines, power plants, etc) and each of these is likely to have the horizontal participation of state entities, project developers, construction contractors and project lenders. Those project arrangements are addressed elsewhere in this book. This chapter contemplates instead the vertical arrangements under which the several contracts of the energy chain relate to one another.

The growth of international energy trade over the last decade or so, particularly in relation to LNG, means that this type of chain is becoming a rare model for new developments. The moves of energy markets towards competition and the presence of commodity traders in many parts of the energy chain have meant that flexibility of contractual arrangements is prized. Also, those arrangements are of increasingly short duration. Perhaps most significantly, the presence of aggregators and portfolio participants in the LNG business has meant that interests are becoming more disintegrated. However, that is not to say that the issues of the energy chains are any less important. Whereas they might not be the precedent for new developments in the international energy sector, these arrangements form the basis on which a great deal of the world's energy is bought and sold, and this will remain the case for many years to come.

2. Consistency along the chain

In principle, the parties to the several contracts in the energy chain will be seeking to achieve an alignment of their respective rights, obligations and liabilities under those connected contractual arrangements. Many matters are, however, likely necessarily to militate against achieving this aim.

2.1 Regulatory arrangements

There is likely to be little consistency of regulatory arrangements along the energy chain. There may well be direct state or government participation in relation to production of petroleum; state ownership or industry or competition regulation in relation to the transportation of gas and the production of LNG; state and treaty (state-to-state) arrangements in relation to maritime transportation of LNG by tanker; and state ownership or industry or competition regulation in relation to regasification, gas transportation, and power generation and distribution. It is also likely that different elements of the energy chain will see different balances of domestic and international interests.

2.2 State participation

State participation, fiscal arrangements and taxation will be different under each of the separate elements of the chain or in respect of each interested state. These differences may give rise to potential commercial gain or loss and will be likely to influence the overall contractual structure, not least by reference to the points of transfer of title to the respective commodities. In addition to this participation by a host state, there may be considerations of participation by other states, particularly by those having consumer markets along the energy chain. For example, it may be that state entities of those other states take complementary interests in the host state in order to facilitate the trade of petroleum products.

2.3 Duration

Among these several contractual arrangements, there is also likely to be little uniformity of contract duration. The duration of production interests is likely to be different from those of transportation and processing arrangements, and the sale and purchase arrangements may well be different again, with certain matters (eg, power supply) being provided for under regulated arrangements of very short duration. The highly capital-intensive nature of much of the related infrastructure will invite the participation of third-party providers of capital, and they will have their own views on the duration of the relevant arrangements.

2.4 Changing circumstances

Even if all these diverse arrangements are aligned at the outset, the necessarily long-term nature of the creation and operation of this value chain will mean that circumstances will necessarily change over time. Matters such as forced access to pipelines and other facilities and the introduction of competition and shorter-term trading arrangements over the long duration of these arrangements will have effect to falsify many of the assumptions on which the earlier contracts and investments were made.

2.5 Confidentiality

Each of the many parties to the several contracts of the energy chain will be looking to enhance its potential profits and minimise its potential risks and costs, in the context of the overall energy chain. Events happening further up the energy chain are likely to have an effect on the rights, obligations and liabilities of those further along the energy chain. These effects under adjacent contracts may be direct, while others may be indirect. The ability to respond to these events will be enhanced by proximity in the energy chain but, even then, the parties may be poorly informed of those events. The contracts of the energy chain are typically of high value and of commercial and operational sensitivity. They are likely to be cloaked in confidentiality and secrecy provisions which inhibit the movement of information along the energy chain.

2.6 Laws

Each of the contracts in the energy chain will be negotiated among the relevant parties and will be reflected in writing, in detail and at length. The interpretation of each of these contracts will be made in accordance with the law chosen by the parties to govern their contract or, in the unlikely event that none is chosen, then in accordance with the applicable rules on conflict of laws. Even where the parties from one contract to another are able to achieve an alignment of their connected commercial arrangements, the construction and interpretation of the terms of those arrangements from time to time may come to frustrate them under the application of different governing laws of those contracts.

2.7 Dispute resolution

Whereas parties to connected energy contracts along the chain may look to bring disputes with common elements to a common forum for resolution, this consolidation will rarely be achieved. A more likely circumstance is that these linked contracts along the chain may provide for litigation or arbitration and with bespoke references to expert determination for more technical matters and mediation or other non-binding processes in particular circumstances. Although it is the case that parties to contracts in the international gas business will almost always choose arbitration for the resolution of their disputes, the nature and extent of those respective arbitration agreements will differ markedly in relation to the relevant law, seat, institutional participation and other applicable arrangements.

2.8 Relationships

The alignment and consistency of these multiple contracts and relationships are difficult to achieve at the outset and in circumstances of performance in accordance with expectations. These difficulties are multiplied over time and are likely to become unbearable in circumstances of material events beyond the parties' control, and of breach, failure to perform, or insolvency. Further, the resolution of these matters may be made more difficult along the energy chain as a buyer under one contract becomes a seller under the next one, and so on.

3. Some particular considerations

In seeking to manage these risks and to effect a set of contractual arrangements that is most likely to minimise the risk of loss and maximise the prospect of gain over time, the parties to each of these contractual arrangements are likely to have particular regard to the following matters, among others.

3.1 Alignment of revenues, costs and remedies

The risks along the energy chain are reduced where the various parts of the chain are aligned and the risks, costs and rewards of the several projects are distributed across the chain through consistent, back-to-back arrangements.

There are arrangements under which the provisions of one contract are responsive to the circumstances under other connected contracts. For example, if a seller is relieved from liability for non-delivery by reason of *force majeure* under the LNG Sale Agreement, will that relief entitle the buyer to corresponding relief in relation to the same non-delivery under the Regasification Agreement? At a more prosaic level, will the delivery flexibility and related notice provisions under the LNG Sale Agreement be such as to enable the buyer to benefit from corresponding flexibility under the Regasification Agreement?

The less integration there is of participation in the several elements of the energy chain, the greater will be the challenge of effecting these aligned, back-to-back contracts. The greater the extent to which contract terms are reflected through the several contracts of the energy chain, the greater will be the parties' opportunity to respond to delays, failures, disruptions and changes of circumstances in relation to the several commodities, services and contracts of the energy chain.

These considerations of integration may also extend to matters of failure or even termination along the energy chain, in the manner of similar considerations of cross-default or other rights at the horizontal, project level.

3.2 Payment and 'pay when paid'

In connected, contractual arrangements such as those in the energy chain, it can be argued that it is the price paid by the final consumer (in this case, of power in the final market) which then percolates up through the chain, enabling the supplier under the Power Supply Agreement to pay the seller under the Gas Sale Agreement, enabling the seller under the Gas Sale Agreement to pay the transporter under the Gas Distribution Agreement and the terminal owner under the Regasification Agreement, and so on.

In closely connected circumstances such as these, a party may take the position that its obligation to pay a supplier of a commodity or a service is dependent on its receipt of revenues from the parties next along the chain. The usual provisions for billing and payment may be subject to supplemental clauses providing that what would otherwise be an obligation to pay will be subject to related receipts under identified contracts along the chain.

This type of 'pay when paid' clause is perhaps more prevalent in the horizontal arrangements of each project and particularly between project developers and sub-contractors. But even in those circumstances, these provisions are emotive and, in some jurisdictions, subject to legal restriction. Also, in a sector where debt finance is customary in project development, the restrictions imposed by lenders on flows of money are likely to reduce the presence of these provisions.

3.3 Letters of credit, guarantees and escrows

The energy chain is constituted by a series of commodity and service contracts which are of long duration and high value. In arrangements such as these, the respective suppliers will be concerned to ensure that payments will be made as required under those contracts.

As a result of the long duration and high value of contracts in the energy chain, suppliers will be particularly focused on the creditworthiness of their counterparties. An assessment will be made as to whether additional credit support in respect of payment obligations will be required. This assessment will often be carried out as part of the initial financial and credit due diligence. Based on this assessment, credit enhancement in the form of letters of credit, guarantees or escrow arrangements may be negotiated.

Credit enhancement may also be required where there are specific jurisdictional risks around certainty of payment or if a project is debt-financed. Lenders, as part of their bankability requirements, may demand acceptable credit protection in respect of payment obligations.

The choice of credit protection will typically reflect particular jurisdictional circumstances and relevant counterparty commercial preference. For example, where a guarantee from a creditworthy counterparty is not possible, a letter of credit from an appropriately rated financial institution may be procured instead.

An escrow held with a neutral third-party agent will provide surety to both purchaser and seller. The payment funds will be held by the third-party agent subject to the terms of the escrow arrangement. Typically the payment will be released to the supplier only upon the third-party agent receiving evidence that the supplier has met the contractual delivery requirements of the relevant commodity.

As the energy chain is interconnected, a failure by one party to pay could disrupt the chain. The commercial effect of a letter of credit, guarantee or escrow is similar. Suppliers seek to ensure that a creditworthy third party will fulfil payment obligations if the counterparty fails to do so. A benefit of an escrow arrangement, from the buyer's perspective, is that as part of the escrow release conditions, the buyer can also seek protection that the relevant payment will be released from escrow only if the relevant commodity is delivered in accordance with the contractual agreement.

3.4 Commodities to be sold and purchased

Contracts along the energy chain will establish the quantities of the relevant commodity to be sold and purchased over time. The overall quantity to be delivered over the course of the contract, as well as the monthly and yearly delivery schedules, will often be predetermined.

Each of the participants in the chain will be looking to perform its obligations, whether as the supplier or recipient of commodities or services. The energy chain includes contracts in respect of petroleum products and electricity. These are complex commodities in themselves, and the complexity is increased by the connected nature of those contracts. The establishment and enforcement of obligations of delivery and acceptance will be dependent on the specification and quantity of that commodity. For example, the Gas Tolling Agreement will entail the delivery and taking of natural gas at entry to the liquefaction plant and the delivery and taking of corresponding specifications and quantities of LNG at the loading arm from the liquefaction plant. This LNG will not only be a matter under the Gas Tolling Agreement, but also a matter under the LNG Shipping Agreement and the LNG Sale Agreement.

The point of production will see raw petroleum which will be processed to the extent required to produce natural gas of a composition and quality appropriate for delivery to the transporter under the Gas Transportation Agreement. The redelivery by the transporter is likely to be subject to the requirements for natural gas as specified in the Gas Tolling Agreement, and so on. The composition and quantities of these hydrocarbons will be provided for at each stage of the energy chain with account being taken for necessary uses and losses along the way. The respective base quantities under each of the contracts are likely to be established some time in advance, with shorter-term flexibilities. Obligations of delivery and acceptance of commodities and provision of services levels are likely to have tolerances in relation to contractual performance and these will vary from contract to contract. In addition to these matters, the necessary measurements themselves may be subject to different standards or procedures, with provision for retrospective adjustment at times of inaccuracy. The management of these connected operations along the energy chain is a difficult task, with visibility along the chain being often restricted.

3.5 Failure to deliver or take

The establishment of the respective commodity obligations and their integration along the chain will be difficult in the context of contractual performance. These matters will be more difficult still in circumstances of commodity failures, whether of delivery or acceptance. For example, in a case where LNG is not made available for delivery under the Gas Tolling Agreement, then that non-delivery will have consequences under the LNG Shipping Agreement and under the LNG Sale Agreement, and so on. The nature of any resultant breach or non-performance will differ under each of the contracts in the chain – for example, the non-delivery of gas, the non-delivery of LNG, the non-performance of transportation or throughput commitments and the non-delivery of electricity. Also different will be the negotiated flexibility or tolerances applicable in those circumstances and the steps of alternative performance or mitigation to be taken in each case.

Looking at each contract individually, it will be usual for the parties in international gas and energy contracts to favour defined or liquidated compensation in the event of non-performance. Not only do these provisions enable a simple calculation of the resulting payment, but they also provide for any recovery of sums due. However, such provisions are not ubiquitous and within contracts and from contract to contract matters may be left open, with the parties pursuing damages at large, whether in court or pursuant to the applicable arbitration agreement. The sector is also noted for the long duration of its contractual arrangements and the prevalence of 'take-or-pay' or 'ship-or-pay' structures to the effect of enhancing the reliability of returns on the considerable capital expenditures involved. These structures entail an analysis of debt claims or damages at large.

Liquidated damages are fixed or ascertainable sums expressed in a contract as sums payable in the case of specified breaches of obligations. They can be distinguished from general damages at large and this distinction is particularly relevant for the purposes of this chapter, as liquidated damages provisions are commonly found in the contracts of the energy chain. In circumstances where the proof of actual damage may be difficult or time consuming and there is a continuing obligation of delivering and taking further supplies, the parties are likely to favour a means of recovery that is easy to operate and prompt to apply. Where obligations of delivery and taking occur regularly over long periods, it is seen as unappealing to have to prove breach and demonstrate loss in respect of each potential failure to deliver a contractually agreed instalment of, say, LNG.

In relation to many of the contracts of the energy chain, the difference between a claim for damages for breach of contract and a claim for payment of a contractual debt may be significant. Many of these contracts will have takeorpay provisions or throughput or capacity commitments which could give rise to either characterisation, depending on their particular terms. A debt is a sum of money established under an agreement as payable by one party to the other in respect of the performance of a specified obligation, or the occurrence of a specific event. A claim for damages will arise where a party has failed to perform a primary obligation under an agreement, other than an obligation to pay a debt. The rules in relation to damages do not apply in relation to a claim for a debt. A party claiming payment of a debt will have to show that it has performed its obligations (ie, that the debt is properly owing), but has no need to prove loss, and questions of remoteness and mitigation, and considerations of penalties, do not apply.

These are among the considerations which will militate against a consistency of like provisions under connected contracts. That is the case at the outset and more so over time. The growth of trading and portfolio development in the international LNG business over recent years may have enhanced flexibility at times of non-performance, but it has done little to enable a predictable linking of remedies along the energy chain.

3.6 Take-or-pay

In a number of the commodity contracts of the energy chain, the buyer's obligation will be expressed not by reference to individual instalment deliveries, but to certain greater quantities over time. Such 'take-or-pay' commitments will relate to the buyer's taking of a quantity of, say, LNG tendered for delivery by the seller or, to the extent not taken, the payment for such LNG in any case, by reference to the price provided under the LNG sale and purchase agreement (SPA) in respect of delivered LNG. This obligation is, in the alternative, capable of being performed by the buyer either by (i) taking and paying for LNG; or (ii) paying for LNG not taken.

In the case where the buyer is obliged to make such a payment, the grounds for that obligation will usually be expressed not as a failure to accept LNG, but as the operation of an obligation to make payment where the quantities of LNG taken over time fall short of identified minimum quantities.

Having established the quantity of LNG to be delivered and taken under the LNG SPA over the relevant period, if the buyer then takes a lesser quantity of LNG, the deficit will, on the face of it, represent the measure of the buyer's failure to take delivery. Without more, breach by the buyer of an obligation to take delivery would entitle the seller to recover its damages ordinarily arising as a result of that breach.

However, an LNG SPA will typically provide for more and the provisions will go beyond simple reciprocity with the provisions concerning shortfalls in delivered LNG and the shortfall remedy applicable to the seller's failure to deliver. They will provide for a 'take-or-pay' obligation on the part of the buyer. Such a take-or-pay obligation has traditionally been expressed by reference to a period of a year, the aggregate of the LNG cargoes scheduled for delivery during that period, or both. More recently, the presence of portfolio participants and the growth of commodity trading influences more generally have led to these take-or-pay commitments being expressed for shorter periods or in respect of individual cargoes, and with obligations of mitigation but no rights of make-up.

On the face of it, a take-or-pay clause represents an onerous obligation on the buyer. In the extreme, the buyer is committed to paying the seller a sum of money equal to the product of the prevailing agreed price and the aggregate of the minimum quantity commitments throughout the term of the contract, whether or not it takes delivery of (in this example) LNG which it can use or resell and regardless of any sales of that LNG made elsewhere by the seller. A buyer's confidence to accept such an onerous commitment will be related to its market and will be influenced by its means of managing this risk under the terms of the relevant contract.

One usual means of managing such risk (although not an inevitability) is the agreement by the seller of a right of 'make-up' on the part of the buyer. This right will often be expressed by reference to the take-or-pay obligation and will provide that, to the extent of the buyer's payment for quantities not taken, the buyer will have a future right to take (or recover) corresponding quantities without payment. This right will ordinarily apply in excess of the taking by the buyer of the applicable take-or-pay quantity for the period of that recovery, thereby maintaining the seller's expected flow of commodity and cash over time, despite the buyer's takes varying from the schedule of taking envisaged under the relevant contract.

In the case of a commodity such as LNG, where scheduling under an LNG SPA is done long in advance and each cargo delivery requires cooperation between the seller and the buyer, the physical exercise of such rights of make-up is unlikely to be straightforward. For example, the relevant make-up cargoes will have to be accommodated within the seller's overall business and operational requirements of the relevant projects and vessels. As a result, the buyer's right of make-up is likely to be expressed in terms of reasonable endeavours rather than firm obligations and to be subject to limitation, typically by reference to its duration, its quantity application, or the prices to be paid at the time the take-or-pay payment is made and when the corresponding right of make-up is exercised.

Take-or-pay clauses also present risks for sellers across the energy chain. The seller will receive payment of the contract price for the specified quantities subject to the take-or-pay commitment, whether or not those quantities are sold. However, that payment is likely to suffer tax and accounting disadvantages and that sum may not in fact be sufficient to cover the seller's losses arising from the buyer not taking and, in circumstances where the buyer has rights of make-up available, may provide the seller with no more than the time value of the buyer's take-or-pay payments, over a short period. If a buyer exercises its right not to take the specified quantities and opts to pay the take-or-pay payment, the seller faces the prospect of being paid only once at the end of the year rather than receiving regular payments over a contract year. This outcome could be disruptive to the seller's cash flow and its consequent ability to manage required debt service payments arising under any financing arrangements. For some, these apparently operational matters will also give rise to opportunities for commercial gain, the ripples from which may make their way along the energy chain.

To mitigate this credit risk and the disruption it could pose to the seller's cash flow, the seller can introduce a right to terminate the contract if the buyer's failure to take or schedule gas reaches a certain level. Alternatively the seller can provide that the take-or-pay quantity and performance regime be calculated on a shorter period. However, even these alternatives could still leave the seller with exposure to the buyer's credit risk.

3.7 Nature of breach

The chain of contracts to effect the movement of energy from a point of production to a distant point of consumption over the course of many years will consider not only the periodic failures to deliver or take commodities or provide transportation or processing services, but also the continuation of fundamental matters of petroleum reserves and available markets as the contracts run their courses. Petroleum reservoirs are not necessarily predictable or well behaved, but assumptions about their productivity and resilience will have formed the basis of the provisions of many of the contracts along the energy chain. In different ways, end-markets are resistant to reliable prediction, although their continued operation will have been assumed in terms of consumption quantities and prevailing prices.

The consequences of reserve failure or market failure will have been considered by the parties and the relevant contracts are likely to provide for corrective or mitigating steps in these circumstances. Failures of reserves or markets are likely to lead to commodity failures (of delivery or acceptance) but the consequences may be more fundamental and lead towards termination, perhaps regardless of available contractual relief.

At the time the contracts of the energy chain are made, there may not be an alternative, available market by reference to which damages can be assessed in the case of commodity failure. However, over the many years of those contracts, markets may emerge and what was once a fixed and faithful connection of seller and buyer may develop into a multi-connected environment of those buying, selling and trading commodities, with markets tending to move and change over the long period of those contracts. In addition to their importance in the calculation of damages in the case of breach, these circumstances are also important in relation to commercial opportunity for the parties over time.

For example, the making of an LNG SPA entails an enduring commitment of fidelity by the seller and the buyer. Initially, that fidelity is supported by a shared commercial benefit, and unfaithful behaviour is discouraged by the sanctions of the agreement, ordinarily the shortfall remedy and the take-or-pay provisions. Over time (and typically the term of an LNG SPA will be many years in length), the nature and extent of the commercial benefit will shift as alternative markets may emerge and operate on the LNG SPA. Where these markets are available to a seller, there may be circumstances in which its fidelity to the contractual relationship formed by the LNG SPA comes to be tested, particularly in the case where the traditional form of shortfall remedy under an LNG SPA results in the calculation of a money value which is unrelated to those available markets.

A buyer may well see such behaviour as wrong in itself, as well as being in breach of the seller's contractual delivery obligations. It may also see it as inconsistent with broader promises in the LNG SPA relating to matters such as commitment of certain reserves over time to the buyer. The compensatory or restorative principles of English law, allied to the undoubted benefits of establishing (at the time of making the LNG SPA) a liquidated damages provision, will have served the buyer poorly in the changed markets and times. In such a case, where the seller may be tempted to renege on its promises under the LNG SPA, the buyer's mind is likely to turn towards more onerous sanctions for breach. The identification and operation of these enhanced sanctions in circumstances of 'intentional breach' may not be easily achieved under English law.

With its compensatory and restorative principles of damages and its absence of punitive remedies, English law does not have a developed jurisprudence of intention or reason in respect of contractual breach. Matters of fraud go without saying, but the intentions of the defaulting party are not often important in assessing damages. The traditional leaning of English law against the idea of a general duty of good faith in the making or performance of contracts or the exercise of remedies may be subject to current debate, but is yet to be materially threatened.

As the gas business has moved from regionalism to globalism, and as alternative markets have developed, parties have sought to create remedies to apply in the case of intentional, deliberate or wilful failures on the part of the other to meet its delivery obligations.

Matters of intentional failure will often give rise to considerations of displacing what would otherwise be expressions of limitation of liability. In this way, the benefits of an agreed scheme of contractual limitations of liability may be lost in circumstances of a party's negligent, reckless or intentional non-performance of its obligations. The consequence of this loss will usually be exposure to a claim of damages at large. It will not be unusual for the terms of the relevant contract to go beyond this, and to provide a specific, agreed remedy in the event of 'commercial' default.

These contractual remedies tend to provide for greater financial disincentives than would ordinarily apply in the case of commodity failure, or to provide a means of the innocent party recovering the gain made by the other in selling or buying elsewhere. Each of these constructions invites legal scrutiny. In the first example, there are elements that would ordinarily suggest an increased risk of breach of the rule against penalties. In the second example, there is a notable reference to the English law principles of restitution and unjust enrichment – principles applicable in circumstances of fiduciary duties and usually absent from commercial arm's length contracts for the sale and purchase of a commodity.

3.8 Performance of contracts

Despite the breach of an obligation to deliver or take the relevant commodity under a contract of the energy chain, there may be circumstances in which the breaching party will be relieved from the liabilities that would ordinarily arise from that breach. In some circumstances, this relief will arise by operation of the applicable governing law of the contract, and in others by reason of the specific provisions of the contract under which the relevant obligation arises.

Broadly, English law will require the performance of contractual obligations in accordance with their terms regardless of supervening events, save to the extent that the parties have themselves provided for applicable reliefs in certain cases of non-performance. In the absence of such reliefs, the courts will hold the parties to their bargain regardless of the costs, expenses or hardships arising in effecting the performance required pursuant to the specific terms of the obligations in the contract.

There are many examples of a party seeking to imply terms into contractual arrangements for the purposes of alleviating or escaping the consequences of changed circumstances. But English law sets a high hurdle in this assessment and requires that such absent term is necessary to give the contract business efficacy or so obviously intended (although not expressed) that it goes without saying.

Much of the jurisprudence in this area has developed in the context of shorter contract durations and lesser commercial values than those of a typical contract of the energy chain. The long durations of those contracts and the volatility of petroleum pricing over time have put great pressure on the parties' commitment to their agreement in the context of inevitable economic imbalance over time. If the contract price under, say, an LNG SPA is capable of comparison with a prevailing market with which it is not aligned, then it will inevitably be at odds with that market (to the benefit of the buyer or the seller from time to time) over its long duration.

In general, English law is most reluctant to allow a party to escape from a bargain which comes to be a poor one and even where a contract does provide for revision in changed circumstances, those provisions will need to be clear and certain to enable enforcement. English law does not recognise notions of economic hardship or general principles of good faith in the making, performance or enforcement of contracts, although there have been recent developments in relation to implied duties of good faith in the performance of relational contracts.

3.9 Reliefs and *force majeure*

As a consequence of English law's general reluctance to relieve a party from obligations freely entered into under contract, parties to the contracts of the energy claim will instead look to provide for specific contractual reliefs from liability, usually termed '*force majeure*' clauses.

Force majeure is not a term of art in English law and the nature and extent of such relief must be defined by the parties. As a result, it is a rare contract in the energy chain that does not include a *force majeure* clause, and an extensive, detailed one at that. What that clause means and how it operates to provide the expected relief for each party are, however, matters of great variation.

English law adheres firmly to principles of freedom for the parties to agree the nature, extent and effect of their contractual arrangements but which, once these contractual arrangements are made, then requires performance of the resulting terms almost regardless, even – notwithstanding changed circumstances, hardship or the making of a poor bargain – to the point of insolvency, unless, that is, the parties have made contractual provision for relief from liability or from the performance of obligations in certain circumstances. This, typically, is the role of the *force majeure* clause in a contract of the energy chain.

English law does incorporate limited principles of events excusing contractual non-performance such as Acts of God (albeit limited to natural causes) or frustrating events such as impossibility. However, unlike many jurisdictions, English law does not recognise *force majeure* (a civil law idea, and French expression after all). As a result, the parties to an LNG SPA will define in the words of their LNG SPA those events and circumstances which might come to give rise to relief by reason of *force majeure*.

The nature of the relief from liability will vary from contract to contract, with some providing for relief from the liability that would otherwise apply in the event of a breach of an obligation and others providing for the suspension and later reinstatement of the relevant obligations or the deferral of dates provided for performance.

Typically, contractual *force majeure* clauses will also provide for a general test relating to those events capable of giving rise to relief (with examples of those events which may be a basis for relief, subject to fulfilling the relevant tests) and a list of those events which will not be capable of constituting a basis for relief, regardless of the fulfilment of the contractual test. These excluded matters will include matters such as a buyer's loss of market or a seller's loss of gas reserves. In the context of the energy chain, these excluded matters may also include unavoidable commitments of the parties. For example, the owner of a transportation pipeline may seek a payment scheme which separates its fixed, capital costs from its variable, operating costs, to the effect that a user may be excused by reason of *force majeure* from those variable, operating costs but not the unavoidable capital costs of the owner having the transportation capacity available, whether or not it is used.

If a seller is relieved from liability for its non-supply in circumstances of *force majeure* under its sale contract, will its buyer then automatically be relieved similarly in relation to its on-sale contract? Relief from liability for *force majeure* will rarely apply automatically or be a matter of declaration by the affected party. Rather, relief is likely to be dependent on the party claiming relief discharging the onus of proving the entitlement to that relief in accordance with the terms of the contract and fulfilling related obligations, such as providing notice and information to the other party and taking reasonable steps to remedy the cause of the failure and reinstate performance of the obligations in accordance with the terms of the relevant contract of the energy chain.

A typical *force majeure* clause will not be effective to defer or postpone dates set out in the contracts, in the absence of clear words to that effect. For example, contracts in the energy chain will often provide a flexible timetable for establishing a 'start date'. This will be the date of first application of commercial remedies, often following a lengthy period of construction of the respective facilities of the parties, and the commissioning and testing of those facilities in readiness for the parties' respective obligations and commercial sanctions for non-performance first coming into effect. In the case of new production, pipeline or reception facilities, the period between the signing of the relevant contracts and the start date may be several years. During that period, much can happen to falsify the respective construction programmes and to delay a party's readiness for the start date beyond the extent of the negotiated contractual flexibility.

At the time of making their contracts, the parties will have turned their minds to consider whether, in the case of such delays arising for reasons beyond the reasonable control of a party, the start date is to be deferred (thereby deferring the coming into effect of the commercial remedies) or the start date is to occur in any event, with the affected party then claiming relief from the contractual remedies pursuant to the contract's *force majeure* provision.

3.10 Allocation of available quantities

Along the energy chain, it is likely that producers and sellers will have multiple buyers. It will, for example, be a rare LNG development which has a single off-taker at the outset, and even if it does, then the project developers will inevitably be selling to others over time. Each sale will be on its own, negotiated terms and there is likely to be consideration of 'club rules' to have effect in relation to matters of common interest. One of these will be the allocation of available supplies at times when the aggregate of all supply commitments cannot be met, for whatever reason.

These 'club rules' will be matters of horizontal application among the seller and its several buyers, but their consequences will have vertical effect along the energy chain. They will reflect the conflicting commercial interests of the seller and the several buyers: the seller preferring to allocate supplies in priority to those buyers whose contracts offer the most advantageous terms and each of the buyers seeking to have its nominations or fixed quantities met in full and in priority to all others. Whatever the scheme which comes to be agreed, the consequences of its application will require incorporation into each buyer's contracts of sale, and so on along the chain.

3.11 Contract administration

In negotiating contracts along the energy chain, each party will wish to make sure of consistency of time periods, notice provisions and other matters of contract administration so as to be able to exercise its rights and perform its obligations. This will be the case in relation to those contracts above it and below it in the energy chain. For example, the supplier under the Power Supply Agreement will want to make sure the notice periods under that agreement are aligned with the notice periods under the Gas Sale Agreement, where it is the buyer of gas. The power supplier will wish to ensure that there is enough time to receive a notice given by the seller under the Gas Sale Agreement and to give a notice under the Power Supply Agreement.

Each of the elements of the energy chain will involve facilities of considerable scale, value and operational complexity. The proper operation of these facilities over time will demand maintenance and repair. There will be benefits to the coordination of these planned requirements, both among the parties to individual contracts, and along the energy chain.

Although the contracts of the energy chain will be of long duration, their provisions may also provide for potential extension. An example here would be an LNG SPA and its likely provisions for the recovery of accrued entitlements beyond the specified contract duration. Consideration will need to be given to how such provisions are to be applied and their effect up and down the energy chain.

3.12 Operations

In the case where the energy chain relates to the beginning of supplies from a new development or the use of new facilities, the parties will usually contemplate that either or both of them will not be in a position to begin commercial operations by the agreed start date. This date is likely to be subject to limited flexibility and may be the date for the coming into effect of contractual remedies or the beginning of a period of commissioning or testing of facilities prior to that date.

In the event that the parties are not in a position to perform by the due date and that failure to perform is not subject to relief or a grace period, then the relevant contracts may provide for either a liquidated monetary remedy (perhaps for each day of delay) or the beginning of operation of the applicable commercial remedies under the relevant contract. It is also likely that the parties will provide for limitations of these liabilities and rights of termination in the case of delay beyond certain periods.

On the face of it, a failure by the seller to tender for delivery quantities which comply with the quality specification under the relevant contract will be a failure giving the buyer a right to reject the goods which do not comply with the contractual specification. However, the contracts of the energy chain (and particularly LNG SPAs) will often provide for a set of rights and obligations which arise in these circumstances, and these provisions will be reflected in the limitations of liability.

These provisions are notable as they will usually be cast in terms of endeavours and result in the buyer (as the innocent party) becoming subject to obligations which arise from the seller's breach in the case where the buyer is aware of the nature and extent of the non-compliance with the required specification of LNG. These obligations are likely to relate to the buyer using reasonable endeavours to take delivery of and treat the LNG, or to reschedule the delivery, or to acquire replacement supplies from elsewhere. It is also likely that limitations of liability will apply in these circumstances, with unknowing acceptance of non-compliant LNG being a particularly difficult matter to address.

3.13 Disputes and consolidation

Disputes that commonly pass along the energy chain include those relating to performance failures and delays. The parties to each of the contractual arrangements in the energy chain will seek to align the dispute resolution mechanisms as far as possible. For example, the parties may require that all disputes in relation to or arising out of all agreements be settled by arbitration, in accordance with common applicable rules of arbitration, at a common venue and with other related details.

It will be difficult to consolidate dispute resolution processes in respect of large multi-faceted projects (and their related contracts) which span jurisdictions. For example, an LNG SPA is a divisible contract made up of many separate sale and purchase obligations. It is difficult to draft an umbrella agreement from the outset which consolidates not only the choice of jurisdiction, but also the dispute resolution process.

The contracts of the energy chain will usually be international and will provide for dispute resolution by means of arbitration. Whereas joining others to an action tends to be facilitated in litigation before the courts, consolidation of disputes or joining third parties to arbitral proceedings is likely to be much more difficult.

3.14 Political risks

A consideration when negotiating contracts along the energy chain will be so-called political risk (eg, change in law, change in tax, and political risk events such as attacks on infrastructure) and where the consequences of those risks should fall. Managing these risks within the context of the contracts of the energy chain will give rise to considerations similar to those applying to the question of *force majeure* generally, and the relevant provisions will often appear as a part of the *force majeure* clause. A particular area of difficulty will be the resistance of investors to accept the consequences of actions by a host state or so-called 'in-country risk'.

The parties may also look to manage such political risk through means which are external to the relevant contract although related to it.

In the case of a sovereign entity, the parties may look towards agreements with the host government and ratification by domestic legislation, making those agreements enforceable. Such agreements may enable allocation of risk to the host state and include stabilisation provisions which allocate change in law or change in tax risk to the host state.

Another mitigating instrument where the counterparty is a sovereign entity may be a sovereign guarantee, making the sovereign state liable for payment if the sovereign entity fails to pay. Where both contracting parties are private entities, they may look towards risk guarantees or risk insurance of the types offered by multilateral organisations in these circumstances. However, these are typically matters more of project development than the energy chain and are covered elsewhere in this book.

3.15 Insurance arrangements

Parties along the energy chain are exposed where damages under one or more contracts are not adequate to offset liabilities under other contracts. In those circumstances, parties may see insurance cover as a means of managing that risk.

However, insurance provisions will be rare provisions in the contracts of the energy chain. Matters of insurance arrangements, claims, proceeds and the application of those proceeds will be central matters in the development of the general infrastructure projects which punctuate the energy chain and are therefore considered elsewhere in this book.

3.16 Termination

Many of the contracts of the energy chain will provide specific rights of termination in the event of material failures, with materiality often being assessed by reference to the commodities not delivered or taken, or the duration of the failure, or both. What will rarely be provided for is a specific measure of the liability of the parties in circumstances where one of them exercises such rights of termination, or the detailed manner in which that liability is to be assessed. In the absence of a specific measure of liability, the parties may claim damages for any breach of the contract which fell to be performed prior to termination, but may not be entitled to 'loss of bargain' damages under English common law.

In some of the contracts of the energy chain (eg, LNG SPAs), the presence of a buyer's take-or-pay commitment may mean that a seller is relatively unconcerned if the buyer does not take the contractual quantities. The buyer will be committed to pay for those quantities in any event other than where contractually relieved – for example, in the case of *force majeure*. Further, while there may be accounting disadvantages for the seller in this case, the seller can assess its position by reference to receiving the contract price for all contract quantities in any case, and with any corresponding rights of make-up for the buyer being largely at the buyer's risk. Also, the seller will potentially have that LNG available for sale elsewhere. Nevertheless, there may be circumstances in which it may be in the seller's interests to exercise contractual rights of termination. Again, the measure of the buyer's liability in this case, or the detailed manner of its calculation, will often not be provided for under a contract of the energy chain.

In addition to contractual termination structures, a party may be able to terminate a contract in the energy chain under the general law if the other party breaches a condition of, repudiates or renounces that contract. The significance of these common law rights of termination is that they give the innocent party the right to claim loss of bargain damages upon termination, that is to say losses which accrue as a consequence of the premature termination of the contract. Given the long-term nature of the contracts of the energy chain, this right may be a very substantial one.

Other circumstances which will be expressed as giving rise to rights of termination of the contracts of the energy chain include the insolvency of a party. Given the geological scope of the energy chain and the diversity of the nationalities of its participants, there may be difficulty in framing the appropriate test of insolvency. Also, the rights arising in the event of a party's insolvency are likely to be matters of individual negotiation in each case, with rights of termination perhaps applying differently to a seller and a buyer.

In addition to rights of termination, the arrangements between the parties may include rights of 'step-in', or one of the parties taking the interest of the other in certain circumstances, such as insolvency. If these provisions are included, they will be closely negotiated and probably complex, particularly in relation to the resulting commercial arrangements and their duration. Looking beyond the parties themselves, there may also be applicable 'direct agreements' which will have a bearing on the rights of the parties in circumstances of potential termination. These are likely to apply to the benefit of third-party lenders and give them rights to protect their position by means of stand-still periods, rights of temporary control and potential acquisition of the interests of the insolvent party. They may also apply to the benefit of related or dependent third party trade counterparties.

Within the energy chain, direct agreements are potentially troublesome as they require the participation of the contracting party which will have its own, competing rights in these same circumstances. For example, in the case of the LNG Sale Agreement it may be that the seller has taken debt finance for the purposes of its developments. Those lenders will wish to protect their position in the event of the seller's insolvency and one way to do this will be to require the ability to adopt the rights of the seller under the LNG Sale Agreement. In those same circumstances, the buyer is likely to wish to pursue its commercial interests, including its protection in relation to its obligations along the energy chain. The terms on which these interests can be reconciled in the short term pending an enduring resolution are likely to be set out in the LNG Sale Agreement and the direct agreement, and to be binding on the seller, its lenders and the buyer. The implementation of these provisions in circumstances of insolvency will be much affected by the prevailing markets and prices and the respective positions of the seller and the buyer in the energy chain at that time.

3.17 Consequences of termination

The consequences which follow from a valid exercise of an express contractual right of termination are, in principle, whatever the contract says they are. However, in the absence of a specific measure of liability, the terminating party may claim damages for any breach of the contract in the energy chain which fell to be performed prior to termination, but will not be entitled to 'loss of bargain' damages at common law unless the termination event relied on was also a repudiatory breach of the contract and there was no express exclusion of that remedy.

Upon a valid termination for repudiatory breach, both parties are released from their primary obligations which are not yet due for performance and there is substituted by implication of law for the primary obligations of the party in default which remain unperformed the secondary obligation to pay monetary compensation to the other party for the loss sustained by it in consequence of their non-performance in the future (ie, damages for loss of bargain).

The principles governing the assessment of damages under English law are complex and such damages on termination of a contract in the energy chain will be difficult to assess. In the case of an LNG SPA, the loss will ordinarily be ascertained as a current capital sum by reference to the difference between the contract price for the agreed quantities of LNG over the life of the LNG SPA and the market or current price of such LNG at the times when it ought to have been delivered, subject to adjustment to take into account the time value of money. Where there is an available market on which the terminating party can enter into a substitute LNG SPA on or shortly after termination on the same or similar terms to the terminated contract, the market price is likely to be assessed by reference to such replacement contract, whether or not the terminating party chooses to enter into such contract. Where there is no such available market, the assessment will be more difficult and damages will be assessed by reference to loss and damage caused to the terminating party.

4. Conclusion

In the case of an interconnected set of projects and commercial arrangements of the type contemplated in the energy claim which is the example in this chapter, it will be usual for a robust and durable set of contractual arrangements to be put in place at the outset and across the many links in the energy chain. The strength of those arrangements over time will be dependent on the performance of others and the continued application of the circumstances and assumptions prevailing at the outset. However, those circumstances and assumptions are likely to be falsified before long, not least by the continued and rapid change of the technologies and markets surrounding gas, LNG and power, the moves of governments and regulators which inevitably feature along the links of these chains, and the changes of trading patterns, including shorter-term arrangements and portfolio aggregators. This chapter has sought to discuss some of the many considerations to be taken into account at the time that these arrangements are first put in place, and over time.

Risks in the development and ownership of wind and solar projects

Antony Skinner
Ashurst LLP

1. Introduction

The focus of this chapter is to identify and analyse risks associated with the development, construction and operation of wind and solar projects around the world. We acknowledge that wind and solar technologies are fundamentally different and the risk profile and quantum of certain risks will be far greater for offshore wind than ground mounted solar, for example. However, the type of risk and the way in which the projects for solar photovoltaic (PV), concentrated solar power, onshore wind and offshore wind are structured are substantially similar.

We will review these risks from the perspective of a developer, but the same risks will also apply to funders. Indeed, funders will have a more conservative view of risk than developers. Developers and funders alike will also look to mitigate risks as much as possible. Once a risk is identified, all relevant parties will consider how best to mitigate the risk and identify and agree upon who is best placed to accept it. It may be that contractors (eg, the construction contractor or operator) are best placed to accept and manage a certain risk; it may be that insurance is available to cover that risk; or it may be that a risk simply exists and has to be accepted and quantified as part of the risk profile of the project.

The types of risk may vary depending on the jurisdiction of the relevant project, but in short, if a developer is looking to develop a solar or wind project of any type, it will need to have the following key arrangements in place in order to progress the project:

- land rights;
- grid connection;
- planning consents;
- construction contracts;
- operating contracts (including management services);
- power offtake arrangements; and
- debt and equity funding.

All of the above have associated risks, which we explore further below.

Projects tend to develop in four key phases:

- Phase 1 – Development;
- Phase 2 – Construction;

- Phase 3 – Operation; and
- Phase 4 – Decommissioning.

Each phase has its own risk profile, which again we will explore further below.

From an investor perspective, the development phase is the riskiest of all phases and is the phase when the project is most likely to fail. Therefore, only developers and investors with a high risk appetite are likely to be involved at this stage.

2. Site selection

2.1 Meteorological conditions

During phase one of the project, the developer will need to identify a parcel of land which is suitable for the proposed project. For wind and solar projects, the choice of site is absolutely key because appropriate meteorological conditions are needed for the chosen technology in order to generate electricity. It is important to note that for solar projects, irradiation data is more readily available on a regional basis, and this data is usually useful for assessing individual sites. Clearly the developer will need to ensure that there are no trees or surrounding buildings which either now or may in the future create shade on the site, but otherwise regional irradiation data should be sufficient to determine the suitability of a site, whether this is for ground mounted or roof top solar.

However, wind projects require site-specific data because wind is a very localised resource. Therefore, a meteorological mast (or 'met mast') will need to have been erected on a site for several years in order to record the wind speeds and direction. It may be that a landowner has procured this data as a marketing tool in order to attract potential developers to buy or lease his land, or it may be that a developer has requested permission to erect a met mast on one or more locations in order to establish data and to decide whether, and if so where, to develop a wind farm.

Once the meteorological data is available, it will be analysed and a future profile will be developed so that the probability with which the wind will blow or the sun will shine at certain levels can be determined. This will then be used in the financial model of the project. For example, the 'P50' case will be the probability that the level of generation will occur with a 50% certainty. The 'P90' case will be the probability that the level of generation will occur with a 90% certainty and is therefore more conservative.

2.2 Grid connection

Another key factor to take into consideration when looking for an appropriate site is the proximity to the nearest appropriate grid connection point. This is likely to be in the form of an existing sub-station, but it may require a new sub-station to be built. Depending on the size of the project and the availability of a sub-station, the developer will need to decide whether to connect to the high-voltage national transmission system or the medium-voltage distribution network.

There may be some benefits to connecting to a distribution network rather than the national transmission system. These may be in the form of:

- fewer industry codes to accede to and comply with;
- lower costs of connection both upfront and ongoing; and
- other benefits which will be specific to each jurisdiction.

These are often called 'embedded benefits'.

However, there may be other grid factors which impact a developer's decision as to whether and where to develop a wind or solar project, and these relate to the availability of a grid connection and the potential for a lengthy wait to be connected. By way of example, in the United Kingdom, an Ofgem report (*Unlocking the capacity of electricity networks*, December 2016) stated that "customers are not expecting to connect until the early 2020s". This is due to the congestion of grid connection applications. Not all grid connection offers accepted/not yet accepted will lead to an actual connection, and this fact only adds to the connection queue congestion. Further delays may be caused where connection offers are subject to significant reinforcement of the relevant grid.

In the UK context, flexible connections have been used by distributing network operations (DNOs) to alleviate congestion by offering flexible connection agreements to generators. Under this mechanism, generators are offered a cheaper connection at an earlier date, but are subject to generation curtailment and import adjustment. While not commercially attractive due to the curtailment and instability of power supply, this offers an alternative route to allow generators to gain access to the grid in congested areas and has been increasingly rolled out by DNOs. However, this type of arrangement will give rise to bankability issues due to the risk of being curtailed unless this risk can be accurately quantified and reflected in the financial model for the project.

2.3 Land rights

Once a site has been selected on the basis of satisfactory meteorological conditions and data and grid connection options, negotiations will need to take place with the landowner to secure appropriate land options. The developer will need to decide if it would like to own or lease the land and will need to agree the land option fees and ultimately the price for the land (whether a sale or lease). It is more common for developers to lease the land and for the rent to be linked to the revenues generated by the solar park or wind farm.

The above are all independent factors which will need to be resolved in a favourable manner in order to progress to the next phase of development. This is why the risks of a project failing during this first phase are higher than during other phases.

3. Planning

The developer will need to apply for planning permission once the land options have been secured. In all likelihood, the developer will start the planning application process in parallel with its investigations into the site, meteorological conditions and grid connection in order to ascertain if the site is likely to receive planning permission and therefore whether it is worth continuing to pursue all elements of the development process.

Clearly, every jurisdiction will have its own regime which will apply to planning regulation. We set out below a brief summary of the planning regime in England and Wales. While there are risks involved in not obtaining planning permission, there are also risks of the planning regime changing while a developer is going through the planning process.

All development in England and Wales that is not a permitted development needs planning permission under the Town and Country Planning Act 1990 (1990 Act), authorised by either the local planning authority or the secretary of state. For wind and solar power projects in England and Wales, it follows that planning permission is one of the main regulatory requirements that developers must satisfy in order to secure a bankable project and before carrying out any development works.

In England, there are two broad exceptions to the above rule for wind and solar power projects:

- first, where a project is authorised by the secretary of state under the Planning Act 2008 (2008 Act); and
- secondly, where consent by the secretary of state for a project is granted under section 36 of the Electricity Act 1989 (1989 Act) and an associated planning permission is deemed under section 90 of the 1990 Act.

Similar principles apply in Wales, albeit that recently devolved planning powers mean that wind and solar projects are increasingly falling within the jurisdiction of the Welsh ministers as opposed to the secretary of state.

Whether or not a project fell within one of the two exceptions above used to be determined largely by its size and whether it was onshore or offshore. However, the consenting regime for these types of project has been subject to numerous changes in recent years, reflecting the inherent tension between central government's twin objectives of (i) fast tracking development and (ii) promoting local input into and control over the planning process. A short summary of the principal planning consents required for wind and solar projects in England and Wales is provided below.

3.1 Onshore wind

Onshore wind projects in England and Wales, whatever their generating capacity, require planning permission under the 1990 Act from the authority. Until recently, onshore wind projects whose capacity met or exceeded 50 megawatts (MW) would have qualified as 'nationally significant infrastructure projects' (NSIPs) under the 2008 Act, thereby requiring a development consent order (DCO) (a unified consent granting planning permission as well as various other consents a project may require, including consents under the Electricity Act 1989 and compulsory acquisition powers). However, through a series of interim orders and then the Energy Act 2016, the Conservative government made good on its 2015 election manifesto promise of giving local people the "final say" on onshore wind projects: these projects were expressly carved out of the regimes within the 2008 Act and the 1989 Act, thereby returning the decision-making process back to local planning authorities in the first instance. As with all ordinary planning applications, it remains possible to appeal to the secretary of state in the event of a refusal by the local planning authority, but this may not be of great comfort given the current priorities of central government.

Given the unpopularity of onshore wind farms among many local communities, the effect of the recent decentralisation of the consenting process is likely to make it more difficult for onshore wind farms of any significant size to obtain planning permission (particularly in England).

It should be noted that in addition to planning permission, separate consents may be required for any associated works affecting highway or public rights of way, listed building or scheduled ancient monument consents, health and safety and environmental permits and wildlife licences. Furthermore, any statutory authorisations are completely separate from any requirement to obtain landowner rights or consents.

3.2 Offshore wind

Offshore wind projects that are located in waters adjacent to England or Wales up to the seaward limit of the territorial sea or in a renewable energy zone (excluding any part over which the Scottish ministers have functions) and which exceed 100MW currently qualify as an NSIP under the 2008 Act. They require a DCO, for which an application is made to the National Infrastructure Planning Unit. Inspectors appointed on behalf of the secretary of state must examine the DCO application following a set statutory timetable. The result is a report making a recommendation as to whether or not to grant a DCO and the secretary of state then makes the final decision. In making a decision, consideration is given to the applicable National Policy Statements as well as local planning policy. As mentioned above, a DCO is a unified consent which could encompass a range of statutory consents required by an offshore wind project, including: planning permission for onshore and offshore elements; removing navigational rights which may pass through a wind farm; marine licensing; and compulsory acquisition. The process is front-loaded and requires a great deal of community engagement and consultation before an application is even prepared and submitted. The examination process itself typically involves a series of hearing sessions focused on particularly sensitive issues and these are usually run in a manner akin to a public inquiry.

Where an offshore wind project has a capacity of less than 100MW, it will not qualify as an NSIP. Currently there would be a requirement for a consent under section 36 of the 1989 Act from the Marine Management Organisation and this is usually accompanied by a section 36A declaration removing public rights of navigation. Any associated onshore development is typically authorised by an ordinary planning permission from the relevant local planning authority. Any further consents which may be needed for the project would need to be secured separately.

3.3 Solar

To date, solar projects have been firmly based on land and so there is no offshore consenting regime to consider.

Where a solar project's capacity is less than 50MW, ordinary planning permission will be required from the local planning authority. It should be noted that any statutory authorisations are completely separate from any requirement to obtain landowner rights or consents. Where a solar project's capacity is 50MW or greater, it will qualify as an NSIP and require a DCO.

3.4 Conclusion

The above highlights the planning risk associated with developing wind and solar projects in England and Wales (although we note that the regime in Wales is slightly different to that in England). The likelihood of securing a planning permission will depend very much on the particular facts of any given case: the site's location and its constraints; a proposal's anticipated impacts relevant to that context; which consenting regime applies; local host communities' receptiveness to the proposals; and a local planning authority's applicable policies and political objectives, together with those of central government. These are not insurmountable and are issues that would need to be addressed by any type of development proposal; early engagement with local stakeholders and statutory consultees is often key. However, as the recent changes to the regime for onshore wind demonstrate, procedural complexity and political uncertainty are the big risks associated with securing planning approvals for solar and wind projects. The process for and prospects of securing a consent may change from when a developer first sets out to develop a project to when it comes to applying for planning approval and/or building out.

4. Regulatory risk

Historically, wind and solar projects have relied on subsidies in order to make projects economically viable. As these technologies have developed, prices have decreased dramatically. For example, solar PV panel prices dropped by 75% from 2010 to 2017. Nevertheless, most renewable projects still rely on some form of subsidy and subsidies rely on government policy, which is subject to change. Subsidies generally take the form of a feed-in-tariff, which is a fixed tariff paid to generators of power from a renewable source; or green certificates, which are certificates awarded to generators of power from a renewable source which can then be sold to realise the value of the subsidy.

Therefore, the subsidy regime and levels available at the inception of a project may change (and in some cases change dramatically) during the course of development. We set out below a case study on changes to the subsidy regime in the United Kingdom and in Italy in order to demonstrate the regulatory risk associated with wind and solar projects.

4.1 United Kingdom

(a) Regulatory risk – general principles

In the early years of the UK renewable energy industry, the main challenge for the UK Government was ensuring that it had appropriate policies in place to encourage investment. However, as time has gone by, arguably the greater challenge for the government has been the need to strike a balance between its policies in support of renewable energy, and the need to manage the rising cost of that support, which is passed on to consumers. This is a position that has been repeated in many other jurisdictions: governments introduce support schemes but over time find the cost to be untenable.

The various steps taken by the UK government in recent years to cut support to renewables – both by way of changes to support levels and changes to the technologies eligible for support – have dealt harsh blows to the UK renewable energy industry and developers in part. However, as discussed in more detail below, in general the government has shied away from cuts that have a retrospective effect on existing projects – that is, changes that have an impact on projects that are already receiving support. This is in contrast to some other jurisdictions, such as Italy (discussed further below), where governments have introduced changes which withdraw or reduce support for existing projects. Nonetheless, this is of course of little comfort to projects being planned for the future, where a level of regulatory risk remains.

(b) Grandfathering under the Renewables Obligation

Until recently, the Renewables Obligation (RO) – a green certificate scheme – has been one of the main forms of support for renewable energy projects in the United Kingdom, offering support over a 20-year period. 'Grandfathering' under the RO maintains a fixed level of support for the duration of a generating station's support, regardless of future changes. It is a 'statement of policy intent' and is not enshrined in legislation, although it is a key policy principle underpinning the RO regime – that is, subject to some exceptions, there is an expectation by investors that the level of support locked in at the time a project is accredited will be maintained.

It should be noted, however, that there have always been some exceptions to grandfathering under the RO. The fact that there are specific exceptions to grandfathering gives further weight to the expectation that grandfathering will be applied for technologies which are not within the specific exceptions.

(c) The Feed-in Tariff

The Feed-in Tariff (FIT) scheme was introduced in April 2010, as a new financial incentive mechanism for small-scale (up to 5MW) renewable energy installations. Under the FIT scheme, accredited installations receive a generation tariff (for any electricity generated) plus an export tariff (for any electricity exported to the grid) over a 20-year period (10 years for combined heat and power). An important principle of the scheme – similar to that under the RO – is that the level of support is fixed once an installation is accredited for support.

The level of support provided when the FIT scheme was first implemented was particularly attractive for solar PV projects and led to the development of a growing solar industry in Great Britain. By its own admission, the government underestimated the level of take-up of the scheme, and less than a year after its inception, began to take steps to reduce the rate of support. A fast-track review of FIT support for larger solar installations was first announced in February 2011 and was followed by various other changes to the scheme. The support for large-scale solar projects (more than 250 kilowatt (kW) to 5MW) was cut from 30.7 pence per kilowatt hour (kWh) to 8.5 pence per kWh on 1 August 2011. The initial cuts were justified by the government on the basis that it had not been contemplated that the scheme would support the growing number of 'solar farm' projects and that the scheme was intended to incentivise microgeneration only.

On 31 October 2011, the government launched a consultation, this time primarily aimed at reducing FIT rates available to smaller-scale (250kW and below) solar PV installations. The new tariff levels were intended to apply from 1 April 2012. For solar installations of 4kW or less, for instance, this was to result in the level of support per kWh being halved, reduced from 43.3 pence (37.8 pence for new build) to 21 pence. Significantly, the government stated in the consultation that its preferred option was for the new rates to apply to all installations that became eligible for FIT payments from 12 December 2011 onwards. Effectively, the government proposed that the lower rates should apply retrospectively to installations completed even before the consultation closed on 23 December 2011.

Two solar PV companies, HomeSun and Solar Century, together with environmental group Friends of the Earth, decided to seek judicial review of the government's proposals. The full details of the High Court and Court of Appeal judgments in the case are outside the scope of this chapter, but the aspect of the case that is useful to focus on is the court's approach to the question of whether the proposed change to the FIT scheme was in fact retrospective and/or unauthorised by the relevant legislation. The High Court confirmed that there is a strong presumption against retrospective legislation or decisions, unless the relevant legislation permits retrospective effect, either expressly or by implication. Mr Justice Mitting pointed out that "changes made by reference to a date earlier than the date on which they come into effect are not... calculated to further the statutory purpose" of the Energy Act 2008. While he did not say so expressly, he implied that such a change would be retrospective.

Mr Justice Mitting also considered that it was outside of the secretary of state's power to make a modification to the scheme which had a significantly adverse impact on solar panels installed before the date on which the modification was made and came into effect.

The Court of Appeal's remit was narrower. In rejecting the government's appeal, the Court of Appeal focused on the issue of whether:

it was within the power conferred on the Secretary of the State by the Energy Act 2008 to make a modification which reduced the tariff in respect of installations becoming eligible for payment prior to the coming into force of the modification.

The court concluded that the proposed modification would have a retrospective effect and so was unlawful. Lord Justice Moses reached that conclusion without reference to the "statutory purpose" analysis adopted by Mr Justice Mitting. Lord Justice Moses focused on the question of whether the FIT scheme provides for a rate of tariff fixed for 25 years from the date the installation becomes eligible for payments. He concluded that the answer is "yes" and therefore the secretary of state did not have power under the Energy Act 2008 to take away an existing entitlement to a fixed rate of return.

The case was seen as a much-needed recognition of the fact that capital investments are made on the basis that the government will not retrospectively withdraw the support that makes such investments viable, and any decision to do so will generally be unlawful.

(d) *The Contracts for Difference regime*

The Contracts for Difference (CfD) regime was implemented in 2014 to replace the RO regime as the main form of support for renewable energy projects (other than those eligible for support under the FIT scheme). Under a CfD, a low-carbon generator is paid a top-up payment above the wholesale price (the reference price), up to a set strike price. The CfD takes the form of a private law bilateral contract between the CfD counterparty and each low-carbon generator, generally with a term of 15 years for most renewable energy technologies. A government-owned limited liability company – the Low Carbon Contracts Company – has been established to act as the counterparty to CfDs, and to collect from suppliers a levy to fund CfD payments and administer payments under CfDs. The fact that the CfD is a private law bilateral contract is considered to be significant in terms of regulatory risk because it means that the terms of it cannot be amended by the government unitarily.

The first allocation round commenced in October 2014 and was open to a wide range of technologies. It was originally intended that the next allocation round would follow in 2015 but that was postponed, with the second allocation round taking place in 2017. However, the second allocation round is open to a much more limited range of technologies – in particular, onshore wind and solar PV projects are not eligible to take part. The way the budget for this allocation round is structured also means that offshore wind is, arguably, in a more favourable position compared to other technologies eligible to take part in the allocation round.

Therefore, the CfD regime presents a low level of risk for projects which are successful in being granted a CfD (particularly once the plant is capable of operation, because before this, there is a risk that the CfD may be terminated if there are significant delays in its construction timetable). However, for developers in phase one of a project, the risk is that they may not be successful in being granted a CfD.

(e) *General approach*

To date, the UK government's approach to changes to the regulatory regime for renewable energy has adhered to the following general principles:

- changes to the rate of support available do not apply to projects already receiving support;
- changes to the rate of support available apply to all new projects which qualify for support after the date of the changes coming into effect, although in many cases special treatment is available to projects already under development at the time the changes are announced (which meet the relevant criteria for special treatment, which generally means a developer has to demonstrate that its project has land, planning and grid connection in place); and

- changes that relate to matters other than the rate of support (eg, relating to feedstock sustainability for biomass projects) may be introduced to apply to all projects from the date they come into force, including existing projects.

4.2 Italy

In Italy, the Italian government took a different approach to the United Kingdom and in 2015 introduced retrospective solar tariff cuts which applied to projects that had already been built and were in operation. The Constitutional Court gave a judgment in December 2016 confirming the legality of such cuts.

The retrospective cuts applied only to solar plants and not to other renewable technologies, such as onshore wind farms. One reason given to justify the retrospective cuts was that solar projects had developed in the absence of controls over the number of megawatts of capacity that could be installed at each tariff rate, so that approximately 19,000MW of solar projects had been installed in Italy. As a result, the cost to the consumer for the green tariff for such installations was overwhelming and the government needed to intervene.

Further, the Italian government clearly gave significant thought to the level of the tariff cuts and was careful, at the time of sizing the cuts, to ensure that the projects would not default under their loans. Lenders would therefore not be hit directly by the tariff cuts. Indeed most projects the author is aware of went into what is called a 'lock-up' under their finance documents, which means that the owner of the project is not permitted to make any distributions to its shareholders. However, the projects did not go into an event of default scenario as a result of the cuts, because the projects could still generate enough revenue to service their debt. Clearly this approach benefits lenders, but not project owners.

Although there was an initial negative reaction to the retrospective cuts in Italy, investors and lenders alike have again started investing in Italian renewable projects. There are various reasons why investors have achieved a degree of comfort in this respect, including the following:

- unlike in other countries perceived as similar, such as Spain, Italian subsidies to renewables are not paid by the government but by the consumer through electricity bills, so the government is not incentivised to cut subsidies as a tool to improve the public finances;
- the rationale for the cut was therefore to reduce electricity bills (ie, improve the competitiveness of doing business in Italy). With the oil price at current low levels and no expectations of material increases in the near future, there appears to be no compelling reason for the government to make further cuts;
- the aggregate curve of incentives paid to renewable energy producers has started to decline in any event, due to the natural expiry of old incentives and the phasing out of or material reduction in new incentives for new plants; and
- paradoxically, the Constitutional Court decision confirming the tariff cuts has brought a degree of stability to the market because many market players actually feared that a declaration of unconstitutionality of the cuts by the court could have prompted the government to take other indirect measures to react to the reinstatement of the old higher tariffs.

Despite all of the above, Italy is still perceived as more risky than other European countries and this risk commands a premium for investment in the country. There is a perception by some market players that this premium is worth the risk, especially given the demand for solar and wind assets in northern Europe, which are driving up prices and consequently driving down equity returns.

5. Construction risk

While the contracting strategies for construction will vary, depending on whether the project company is developing a solar park, onshore wind farm or offshore wind farm, the associated risks and the contracts that are put in place to construct the asset and mitigate the risks will share a number of common themes. At the most basic level, any developer will be looking to ensure: certainty as to the quality of the asset to be constructed; certainty as to programme and completion date; and certainty of price and final outturn cost.

A typical construction contract will clearly define the scope of work to be undertaken and require the contractor to complete that work within a specified time period and for a fixed price. In the event that completion of the asset does not occur by the planned completion date, the contractor, in the absence of an event entitling it to an extension of time to that planned completion date, will be liable to pay the project company delay liquidated damages. The purpose of these delay liquidated damages is to address the risk of a project company cash flow shortfall as a result of completion occurring later than expected. Simply put, the lenders will expect to be repaid and if the asset is not complete, the likelihood is that the project company will not be able to generate the required level of income from the relevant asset in order to pay debt service. In the absence of this income, the project company will need an alternative revenue stream in order to be able to service its debt repayment obligations and avoid default under its finance arrangements – delay liquidated demands are one such alternative revenue stream.

Similarly, to the extent the facility does not meet its quality requirements as set out in the construction contract, the project company is likely to have rights of rejection/termination or an entitlement to levy performance liquidated damages to compensate itself against any shortfall in asset performance.

The right of rejection is controversial for a contractor because it means the contractor has to give back all money received under the construction contract and restore the site to its original condition. Rejection can be used only if the performance of the project is so bad that it has deprived the project company of substantially all of the benefit of the contract. This remedy is often used as a bargaining tool for the project company and is rarely exercised.

Performance liquidated damages are used to compensate the project company for any shortfall in asset performance over the expected useful life of the asset. Performance liquidated damages are often calculated as the net present value of projected lost revenue over the expected useful life of the asset.

There are likely to be caps on the liability of the contractor with respect to delay and performance liquidated damages, often in the region of 15% to 20% of the total contract price. The contractor will also look to cap its overall liability at 100% of the contract price subject to certain exclusions (eg, indemnities and insurance recoveries).

Beyond the construction phase, we would also expect any typical construction contract to include provisions regulating the contractor's liability for defects in the asset. It is standard for the contractor to be obliged to return at its own cost to remedy any defects which appear within the constructed asset during the defects rectification period. The defects rectification period will vary according to the market and type of asset, but periods between 12 months and five years are fairly standard.

In terms of market practice in relation to the contracting strategy for solar projects, we see the use of engineering, procurement and construction (EPC) contracts within the solar space. These fixed price EPC contracts provide the project company with a single point of responsibility in respect of design and construction risk and mean that the contractor is by and large bearing the risk of any cost overruns and programme delays.

In terms of the testing regime, it is relatively common to have a phased testing regime for solar projects. The first stage is to achieve provisional acceptance. Provisional acceptance involves the solar park being physically and mechanically complete and having achieved the minimum performance requirements. Once provisional acceptance has occurred, the contractor is no longer liable for delay liquidated damages. The second stage usually occurs 12 months after provisional acceptance and is intermediate testing. Here the performance of the solar park over the 12-month period is tested against a guaranteed performance ratio. Failure to meet the guaranteed performance ratio results in a performance liquidated damage liability to cover revenue shortfall for that 12-month period. Finally, and usually 24 months after provisional acceptance has occurred, final acceptance testing will be carried out. Again, there is a test of the solar park's performance against the guaranteed performance ratio; however, if the test is not passed this time, the performance-based liquidated damages will compensate the project company for the reduction in the value of the solar over its future life and the previous 12 months' performance shortfall.

With regard to wind farms, there are different approaches to procurement for onshore wind farms and offshore wind farms. With onshore wind farms, it is usual to see two contracts being let: the turbine supply agreement for the supply and erection of the wind turbine generators, and a balance of plant contract for the associated civils, foundation and access works. The project company will usually manage the limited interface risk posed by such arrangements.

Developers of offshore wind farms have considerably more interface risk to consider and their procurement strategies reflect both this and the fact that there are a limited number of contractors with either the skill set or appetite to sign up to fully wrapped EPC contracts. Offshore wind farms tend to adopt a multi-contract procurement approach, with the project company entering into many different contracts for the different work packages (eg, turbine supply agreements, high- and low-voltage cabling contracts, electrical systems, foundations and topsides), and leave the project company to manage that interface risk. The recent trend is to seek to reduce the number of discrete contracts and try to bundle related disciplines together into the same package. This helps to reduce the interface risk.

6. Operating risk

Once a project moves to the operating phase, the generally accepted view is that there is a material step down in the risk attached to a project. Certain funders and equity investors will only invest after commercial operation has been achieved.

The purpose of this section is not to analyse the technical risk at a granular level, but rather to look at the types of risk that might arise during operation and how they are best mitigated.

The presence of an operation and maintenance (O&M) contract is important to define the parameters for the operation and maintenance of a project during its life. If an O&M contractor is being employed to undertake these tasks, it is important to cover all the requirements relating to preventative and corrective maintenance, performance monitoring and reporting, together with the frequency with which these activities are to be performed. This allows contractor performance to be measured.

It is usual for an O&M contractor to guarantee plant performance during the contract term. This is typically achieved through the presence of an availability warranty covering the entire plant. In the event of the contractor not honouring its obligations, resulting in the plant performing below the guaranteed value, the project company would be eligible to claim for compensation to cover lost revenues. The terms of the O&M agreement will vary from sector to sector. Where the term is long, say over five or more years, then there are likely to be bench marking/market testing provisions and associated break rights. Where the term is short, we would expect to see provisions allowing for term extensions.

The core obligation of the O&M contractor will be to maintain the plant. Maintenance falls into two broad categories. The first is scheduled maintenance. This maintenance is planned in advance and aimed at fault prevention, as well as ensuring that the plant is operated at its optimum level. The second is unscheduled maintenance, which is carried out in response to failures. In order to facilitate a rapid response in the event of equipment failure, a suitably stocked spare parts inventory is essential. Where an O&M contractor uses items from the spare parts inventory, it should be responsible for replenishing the stocks.

7. Power offtake risk

The key for any wind or solar project is the revenue stream. As discussed above, most wind and solar projects rely on some form of subsidy, whether by way of a FIT or green certificates. If the FIT is all-inclusive, then the project company/generator will not need to sell the power generated by the wind or solar plant separately. However, a number of subsidy regimes provide a FIT or green certificate linked to the renewable element of generation, but leave the generator to sell the power (also known as the 'brown power element') separately.

Where the generator has to sell the 'brown power', it will need to enter into a power purchase agreement (PPA). The form of PPA will vary accordingly in each jurisdiction, but the key features of the PPA will be similar and will include price, term and imbalance risk. We will deal with each of these in turn.

7.1 Price

The price can be fixed; fixed but subject to inflation indexation; variable and attached to a market price index; or the generator might have the option to fix a price for a period of time in the future (eg, for the next year). Finally, the offtaker may offer a floor price so that if the market price goes below the floor price, the offtaker will be required to pay the floor price. This is very helpful for funders as it offers them a minimum price downside scenario.

For index linked pricing, the offtaker will, in all likelihood, offer a discount to the market price so that it will make its profit on the difference between the market price and the contract price. The offtaker is also taking risk in relation to the project (including imbalance risk and change in law risk described below and, if applicable, the floor price described above) and will therefore require a return for taking this risk.

7.2 Term

The term of the PPA will have a strong influence on the term of any debt that funders are willing to lend. Generally, the term of the debt will be shorter than the term of the PPA or will expire at around the same time as the debt is repaid. However, in more sophisticated markets such as the United Kingdom and the United States, it may be that more favourable terms are available for shorter-term PPAs. The reason for this is that the offtaker will have greater visibility and certainty on how power prices and market structure will be maintained for a shorter period of time. For longer contracts, the offtaker will need to price in a greater risk and will therefore offer a lower price for the power.

7.3 Imbalance risk

Imbalance risk is where the generator does not generate electricity at the level it has promised to do so under the PPA. Electricity cannot be stored (subject to certain storage solutions which are beyond the remit of this chapter). Therefore, the electricity grid needs to be balanced so that generation matches power consumption at all times. This is a huge undertaking for grid operators. One way they manage this risk is to require grid users to notify their expected electricity generation and consumption for specified periods (eg, 30-minute settlement periods in the United Kingdom). Failure to deliver or consume the notified volume of electricity will result in imbalance payments being made to the grid operator.

For intermittent generation such as wind and solar, imbalance risk would provide too great a risk to the project for a funder and maybe even an equity investor. Further, a single asset which is dependent on the sun or wind to generate has no way of mitigating its exposure to imbalance. However, large utilities with a portfolio of generation available to them will be able to mitigate this imbalance risk to an extent. Therefore, it is common in renewable PPAs for the offtaker to take imbalance risk *vis à vis* the grid operator. The only risk to the generator is that it has to notify the offtaker in advance as to the level of availability of the plant. So long as the plant is available at the level notified, it is for the offtaker to monitor the output of the plant based on current meteorological conditions.

8. Financing risk

Onshore wind, offshore wind and the various forms of solar are generally seen as proven technologies by a majority of funders. However, for offshore wind in particular, not very long ago funders were reluctant to lend on a limited recourse basis due to the perceived risk of constructing and operating a wind farm in an offshore environment and in salt water.

On a global scale there is now 14 gigawatts (GW) of offshore wind installed and operating. Of this, 12.5GW is located in Europe and 5GW is located in the United Kingdom alone. Therefore, funders have become more comfortable in accepting the risk of financing an operating offshore wind farm. However, they will require a robust contractual structure to be in place with respect to the operation and maintenance of the wind farm, together with availability guarantees on the turbines and also evidence of the availability of appropriate vessels at short notice in order to carry out unplanned maintenance of the offshore wind farm.

With respect to construction, as discussed above, the offshore wind market has evolved such that there is not a single contractor who is willing to wrap construction risk. The reason is that there are so many different and independent elements to the construction of an offshore wind farm that a single contractor would have to charge a large premium in order to wrap this risk. The developers of offshore wind farms are often large utilities (eg, DONG Energy, RWE or SSE) who consider that they are best placed to manage the interface risk and are unwilling to pay a third-party contractor a material premium to manage the risk.

However, funders (being conservative in nature) are unwilling to accept the interface risk simply because of the involvement of a utility. Therefore, funders will require some form of formal construction management agreement to be in place under which the utility is contractually obliged to manage the construction interface risk and will be liable for at least a portion of the debt in the event that construction is late or never completed.

It is the author's view that the construction management agreement and liabilities of the utility thereunder often falls short of the completion guarantee that is seen on the large international petrochemical deals which in effect guarantees repayment of the debt in full if the project does not complete, but is a risk sharing arrangement to ensure that the developer (in this case being a utility) has put at least some of its balance sheet at risk to share in any losses that may arise in the event that the construction of an offshore wind farm does not go smoothly.

For onshore wind farms, there are clearly risks associated with their construction, but funders are much more comfortable with this risk. Generally there will be only two construction contracts – the turbine supply agreement and the balance of plant agreement. The interface risk is therefore much more manageable. Nevertheless, to date, there have often been material risks with respect to completion of onshore wind farms (and indeed offshore wind and solar projects) with respect to the subsidies available. Most onshore wind, offshore wind and solar developments to date have relied on some form of green subsidy in order to make the project economically viable. It is sometimes the case that the subsidy will be awarded only once the project has achieved completion by a certain date. If the project is late, it may be that the subsidy is available at a reduced rate or is not available at all.

In the United Kingdom, for example, the RO regime expired on 31 March 2017 with respect to new entrants (subject to certain grace periods which are beyond the scope of this chapter). Therefore, if a project achieved its completion date after the so-called 'RO cliff date' it was at risk of not receiving the RO subsidy, thereby making the project uneconomic. Most construction contractors were not willing to wrap this risk and said this should be an equity risk. For funders, the closer the scheduled completion date for a project was to the RO cliff date, the more reluctant they were to lend. By way of general comment, if there was less than a six-month buffer between scheduled completion and 31 March 2017, funders refused to lend on a limited recourse basis because they too viewed the RO cliff as an equity risk.

Further, as subsidies are reduced, it may be that a project will receive a lower subsidy on completion than the subsidy which the developer understood it would achieve when the project was at its inception phase. This is clearly a developer risk. Funders will be reluctant to lend if there is a risk of a reduction in subsidy by the time the project is completed. One way to mitigate this risk for funders is to size the permitted debt based on the lower subsidy level, with the ability for the developer/borrower to increase the size of the debt if it completes the project in time in order to achieve the higher subsidy level. This places the subsidy risk with the equity investor, which would appear appropriate based on project finance principles.

9. The future of renewables

Based on REN21's 2016 report, renewables contributed to 23.7% of global electricity generation in 2015. In the latest edition of the *Medium Term Renewable Market Report* prepared by the International Energy Agency in 2016, the agency upped its five-year renewables forecast by 13%, due in large part to stronger policies in the United States (pre the Trump era), China, India and Mexico. The report projects global renewable electricity capacity will increase by 42%, or 825GW, between 2015 and 2021. Therefore, renewable energy provides a material contribution to the global energy supply and this is projected to increase in the future.

All the risks identified above will continue to apply in the future, but the risk weighting attributed to each identified risk may change as the deployment of renewable technologies increases around the world. In particular, as the cost of renewable technologies has decreased, there is increasing pressure on renewable projects to achieve 'grid parity' and to be 'subsidy free'. This means that a renewable project will sell its power on a merchant basis and will receive a market price for its power and is therefore competing with other forms of generation such as gas-fired and nuclear. This may increase the risk of a change in law, which might adversely affect the tariffs available to renewable generation.

The onset of renewable energy has resulted in pressure on other forms of power generation and in particular gas-fired generation. Due to the fact that renewable technologies such as wind and solar have an almost zero marginal cost of production, whenever the sun is shining or the wind is blowing, solar and wind power stations will nearly always generate regardless of the prevailing power price (unless perhaps the power price is negative). Therefore, power stations which incur a marginal cost of production (eg, gas-fired power stations) will generally have to switch off when there is a high level of renewable generation. As a result of the increase in renewable generation, the economics for running a gas-fired power station have fundamentally changed.

Gas-fired power stations used to be high up the merit order for power production. This means that because traditionally gas-fired power stations were generally clean and efficient plants with a relatively low marginal cost of production, they used to generate for a majority of the time. This is often referred to as baseload production. Now that gas-fired power stations have to work alongside renewable generation, the generating profile for gas-fired power stations has changed so that they help to balance renewable generation and will be switched on and off more often as intermittent renewable generation peaks and troughs. This makes gas-fired power stations more expensive to run and also means they are generating less often. Nevertheless, they are an essential part of the generation mix and are essential to keeping the lights on when intermittent renewable generation cannot generate (eg, on a cold day with no wind). Therefore, in order to encourage gas-fired power generation, governments around the world are introducing capacity markets whereby a gas-fired generator will be paid a fixed fee for being 'available' regardless of whether it generates or not.

One of the challenges for renewables is that one could argue there is no such thing as 'grid parity' any more. Renewable generators are now competing on a non-level playing field in favour of non-renewable generation. New-build nuclear projects also require a 'low carbon' subsidy due to the cost of construction. Nuclear power stations have to be run as baseload plants because they are not flexible in any way. Therefore, as part of the merit order for generation, nuclear will generally be at the top of the list.

One final point to note is the issue of cannibalisation of wind and solar power pricing. What this means is that as we have more wind and solar power generation capacity in a particular jurisdiction, on a sunny or windy day (or even both) there is a high level of power generation with a low marginal cost of production. Whenever there is a high level of cheap supply and a relatively stable demand, basic economic theory dictates that this will result in a low price. Therefore, for a wind or solar generator, you are likely always to be generating during periods of high supply and low price. This puts further pressure on the financial viability of intermittent renewable generation.

We are starting to see more sophisticated power purchase agreements being negotiated in the United Kingdom for example, which allow a wind or solar project to fix its power price on a forward-looking basis. This helps to mitigate the cannibalisation effect of wind and solar power pricing. However, going forward, the roll out of cost-effective and efficient battery storage projects alongside wind and solar projects could be a game changer and could help wind and solar projects to become more of a baseload form of generation or be flexible to match supply with demand. As a result, if periods of high wind occur during the night, for example, when there is low demand and therefore a low price, the wind farm generator could store this power and export onto the grid in the morning when demand begins to rise along with the price for power.

10. Conclusion

As can be seen from the above, while wind and solar projects are increasingly viewed as low-risk projects in which to invest, they are not without risk. This chapter has focused primarily on risks that arise in the United Kingdom, but this type of risk and how it should be managed will apply in a majority of jurisdictions.

The development phase of a project is the period of the most risk. The risks associated with procuring an appropriate site, planning permission and grid connection are material. Also, during the development phase, a developer often has less protection against changes to law or policy which might affect the project.

Once a developer has contractually locked in the land, planning and grid arrangements for a project, the number of investors willing to invest will increase dramatically. This reflects the step down in risk at this stage.

The risk associated with the construction of a solar or onshore wind project is generally viewed as low to medium and most investors are comfortable with this risk. Construction risk on offshore wind projects is higher and will require much more technical analysis and contractual protection in particular, due to a high number of independent elements which will all need to be aligned in order to ensure a successful construction completion. The fact that construction is taking place to a large extent in an offshore and unpredictable environment compounds these risks.

Generally speaking, once a project is constructed, the operation of a wind or solar park should be relatively straightforward, but extreme weather and political risk will always pose a risk during operation.

Risk in nuclear projects

David Wadham
Ashurst LLP

---

1. Introduction

The development of any large-scale infrastructure project will require project participants to analyse and allocate a whole host of risks. Many of these typical risks apply to the development of nuclear projects. However, the nature of nuclear power and nuclear power projects makes many of these risks quite extraordinary; furthermore, nuclear projects are subject to certain additional risks that are not relevant to other major infrastructure projects. The examples below illustrate this point.

- Following the Fukushima disaster in Japan in 2011, the German government decided to pass a law requiring the immediate shutdown of eight nuclear reactors constructed before 1980 and the shutdown of all of Germany's remaining nine reactors by 2022. The utilities concerned, E.On, RWE and Vatenfall, alleged losses of around €19 billion and brought a case against the German government for expropriation. In late 2016, the German Federal Constitutional Court held that although there had not been an expropriation, the change of law amounted to a restriction of the companies' property rights and they were entitled to reasonable compensation.
- In March 2017, Westinghouse, the large US manufacturer of nuclear reactors owned by Toshiba, filed for Chapter 11 bankruptcy protection in the United States. Toshiba had been forced to write down the value of its US business by some $6.3 billion due largely to massive cost overruns estimated to be potentially in excess of $11 billion incurred in the construction of four reactors across the VC Summer and Vogtle power plants in South Carolina and Georgia in the United States. At the time of writing, the problems of Westinghouse have come close to pushing Toshiba, a company once with a market value of $24 billion, into bankruptcy itself.

The purpose of this chapter is not to provide a comprehensive risk register for nuclear new-build development; rather, it will seek to highlight two broad categories of risk for a potential investor, political risk and construction risk, which play a key part in shaping the contractual structure and risk allocation of any new-build nuclear project.

2. Political risk

Since governments control energy policy, all power generation projects carry some degree of political risk. Carbon taxes can be imposed or increased on conventional thermal generators, and subsidies can be reduced or withdrawn for renewable generators. Indeed, in Western Europe we have seen many governments imposing, and then changing, policies to drive a green decarbonisation agenda.

However, the nature of nuclear projects makes them particularly vulnerable to political risk. Given the size of nuclear projects, the level of government involvement and, in most cases, financial support required by a nuclear project is liable to be quite substantial. Moreover, nuclear power is a politically controversial topic and a change in government can cause a sudden and dramatic shift in energy policy from a government that is strongly supportive of nuclear to one that is implacably against. Again, the same is true to some extent for renewables, where an incoming government might, for example, oppose onshore windfarms (as happened in the United Kingdom), but nuclear is not only vulnerable because of its size but also because of the duration of each phase of the project: development, construction, operation and decommissioning are so much longer than for conventional power projects. The developer of a nuclear plant could have spent hundreds of millions in a pre-development phase, only to find an incoming government is against nuclear. Equally, after a long and expensive construction phase, it will take a significant operational period for an owner to recoup its investment: the owner of a solar farm may have recouped its investment in a matter of a few years, but the operational life of a nuclear plant could be around 60 years, so a curtailment of nuclear generation even after a couple of decades can be financially catastrophic.

What happened in Germany is a particularly good example of how political risk can impact on nuclear power. Through no fault of the German utilities, a sudden and dramatic shift in German government and public opinion post-Fukushima resulted in a fundamental policy and legal change, triggering huge losses for the generators.

2.1 Mitigating political risk

There are two obvious routes to mitigating political risk for nuclear developers undertaking nuclear new-build. The first is to put in place some form of contractual arrangement with the host government. The second is to seek to rely on national or international treaty legislation.

(a) Contractual mitigation

The form of contractual protection that is achievable will very much depend on the extent to which the electricity market in the relevant jurisdiction has been liberalised and the state intervenes in the market. If, for example, a project is being developed in a market where there are long-term concessional-type power purchase agreements (PPAs) with a state offtaker, then it is relatively straightforward to add in appropriate enhanced protections against political risk, either in the PPA itself or in some form of parallel government support agreement. If, however, the project is being developed in a liberalised market, there may be no obvious linkage between the host government and the generator, and so it becomes more difficult to address political risk. Indeed there might also be national or supranational constraints on the ability of the state to intervene and provide support, such as state aid, for example.

The difference is illustrated by contrasting the contractual structures for the Baraka nuclear project in the United Arab Emirates (UAE) and the Hinkley Point C nuclear project in the United Kingdom. In the case of Baraka in the UAE, where power projects are procured by the state entering into long-term concessionary PPAs with private sector developers, the procuring authority, Emirates Nuclear Energy Corporation, entered into a bespoke prime contract which covered all aspects of project delivery, and a suite of supporting documents was developed and entered into to address the relevant risks in the agreed fashion.

However, in the case of Hinkley Point C in the United Kingdom, the UK government is no longer directly present on the electricity market and is (at least until the United Kingdom exits the European Union) constrained in terms of the support it can offer by the requirements of EU state aid legislation. The UK government had previously developed a form of contract for difference (CfD) to support renewables generators (principally wind and solar) and formed a state-owned company funded by a levy on all suppliers, the Low Carbon Contracts Company (LCCC), to act as the counterparty. One key feature of the standard renewables CfD is that there was no ability for the generator to terminate for LCCC default or prolonged political *force majeure* affecting the generator. While this risk allocation was considered bankable for renewables projects in the UK market context, the lack of termination mechanism for fundamental government defaults was not acceptable in the context of a nuclear project. Hence a bespoke CfD, accompanied by a bespoke support document, had to be developed – the so-called Secretary of State Investor Agreement – to accommodate the political shutdown protections described below, as well as certain other concepts. This documentation had to undergo an extensive state aid approval process. The Hinkley Point framework is discussed in more detail below.

Another common contractual framework used to develop a nuclear project is the inter-governmental agreement (IGA). The idea of a government-to-government deal embodied in an IGA makes some sense in the context of nuclear development. After all, nuclear projects are often developed by state-owned generators and such projects require both support from the host government and often some degree of nuclear technology transfer from the home state of the generator. The concept of a state-to-state deal embodied in an IGA appeals to a number of nuclear exporters and indeed is particularly favoured by the Chinese and Russian state-owned generators, which feel more comfortable undertaking project development where the project is backed by a written understanding between governments.

Turkey is a good example of a country that is seeking to develop its nuclear projects under an IGA model. In 2010 it signed an IGA with the Russian government to develop a reactor based on Russian technology at Akkuyu and then again in 2013 signed an IGA with the Japanese government to develop a reactor based on French/Japanese technology at Sinop. These IGAs are essentially inter-governmental memoranda of understanding (MoUs) that record the key terms on which the project is awarded. For example, the Turkish IGAs are in the region of 15 pages and set out fundamental terms such as the award of the project, the base power price, how the power will be sold, the grant of land rights, and confirmation of support for the permitting process. In short, the IGA is meant to provide a support framework that will enable the development of the project within the specified parameters.

However, from a risk perspective, IGAs have their limitations. As mentioned, in essence they are MoUs with broad statements of principle that are not really capable of enforcement as if they were detailed contractual terms. Moreover, they are between the two governments concerned, not necessarily the parties who will undertake the project development, and they are often expressed to have a form of dispute resolution through diplomatic means. Unless the terms of the IGA are then further developed into some form of host government agreement or concession, then the contractual protection they afford is quite limited. It is interesting to note that as of the time of writing, neither the Akkuyu nor the Sinop project has commenced construction and both seem somewhat stuck in a long pre-development phase undertaking feasibility studies and project company formation processes. While the slow development of these projects is attributable to a number of reasons, some commentators would suggest that the IGA framework, with its combination of some very specific requirements (eg, the price per kilowatt hour) and some non-binding statements of principle, is a contributory factor to the pace of development.

(b) Treaty protection

While robust contractual frameworks are essential to support the development of nuclear projects, they are often not, of themselves, enough. Most nuclear project developments are contractually and commercially rooted in the host country. The generator will find itself contracting under local law with local court jurisdiction (or locally centred arbitration) with the host state. While the extent to which the local law and jurisdiction nexus is a concern will vary from country to country, even in countries with well-defined laws and a robust judiciary, the particular political risk that is inherent with nuclear development will cause foreign nuclear developers to seek alternative, non-contractual and international routes to mitigate this risk.

Two obvious routes are the Energy Charter Treaty and bilateral investment treaties.

The Energy Charter Treaty (ECT): The ECT entered into force in 1998 and 52 states have signed or acceded to it. These include many western European countries, but also an increasing number of Eurasian states, including states such as Turkmenistan and Uzbekistan, as well as Japan. In addition to providing a means of resolving disputes between participating states, the ECT provides protection for foreign investment by granting a number of fundamental rights to foreign investors with regard to the investment in the host country. Foreign investors are protected against the most important political risks, such as discrimination, expropriation and nationalisation, breach of individual investment contracts, and damage due to war and similar events. Part III of the ECT deals with investment promotion and protection, and article 10 enshrines the principle that obliges contracting parties to:

> *... create stable, equitable, favourable and transparent conditions for Investors and such conditions shall include a commitment to accord at all times... fair and equitable treatment.*

Under article 26 of the ECT, an investor can bring claims against a contracting party for breach of an obligation involving investment. An investor can choose between a domestic court of the contracting party, the International Centre for the Settlement of Investment Disputes (ICSID) (provided both the host state and the home state of the investor are parties to the ICSID Convention), or international arbitration under UNCITRAL or Stockholm Chamber of Commerce rules. Awards under the ECT are binding and final.

Bilateral investment treaties (BITs): BITs work on a broadly similar basis. While the precise wording of BITs varies, they typically grant investments made by an investor of one contracting state in the other with a number of guarantees, the most common of which is a guarantee of "fair and equitable" treatment. BITs often provide for investor-state dispute settlement via ICSID. Many countries have entered into tens of, if not more than a hundred, BITs.

Thus in the context of a nuclear project, even if the host government is not party to the ECT, an investor may well be able to structure its investment such that it benefits from BIT protection by routing its investment through a particular country. While the language of the ECT and many BITs is very 'broad brush', these international arrangements create a legitimate expectation of fair and equitable treatment that is likely to discourage host governments from taking discriminatory political actions that could negatively affect a foreign investor's investment in a nuclear project.

2.2 Mitigating the risk of political shutdown and change in law: the Hinkley Point experience

(a) Political shutdown

So-called political shutdown is a major risk for nuclear developers and their funders, and indeed following what happened in Germany it now seems inconceivable that a nuclear project could be developed without some form of protection against compensation for political shutdown.

In simple terms, politically caused shutdown is a form of political *force majeure*. Political *force majeure* clauses for power projects vary greatly from jurisdiction to jurisdiction, but for the most part tend to focus on the impact of increased costs arising from a change in law (see the next section), and the politically motivated termination events in a concession tend to focus on the expropriation or nationalisation of the power plant. The idea of a plant being turned off is not usually expressly dealt with.

In the recently closed Hinkley Point C nuclear project in the United Kingdom, the subject was given considerable thought and a nuclear-specific political shutdown mechanism developed.

In that project, a 'Qualifying Exit Event' covered the risk of political shutdowns, dealing with both a politically motivated shutdown and a change in law which effectively prevented economic operation.

A politically motivated shutdown event (a 'Qualifying Effective Shutdown Event') occurs where a government authority causes a shutdown unless the shutdown was for a material reason of "*health, nuclear safety, security, environment, nuclear transport, damage to property or nuclear safeguards relevant to the project*" and where at the time of the relevant event it was "*objectively justifiable by reference to an identified change in circumstances*".

A second limb, a 'Qualifying Change in Law Cessation Event', provides protection for the generator against qualifying changes in law with which it is not technically feasible to comply, or which cost in excess of a (high) threshold cost amount to achieve compliance.

If a Qualifying Exit Event is agreed or determined to have occurred, then this leads to the payment of compensation to debt and equity holders.

The discussion around politically motivated shutdown is always a difficult one. A host government will absolutely require a clear and unfettered right to shut a plant down without the risk of paying billions in compensation for a broad range of safety and security-related reasons. On the other hand, it is a risk of which generators are acutely aware post the events in Germany, and it is worth noting on the Hinkley Point language that the change must not only be objectively justifiable but also be so by reference to an "identified change in circumstances": it is a pre-requisite to the government relying on its rights that something must have happened to trigger the objectively justifiable shutdown decision.

(b) Change in law/regulation

Another area of particular sensitivity for nuclear projects is change in law and the extent to which it affords protection against political risk.

The extent to which change in law protection is available to power generators varies greatly from jurisdiction to jurisdiction. In emerging markets, where the host government (or an entity owned by the host government) commits to take a plant's entire capacity and output over a long period, perhaps 15 or 20 years, the change in law protection tends to be robust, with any change in law that has an impact on the generator above a *de minimis* financial threshold triggering a right to compensation.

However, in more liberalised markets where the sale and purchase of power is between privatised entities, then the concept of change in law is almost wholly absent, save perhaps for a change in law clause that will allow the parties potentially to reassess the contract following a material change in law that has a material impact on the economics of the contract. Where there is some form of government offtake or government subsidy (eg, in relation to a renewables project), some form of change in law protection is likely to be available. But in contrast to the 'belt and braces' change in law concept in developing markets, in more liberalised markets change in law is likely to be more nuanced, with only discriminatory changes in law (ie, changes in law that unduly affect the specific project or all projects of a similar nature), rather than general changes in law, giving rise to relief.

But the extent to which a nuclear project is subject to intense and ongoing regulatory scrutiny makes the negotiation of change in law protection particularly difficult. While it is true that the generation of power is a regulated (licensed) activity in most jurisdictions, those licensing arrangements tend to be relatively straight-forward: a generator will typically apply for, and obtain, a generation licence at the outset of a project that will impose a set of standard conditions. Only rarely will an issue with the terms of the licence arise during the project life.

However, the situation is quite different in relation to the licensing of a nuclear plant. For good and obvious reasons, a nuclear generator will be subject to intense and ongoing scrutiny. Similar to a conventional generation project, a nuclear generator may be issued with a standard form licence at the outset of the project, but in practice on a nuclear project these general licence conditions will be used by the regulator actively to monitor and regulate every aspect of the licence holder's activities. Notably, the holder of a nuclear licence will typically be subject to a number of 'hold points' during construction, entitling the regulator to satisfy itself as to the licence holder's ability to proceed safely – for example, at the pouring of first nuclear concrete and prior to the first load of nuclear fuel.

But this level of oversight and potential intervention in the project is difficult to interpret in the context of a standard contractual change in law clause. Such a clause will typically cover a change in regulation or in the interpretation of any regulation, but it is potentially a very grey area as to whether the myriad of decisions taken by a regulator in the course of its detailed oversight of a nuclear project constitute a 'change in interpretation' or not. Particularly in cases where the technology is newly licensed, many of the specific matters under consideration may well be under consideration for the first time, and the generator will almost invariably want to claim that any requirement of the regulator that causes increased cost and/or time amounts to a change in law. On the other hand, the host government granting the change in law protection will not want to fetter the discretion of an independent regulator in exercising effective independent scrutiny of a nuclear project.

Thus, in change in law clauses on nuclear projects there is a great focus on nuclear regulation and the possible impact of regulatory intervention. One of the particular concerns is that the regulator could change the entire basis of its regulatory approach and in applying different standards could radically alter the requirements imposed on the project. For example, the UK nuclear regulator, the Office for Nuclear Regulation (ONR), regulates on an 'as low as reasonably practicable' (or 'ALARP') basis, meaning in simple terms that the licensee of a nuclear site must demonstrate that the relevant risks have been reduced ALARP by showing that the costs of improving safety any further would be "grossly disproportionate to the safety benefits that would accrue from the relevant improvement compared to the status quo". The ONR also provides extensive guidance as to how this principle should be applied.

It is worth noting that while being based on the change of law provisions in the generic CfD developed by the UK Government as the support mechanism for renewables projects, the Hinkley Point C nuclear CfD contains an additional limb looking at a change in regulatory basis. It looks at circumstances or matters regulated either by the ONR or by the Environment Agency, and in the case of the ONR captures where the ONR no longer regulates such circumstance or matter:

> *... by reference to an assessment of whether a sacrifice required for risk reduction in respect of the relevant matter or circumstance would be grossly disproportionate to the benefit that would be achieved.*

In other words, has the ONR decided to move away from the ALARP basis of regulation?

While this additional protection may be helpful for nuclear generators versus renewables generators, some would argue that it remains a high bar for any claimant to have to prove that the entire basis of independent regulation has shifted.

2.3 Cross-border challenges and state aid

So far when considering political risk we have focused on those issues that relate to domestic political risk, the risk posed by the generator's relationship with the host government. However, more than other generation projects there is an international dimension to the political risk faced by nuclear generators.

Following Chernobyl, countries in Europe became acutely aware of the potentially far-ranging impacts of an inadvertent release of ionising radiation and, as a result, countries, particularly those that do not support nuclear power, are much more likely to try and intervene against a nuclear project in a neighbouring country. For example, the Irish National Trust, An Taisce, sought judicial review before the UK courts of the decision to grant the relevant consents to Hinkley Point, on the ground that the UK Government had failed to undertake transboundary consultation (as required by the EU Environmental Impact Assessment Directive) with the Irish people in respect of a project some 150 miles off the Irish coast. In this instance, the UK court rejected the application on the ground that the relevant secretary of state (government minister) was able to satisfy himself on a reasonable basis that he had sufficient information to enable him to come to a final decision on the planning process, including sufficient information to make a comprehensive assessment of safety.

One particular facet of cross-border political risk that is peculiar to Europe is state aid. In short, state aid is any advantage granted by public authorities through state resources on a selective basis to any organisations that could potentially distort competition and trade in the European Union. EU legislation prohibits the giving by a member state of state aid save in certain circumstances. 'State aid' is broadly defined and can include support such as subsidy payments and loan guarantees. Many nuclear projects benefit from support which could be considered state aid and, as such, there is potentially a need to apply to Brussels to obtain state aid clearance. This process exposes state aid applicants to significant external political risks: submissions can be made for and against the grant of state aid, and the state aid process, if not the final legal decision, can be heavily influenced by the prevailing politics in Brussels. In extreme cases, even once-granted state aid decisions can be appealed.

This is the position that the United Kingdom found itself in with Hinkley Point. Having obtained state aid clearance, the European Commission's decision was subject to the (almost unprecedented) challenge by a third-party state, Austria, which is set against nuclear (in part having regard to the pro-nuclear states that surround it). The appeal is ongoing at the time of writing. Although thought by many commentators unlikely, the impact of a successful Austrian appeal would be dramatic. An indemnity against the repayment of illegal state aid would of itself constitute illegal state aid, and so unless an alternative state aid-compliant solution could be found by the UK Government, the plant owners would potentially be left facing significant losses. This is a risk that is difficult for investors on a nuclear plant to accept, for it is one that lies wholly outside their control and, to some extent, outside the control even of the host government. It requires clear discussion with the host government to ensure that the government is committed at project commencement (to the extent it legally can be) to ensuring that a successful outcome for the project is found.

3. Construction and technology risk

3.1 Background

One area of intense focus for investors when assessing a nuclear project is construction risk. In recent times there have been a number of very high-profile delays and costs overruns. For example, Areva is experiencing significant delays and overruns with its recent projects at Olkiluoto in Finland and Flammanville in France as it seeks to commission its first EPR reactor. Likewise, Westinghouse and its contractors have experienced significant delays at the Vogtle and Summer projects in constructing and commissioning its first AP1000 reactor.

3.2 Construction risk

The sheer liability in dollar terms arising from a delay on a nuclear project means that conventional ways of mitigating construction risk are difficult to achieve. On a conventional gas-fired independent power producer (IPP), for example, the construction risk sits almost entirely with the main contractor: gas-fired plants, even very large ones with costs in excess of a billion dollars, are typically built under a turnkey engineering, procurement and construction (EPC) contract structure with a single construction contractor (or joint and several consortium), who is not necessarily the turbine manufacturer, taking single point responsibility for constructing the plant to a fixed time and fixed price. Under such a scenario, the EPC contractor will typically accept a general limit on its liability equivalent to 100% of the entire contract price and will accept to pay substantial performance and delay liquidated damages, often in the region of up to 20% to 25% of contract price in aggregate, to keep the equity and debt providers whole against the consequences of any under-performance or delay. Thus typically equity and debt can be held harmless against delays of over 180 days or more in commissioning the plant. In an extreme delay or under-performance scenario, where the plant cannot be constructed by a longstop date or cannot meet fundamental performance criteria, it is not uncommon to see the ability for the plant owner to "reject" the plant and be repaid the entire contract price.

This conventional power contract structure and risk allocation does not, however, transfer to the nuclear sector. The first issue is one of cost. Large gas-fired plant are at the limits of what can be procured on the basis of a fixed price turnkey contract structure, but nuclear plants are significantly beyond it. The largest companies do not, therefore, have the balance sheets to be able to undertake the procurement of such a project on a rigid EPC structure and offer up limits of liability and liquidated damages to insulate the investors to the same degree as in a conventional project. The remedy of total plant rejection does not enter the equation.

Another issue is the length of the construction period and the possible length of cost overruns. Whereas the average combined cycle gas plant can be commissioned in 36 months, construction and commissioning of a nuclear plant can take six to seven years. There is not really any ability for the contractor to hold a fixed price for such a large civil infrastructure project over such a long period. Equally, the duration of possible time overruns is extensive: delays on gas-fired plant are typically measured in days and weeks, occasionally in months. Nuclear delay scenarios start in months and can run to years. For example, Olkiluoto in Finland is presently reported to be running some nine years behind schedule. Clearly there is no real possibility of procuring from the contractor delay liquidated damages to hold investors fully harmless for such periods.

3.3 FOAK risk

Another issue is that of technology. There are thousands of gas turbines in operation in the world. Even when a manufacturer introduces an updated model with new features, it can relatively easily deploy the new model at a test site and let it run for a few thousand hours to prove the new technology. So-called 'first of a kind' or 'FOAK' issues with regard to new nuclear technology are much harder to address. The deployment of FOAK nuclear technology will naturally attract intense regulatory scrutiny which will have an impact on the project timeline, and the licensed generator deploying that technology for the first time will undergo an intense ongoing scrutiny during the construction phase and thereafter. Furthermore, given the relative lack of new nuclear reactors under construction in the world at one time, it takes an inordinately long time to prove a new reactor design, meaning that for that time the FOAK reactor will have a risk profile that makes bankability problematic. To illustrate the point, the debt documents for the Hinkley Point financing filed with the European Commission as part of the state aid approval process make clear that Infrastructure UK, the primary funder/guarantor, as a pre-condition of releasing full corporate debt guarantees from the sponsors (and relying purely on project cash flows for repayment), required that the EPR reference reactor at Flammanville in France had entered into commercial operation and proved its performance.

3.4 Regulatory issues relevant to construction

Regulatory issues also have an impact on contract structures. Most conventional plant construction contracts work on very strict turnkey principles: the contractor remains solely responsible for the construction and commissioning of the plant and the owner only assumes responsibility for the plant when it is fully commissioned and ready to go into commercial operation. Even when the plant is being commissioned using the owner's (or the operator's) staff, such members of staff are treated as agents of the contractor, who remains liable for their performance save in very limited circumstances. Such an approach does not sit well with nuclear regulation. Most nuclear regulation requires that there be a single licensed operator who is fully responsible for a licensed site. Thus, devolving total responsibility to a construction contractor is not possible. There must be far greater involvement during construction and certainly there needs to be an acceptance of responsibility from the owner once nuclear fuel is loaded: plant 'take over' cannot be deferred until the cusp of commercial operation. Moreover, in general terms the nuclear site licensee must be adequately staffed and resourced to demonstrate that it is an appropriate owner and operator of the site: the standard IPP concept of a relatively lean owner team effectively administering the turnkey construction contract will not suffice.

3.5 Approaches to nuclear contracting

The risks associated with constructing a nuclear reactor are therefore not only huge in terms of absolute amount, but also complex and unique. If this risk cannot be passed down wholesale to the turnkey EPC contractor, how can it best be mitigated? There seem to be two possible approaches to this issue.

The first approach is, in simple terms, to stick as closely as possible to the risk profile of a conventional power project. Thus the generator may enter into a single EPC contract with a consortium comprising the reactor technology vendor, plus one or two major civil contractors. However, that contract will likely have several noticeable differences from a conventional IPP EPC contract. First, rather than a fixed price lump sum approach, the contract is likely to be divided into different packages, with only some packages adopting a fixed price approach and others being procured on a target cost or perhaps even a 'time and materials' basis. Second, the scope of retained owner's activities is likely to be significantly larger than on a conventional IPP, with, for example, the owner playing a much more significant role in testing and commissioning. Finally, the levels of liquidated damages and liability caps are likely to be greatly reduced versus their conventional equivalents.

The alternative approach (which was the approach adopted by EDF on Hinkley Point) is to adopt a so-called multi-contract strategy where the generator, instead of placing a single turnkey contract, itself places multiple contracts. Some contracts will be large, for example for the nuclear steam supply system with the reactor vendor, but others much smaller. This approach has several disadvantages: it places a much greater burden on the generator to manage the entire construction process and it exposes the generator to very significant interface risk between its various contractors. However, in return, it is argued, the individual contractors do not price the same element of risk that a turnkey contractor would for wrapping the construction risk, and perhaps more importantly the generator has far more control over the plant construction process and can adopt flexible ways of working with individual contractors, perhaps placing certain contracts later in the construction process when the scope is clearer and/or working much more closely with a particular contractor to engineer, design and construct an element of the plant in a particular way. The owner is free to manage and intervene in the construction process in a way that the owner administering a turnkey contract cannot.

4. Conclusion

With the possible exception of the United States, the development of nuclear power plants has traditionally been undertaken by state-owned utilities operating in their home markets. This model is changing, however, and more plants are being developed on a cross-border basis and/or by utilities or other entities which do not necessarily have the state's full balance sheet behind them. In this changing world, there are inevitably a multitude of risks that must be considered, allocated and mitigated, not least matters such as long-term power sale and purchase arrangements and third party nuclear liability; but finding a viable way to allocate construction risk and ensuring that long-term political risk is mitigated to the extent possible still remain two of the biggest hurdles to successful nuclear project implementation.

Financing the energy transition

Deyber Cano
Consultant, Project Financial Modelling
Brian Scott-Quinn
ICMA Centre for Financial Markets, Henley Business School

1. Introduction – the crisis in the energy industry

A key risk to banks, institutional investors and others holding financial assets is the potential impact of global warming on their holdings of energy assets. Global warming will also impact other, non-energy, financial assets. These impacts will reduce the value of investment portfolios and, at worst, could severely impact the ability of banks and institutional investors to finance the energy transition that will be required over future decades. In this chapter we consider how a shift from bank financing to bond market financing, some new regulations on banks and institutional investors, and some new approaches to risk allocation may minimise the impact of global warming on banks, investors and society.

Evidence that institutional investors are starting to think about these issues comes from a warning[1] on climate change issued by Schroders, one of the largest investment managers. Head of sustainable research Andy Howard observes that on the world's current path, global temperatures are likely to rise – not by two degrees above pre-industrial revolution levels, but by as many as four degrees. He goes on to say that a consequence is that investors may not be able to avoid the forces of nature colliding with financial markets in the years and decades ahead. His analysis suggests that 15% to 20% of corporate cash flow, on average, is at risk because of climate change. Within this average, up to 100% of cash flow may be at risk for particular assets.

This belief is echoed by Aviva Investors, one of Europe's largest investors. According to the *Financial Times*,[2] Aviva Investors has warned more than 1,000 companies globally that they face shareholder backlash at their annual meetings next year if they fail to disclose publicly the risks posed to their business models by climate change. The large insurer has said that it will vote against the annual reports and accounts of companies that fail to embrace recommendations set out in June 2017 by the Task Force on Climate-related Disclosures, a group backed by the Financial Stability Board at the Department for Business, Innovation and Skills. Steve Waygood, an Aviva investment officer, noted that:

> *The transition risk, the physical risk and litigation risk will be very material for some sectors. This isn't about people's conscience, or the panda or the polar bear. It's about people's pockets.*

1 "Schroders warns over climate change risk", *Financial Times*, FTFM, 17 July 2017.
2 "Aviva Investors demands greater climate change disclosure", *Financial Times*, 20 July 2017.

Governments around the world are also considering the impact of global warming on the long-term (systemic) sustainability of the financial system – as evidenced, for example, by an EU report[3] on 'sustainable finance'. In the foreword to this report, the EU vice-president for Financial Stability, Financial Services and Capital Markets Union and the vice-president for Jobs, Growth, Investment and Competitiveness include this paragraph:

The commitment to hardwiring sustainability into EU policies and cross-cutting initiatives is already ingrained in the Mid-Term Review of the Capital Markets Union Action Plan. But a deeper re-engineering of the financial system is necessary for it to become truly sustainable from an economic, social and environmental (ESG) perspective. (emphasis added)

In our view, sustainability of the financial system means two things. First, that the finance industry should be structured to ensure that it can make the fullest possible contribution to sustainable and inclusive growth of the global economy while taking full account of ESG factors. This will require a substantial shift from intermediation through depository institutions (banks) to intermediation through debt capital markets to spread risk more widely. Second, ensuring that if climate change impacts more suddenly and severely than expected on global real assets, that the resulting fall in value of the corresponding financial assets does not damage the financial system so severely that it is unable to achieve the first objective. This will be achieved also by spreading risk through the capital markets as well as the banking system, but equally important will be a reduction in investment by both banks and capital markets in financial assets which are backed by carbon-generating real assets.

Ensuring that the financial system can continue to contribute to the sustainable growth of the world economy requires that it makes some adaptations, which we discuss below. These adaptations should also minimise the risk that the financial system becomes unable to perform its main function due to a systemic financial crash arising from global warming.

The manifestation of climate change risks may, in practice, result in a low, medium or high level of impact on the economic system and on human welfare. The global economy might be able to cope with the low- or medium-risk scenario, but the high-risk scenario would be one in which the banking system and capital markets will have become so weakened as a result of the impact of climate change that, unaided, they will be unable to support the level of new financing needed.

At the lowest level of impact, financing for carbon-based energy projects may simply become unavailable in the decade ahead, at least in the West. This risk is not a 'black swan' risk as it can be seen already from the evidence of institutional investors exiting their existing carbon-based investments and refusing to allocate funds to new ones. The risks of holding investments in fossil fuel activities ('stranded assets'), including oil, gas and coal reserves, gas liquefaction, fossil fuel-fired power generation including combined cycle gas turbines (CCGT), space heating and transport assets to which investors are now paying ever more attention, are dramatically greater than at the time the first edition of this book was published in 2011.

3 EU High-Level Expert Group on Sustainable Finance, *Interim Report*, July 2017.

This trend away from investment in carbon-producing assets is being accelerated by regulatory requirements now being imposed on insurance company asset portfolios in a number of countries to force them to avoid the risk of being invested in 'stranded assets' and the consequent possibility of financial loss. Comparable regulations are also likely to be imposed on pension funds and banks. All the major systemic financial risk organisations (including the central bankers in the Basel Committee) are analysing the impact of a sudden fall in value of carbon-based assets and hence the potential for a dramatic climate change event setting off another financial crisis.

At the medium impact level, a move to a more rapid decarbonisation than at present as a way of achieving a new steady state of 'acceptable' carbon emissions (ie, much less than the four degrees scenario) may require carbon capture and storage (CCS) on a large scale in the short term. A large reduction in atmospheric carbon release will require a dramatically increased level of investment in alternative technologies (ie, non-carbon based) and may also have to include CCS from the atmosphere. However, as we explore below, the banking system alone will not be able to provide this level of financing. It will require the participation of the capital markets on a much larger scale than has been the case to date. It is the increase in capacity (liquidity) and hence cost of finance that capital markets can bring, and the additional spreading of risk that results from extending capital market financing, that makes it so important to work towards greater use of bond markets.[4] New mechanisms to alter the pattern of risk allocation in project financing, as discussed below, will also be important. State support is also likely to be required, whether in the form of guarantees or actual financing.

At the highest impact level, there is the possibility of a 'climactic' climate event – a sudden shift in the speed of climate change impact on Earth. This is also not a black swan risk. Its impact will be on not only physical aspects of life on Earth, but also financial. First, it could make much of our existing infrastructure – ports, some railways, some low-lying towns, water supplies and of course much power generation infrastructure and gas-related assets – no longer viable for use, thus resulting in a huge write-off of assets by the pension fund, insurance, banking and asset management industries, as well as by households to an extent well beyond the impact of the current debate on 'stranded assets'. At the same time, it would create a demand for capital for new infrastructure and non-fossil generating capacity from a banking and capital market industry that would have been severely damaged by such a crisis.

The solution to global warming is often discussed in terms of the power generation sector and the elimination of coal and oil power generation. However, gas (CCGT) power stations, while not as polluting as coal, still generate 50% as much carbon dioxide (CO_2) as coal for a given output of electricity. Natural gas is also the main source of energy for space heating of commercial, industrial and domestic

4 A good technical guide to bond market financing for sponsors and developers is the *Guide to Infrastructure Financing* produced by AFME and co-authored by the authors of this chapter in conjunction with the AFME/ICMA Infrastructure Working Group of industry professionals; www.afme.eu/en/reports/publications/guide-to-infrastructure-financing/.

buildings. However, not only is such natural gas combustion a large contributor to total greenhouse gas production, in cities it is also a major source of local air pollution (nitrogen oxides or NOx), adding to that of petrol and diesel vehicles. This type of pollution is a hazard to health and thus, in the long term, natural gas assets such as gas extraction, liquefaction, pipelines and local distribution networks are also under threat.

2. Fundamental factors reshaping the financing of the energy industry

Some of the fundamental factors that are impacting the financing of energy-related assets include the weakening of utility company balance sheets as a result of grid access priority to renewables, bank regulatory changes, subsidy to renewables, ever-more leveraged balance sheets of utilities, and the loss of monoline insurance facilities. On the asset manager side of the equation, the impact of a long-term low interest rate (low yield) environment on institutional investors in both debt and equity markets has been to cause them to seek higher yielding financial assets of which clean energy-related project finance assets (debt and equity) are one example. This is the good news for the transition.

At the same time, the beneficiaries of investment institutions' financial asset holdings (pension policy holders, long-term savers, students benefiting from endowment funds etc) are increasingly holding their agents (institutional investors) to account in terms of ESG factors and especially in relation to carbon-emitting investments. Bank customers may also have regard to the extent to which their bank is financing what they see as environmentally damaging assets, particularly as a result of new regulatory rules on transparency of lending which enables an analysis of the banking book. This is also good news for the transition process.

The key to whether ESG factors, in particular environmental factors, will determine the financial and real investment strategy of banks and investors could depend on the approach to ESG factors taken by the two major powers in the world – China and the United States – and specifically by their presidents. Unexpectedly, perhaps, President Trump's threatened withdrawal from the Paris agreement has seemingly strengthened President Xi's resolve to make his country the world leader in mitigating the impact of climate change. As an article in the *Financial Times* by Nicholas Stern has noted:[5]

> *China has recognised not only the grave risks of unmanaged climate change, to which it is very vulnerable, but also the great attractions of an alternative path for growth which is cleaner, more efficient, innovative and dynamic. At home, its most recent five-year development plan reflected profound changes to its economic strategy that incorporate sustainable development.*

This change is also reflected in BP's 2017 Statistical Review,[6] which reports that:

> *A dramatic decline in the use of coal resulted in global coal use falling by 1.7%. Chinese coal production fell by 7.9% in 2016, while the price of steam coal increased by over*

5 "China is shaping up to be a world leader on climate change", *Financial Times*, 20 January 2017 www.ft.com/content/3f1ba5ba-ddac-11e6-86ac-f253db7791c6.

6 www.bp.com/content/dam/bp/en/corporate/pdf/energy-economics/statistical-review-2017/bp-statistical-review-of-world-energy-2017-full-report.pdf.

60%. China also enforced measures that restricted coal mines to operate for a maximum of 276 days of a year.

It must be noted, however, that China's drive for investment overseas, in Asia and Africa in particular, is in part driven by a desire to obtain minerals – coal, oil and gas – for domestic use, which is not conducive to reducing carbon emissions. According to an article[7] in the *New York Times*, Chinese corporations are building or planning to build more than 700 new coal plants at home and around the world, some in countries that today burn little or no coal. They report that four out of five of these coal-fired plants are to be in China. Provided city dwellers are not being directly affected by the emissions from these new plants, they are likely to be easily financed by the Chinese policy banks. In addition, there are few fiduciary or disclosure responsibilities for banks or investors as in the West.

In the United States, some observers wonder if the Trump effect will wipe out the shifts in energy mix that have been ongoing in that country for many years. This seems to us unlikely as many of the targets already set in the United States are based on shifts in energy use and the energy mix that are largely driven by market forces or environmental laws that a president is unlikely to be able to overturn. For example, energy efficiency – both domestic and residential – is likely to continue improving and an ongoing move from coal to natural gas, solar and wind will likely continue as their costs decline and will not be stopped by regulation. While natural gas is not environmentally friendly, as an interim solution in the United States, its CO_2 output per unit of power produced is approximately half that of coal, therefore providing short-term mitigation benefits. In addition, many cities and individual states such as California will continue with their climate-friendly policies regardless of what Washington might like during any particular presidency.

In the case of the United States, however, it has to be added that obtaining financing for new shale wells for oil and gas production (shale output is now said to be half the US total) has recently proved much easier than some expected, given the sharp decline in price for oil and gas and the traditionally high production cost of shale wells. Producers have, however, been able to reduce production costs better to match falling selling prices, and banks and high yield bond lenders have once again become willing to provide financing. More importantly, perhaps, has been the willingness of private equity funds to support development. Reuters reports[8] that drilling joint ventures, called 'DrillCos', combine cash from investors such as the Carlyle Group LP with drillable-but-idle land already owned by producers. Investors get a promise of double-digit returns within a few years, while producers can raise output without spending more of their own cash. These ventures have raised $2 billion in the last 24 months. DrillCos take control of drillable land and generally turn over 100% of the cash flow from oil and gas production to investors until they earn a 15% return. At that point, control reverts to the producer, with the investor's stake shrinking to about 10% of remaining production.

7 "As Beijing joins climate fight, Chinese companies build coal plants", *New York Times* online, 1 July 2017 www.nytimes.com/2017/07/01/climate/china-energy-companies-coal-plants-climate-change.html?_r=0.

8 "FinTech now financing: US shale firms get creative to pump more oil", *Reuters*, 13 July 2017. www.reuters.com/article/us-usa-shale-drillco-analysis-idUSKBN19Y17R.

2.1 Change in sources of equity for energy financing

In the last five or more years, there have been changes in the sources of long-term equity finance for clean energy and these are expected to continue. In the past, a high proportion of wind farms in Europe were financed on balance sheet by utilities which financed, built and operated them. Today, institutional investors have supplanted a considerable proportion of such investors, although these same utilities may subsequently operate such wind farms.

Much of this switch has resulted from the financial difficulties of many utilities and the fact that their balance sheets are already more highly leveraged than their investors are comfortable with. This has also affected the water industry in some countries such as the United Kingdom and resulted in some water companies being forced to undertake new investment through a regulated project company (see Thames Tideway project at 2.7(e) below).

The increase in the use of project finance and the technological improvements in wind power, specifically offshore, have enabled it to become more established as a relatively safe brownfield investment for equity and debt investors due to the increasing efficiency and lower cost of such technology and a greater experience of on-time and on-budget construction.

2.2 Change in equity mix in wind energy projects in Europe, 2010 and 2015[9]

Although many investors have become comfortable with brownfield projects, many are not yet comfortable with the greenfield stage and hence with taking on construction risk. Most of the infrastructure holdings of such investors, including energy assets, have therefore been obtained by acquiring portfolios of operating projects. In order to be able to finance the volume of investment required for a rapid shift to a non-fossil fuel economy worldwide but at the lowest possible financing cost, it would be necessary for more investors to be involved with greenfield projects. Such a shift is already happening, as more of the larger institutions become direct investors in projects, either alongside investment funds or through co-investment with other institutional investors.

2.3 The impact of new regulations on bank financing – Basel III & IV

It is becoming harder for banks to provide the volume of financing that the transition will require, in considerable part due to increasingly restrictive banking regulation. This regulation is designed to reduce the incidence of individual bank insolvency but, even more, to reduce the probability of a systemic banking crisis through banks lending long term using short-term deposits, which is a key feature of infrastructure lending.

In addition, it is now being suggested[10] by the European Commission and others that banks will be required to improve the transparency and disclosure of 'sustainability factors' and how these influence their risk profile. This would be

---

9 OECD (2016), "Fragmentation in clean energy investment and financing", Business and Finance Outlook 2016, OECD, Paris. DOI: http://dx.doi.org/10.1787/9789264257573-10-en.

10 EU Interim Report, July 2017 by the High-Level Expert Group on Sustainable Finance.

required under the so-called Pillar III disclosures, which are designed to stimulate market discipline (ie, ensuring that investors do not acquire shares or bonds issued by banks which may hold unsustainable portfolios of risk assets). Any carbon-related assets would fall into a high-risk category.

While debt finance can be intermediated either through the banking system or through bond markets and institutional investors, bank finance is much more flexible and has, of course, been the predominant source of financing for all infrastructure projects worldwide at least until today. This flexibility means, for example, that cash can be drawn down to match the cash needs of the construction phase and not in one single draw; covenants can be adjusted relatively quickly (waiver requests) if there are unexpected changes in the project; and a loan may be paid down more quickly if more cash becomes available from the project. In addition, and key in some ways, infrastructure lending bankers get to know their clients and develop long-term relationships, which may result in commercial bankers being more flexible than investment bankers and their institutional investor clients.

On the other hand, regulators are taking steps to encourage banks to reduce asset/liability mismatch on their balance sheet, which is the means by which banks have been able to borrow short term (demand deposits) while lending long term (15 to 25-year loans). Since the financial crisis, which was principally a liquidity crisis which then led to insolvencies of banks, regulators have set about restricting maturity transformation through the banking system. This means that they penalise banks which borrow short term to lend long term. They also do not like 'risky' lending and may classify infrastructure lending as risky ('specialised lending' in the language of Basel III), even though rating agencies suggest that it is less risky than corporate lending at an equivalent rating. As a result, they have raised substantially the capital required to back loans and even more so for what they categorise as risky loans. Moody's analysis[11] is shown in Figure 1 on page 134 and demonstrates that infrastructure loans are in fact less risky than corporate loans.

Since infrastructure projects often have a life of 25 years or more whereas banks now prefer to lend for, perhaps, five to 10 years, there is clearly an immediate mismatch between infrastructure projects and the use of bank intermediation for their financing. If expected loss (according to Basel rules) on infrastructure assets (including energy assets) is greater than for other types of lending, banks may prefer those other types of lending. In addition, the new steps being taken by regulators to discourage investment in carbon-related assets through increasing transparency may further reduce the attraction of energy asset investments for both banks and capital markets.

Standard and Poor's[12] recently analysed some of the issues facing banks in the new regulatory environment and how they have set about trying to retain as much of the business as possible.

11 Moody's Infrastructure Default and Recovery Rates, 1983–2016.

12 Michael Wilkins, Infrastructure Finance Ratings S & P, from FTSE Global Markets, 20 February 2017 www.ftseglobalmarkets.com/news/can-the-capital-markets-step-in-to-plug-the-infrastructure-finance-gap2222222.html.

Figure 1: Overall cumulative loss rate

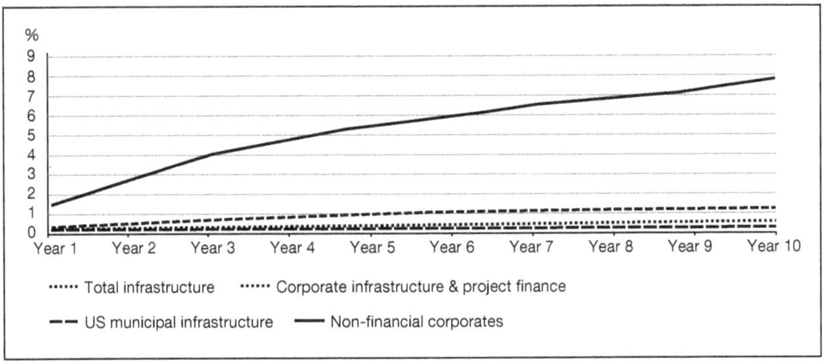

Source: Moody's Investors Service

As regulation compels banks to re-evaluate their approach to project lending, the capital markets may serve to plug the infrastructure finance gap. Global project bond issuance rose by 22% in 2016 (see Figure 2 below), and while this is not yet the take-off that many in the market predicted, the capital markets could play an even greater part in infrastructure finance in the face of falling bank competition.

Figure 2: Global project bond issuance

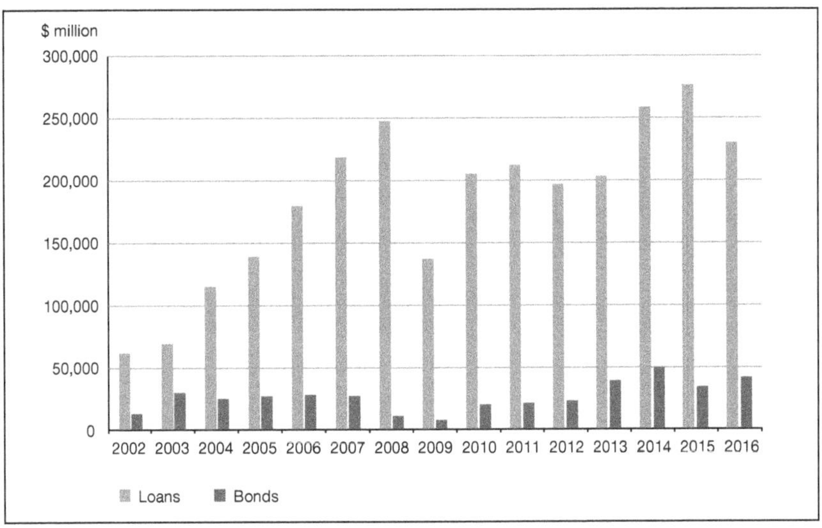

Source: S&P Global

2.4 Increasing role of bond market financing

The transition to greater use of capital market (bond) financing requires a substantial shift in mindset from sponsors and developers seeking to finance projects using project bonds. Investment bankers with whom developers have to deal in arranging a bond issue take a transactional approach to clients rather than the relational approach with which the industry is more familiar. This arises in part from the fact that a debt capital market banker is not providing other services to its client, such as foreign exchange, treasury, interest rate hedging, working capital lending, revolving credit, invoice discounting etc, which a commercial banker might be providing and making a good return on. In contrast the investment banker makes a return only on a single bond issue and a project company is unlikely ever to issue another bond.

In addition, a commercial banker is going to be the investor in the debt, at least initially, and is thus both the arranger (originator) and the investor. In contrast, in the debt markets the arranging (originating) banker is only an intermediary between the developer/sponsors and investors, and consequently, a second key to a successful bond issue is an understanding of the needs of bond investors. Generally, institutional investors seek long-term assets to match their long-term liabilities, such as pension policies, which is in direct contrast to bank lenders, for whom short-term assets are more attractive. Indeed, such assets have become so attractive to investors that at the time of writing many investors believe that the illiquidity premium expected from holding such assets has disappeared.

A bond issued at the time of financial close (rather than at a subsequent refinancing of a bank loan) offers the advantage that it will not require such refinancing because it can have as long a maturity as required by the project company. This therefore mitigates the risk of a future refinancing raising the cost of debt service. This is particularly relevant at the time of writing as interest rates are close to an all-time low and hence more likely to rise than fall.

In addition, one of the key advantages of using longer-term finance (which may be available only from bond markets) is that debt service is spread out over a longer period. This results in a smaller principal repayment each year (amortisation) and hence a greater amount of free cash flow is available to the company in the early years. If, after meeting all prior claims in the cash flow waterfall, there is a larger surplus available to make an equity distribution, then the internal rate of return (IRR) of the project will be higher.

2.5 Corporate bond financing and the Green Bond market

A large energy corporate such as Exxon Mobil would be regularly in the market with new corporate bond issues (both to raise new finance and to refinance maturing issues) in which the 'Use of Proceeds' paragraph in the prospectus would simply state 'For General Corporate Purposes'.

To the extent that such corporates choose to finance new projects on balance sheet, increasingly, this use of proceeds clause is not going to satisfy investors. They will wish to know if any of the proceeds of the issue might leak into carbon-emitting investment projects. If so, many will not buy such securities or the corporate will have to offer a substantial premium. The reason is simple – many of the underlying beneficiaries of institutional investor funds will not permit their fund to make investments that increase global CO_2 emissions.

One (partial) solution to the problem of the use of proceeds clause in a corporate bond is to provide the necessary disclosures on use of proceeds to satisfy the Green

Bond criteria. To help with this process, and in order to make this growing asset class more appealing to institutional investors, the International Capital Market Association (ICMA) developed the 'Green Bond Principles'. These principles are supported by over 115 institutions that participate in the Green Bond market. Traditionally, Green Bonds have been issued by corporates; increasingly, they are also being issued by project companies. Indeed, it is likely that carbon-emitting projects (including projects such as CCGT generators) will find that both new financing and refinancing in the bond markets becomes increasingly difficult as investors choose to hold only Green Bonds and thus invest only in Green Project Bonds.

2.6 Project bond financing and solving potential drawbacks of such financing

While institutional investors like long bonds, whether corporate or project, there are a number of problems which arise when trying to fit project bonds into the capital structure of a greenfield project. The 'sticking point' for bond investors is that project bonds without new credit risk spreading and risk mitigation features may have some characteristics that are not attractive to investors or, to meet the requirements of investors, do not match the needs of projects.

2.7 Credit risk mitigation from sponsor support

Institutional investors generally require a higher credit rating (at least investment grade) than bank investors and are thus likely to require some additional type of credit enhancement if they are to be attracted to investment at the start of the construction phase.

One of the ways in which the investment bankers have tried to overcome this issue is by the use of a construction performance support package (which would include support by creditworthy sponsors), which limits the exposure of bond investors to construction cost overrun or extended construction time and thereby may enhance the bond's rating, as shown in Figure 3.

Figure 3: Construction performance support package

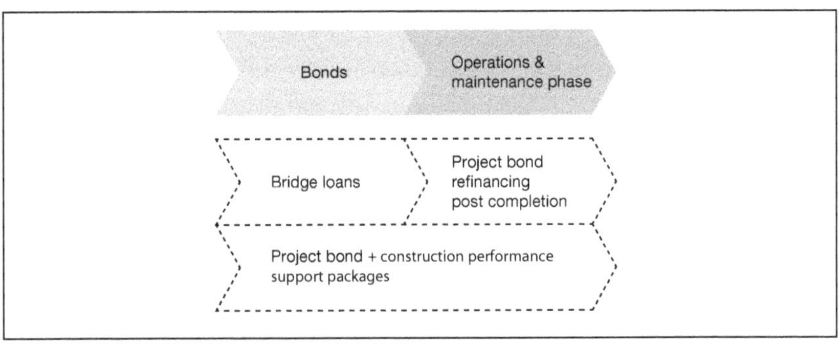

If investors are persuaded that the risk of the construction phase has thereby been mitigated adequately, they may be persuaded to finance the construction phase. Some of these mechanisms are considered in the following sections.

(a) Construction phase – risk mitigation by limited recourse

Project finance is not always non-recourse. Indeed, Dentons[13] notes that:

The expressions 'non-recourse finance' and 'limited recourse finance' are often used interchangeably with the term 'project finance'. In strict terms, non-recourse finance is extremely rare and in most project finance transactions there is some (limited) recourse back to the borrower/sponsor beyond the assets that are being financed... this security may amount to full or partial completion guarantees, undertakings to cover cost overruns or other degrees of support (or comfort) made available by the sponsors/shareholders or others, to the lenders.

Such cost overruns, where the additional funds are supplied by the sponsors, would normally be provided in the form of additional equity. The World Bank views this type of limited recourse as 'sponsor support':

Sponsor support may include:

- *shortfall guarantees, where the banks, after enforcing all other security rights, experience a shortfall;*
- *buy-down undertakings, a promise to prepay project debt to ensure specified ratios, in certain circumstances;*
- *price guarantees, to ensure the price of off-take;*
- *market price purchase guarantees, to purchase a minimum quantity of product at market price over a set period;*
- *tax loss purchases, where a shareholder agrees to purchase certain tax losses from the project company;*
- *technical support, extended warranties and maintenance arrangements; and*
- *contingent equity or subordinated debt commitments to cover construction or other price overruns.*[14]

(b) Non-payment insurance to mitigate credit risk

Banks are taking steps to ensure that they are not competed right out of the infrastructure and energy project financing markets by altering their business model, including the use of non-payment insurance (NPI), as explained by Standard & Poor's:[15]

For instance, getting NPI for 35% of a loan, a lender may be able to reduce the risk of default, constituting a 'BB+' project to one which could be rated 'A'. As a result, banks can put aside less capital for the same loan amount. Furthermore, credit insurance is typically less expensive than credit default swap protection and – unlike bank syndications – averts the need for the lender to introduce clients to competing banks.

To meet stricter capital requirements, banks may also continue to build on their "originate-to-distribute" models; issuing loans to sell rather than retaining until maturity. Société Générale, for instance, is increasingly selling its infrastructure loans to

---

13 Neil Cuthbert, Dentons, *A Guide to Project Finance* www.dentons.com/~/media/6a19989441 7f4877adea73a76caac1a5.ashx.

14 World Bank Group PPPIRC, http://ppp.worldbank.org/public-private-partnership/financing/sources.

15 Michael Wilkins, Infrastructure Finance Ratings S & P, from FTSE Global Markets, 20 February 2017 www.ftseglobalmarkets.com/news/can-the-capital-markets-step-in-to-plug-the-infrastructure-finance-gap2222222.html.

institutional investors rather than syndicating loans between banks – a shift from its pre-crisis strategy. Natixis and Crédit Agricole are executing similar strategies.

NPI, which is also called structured credit insurance, enables banks to claim for non-payment of interest or capital by the borrower. It should result in a higher rating for the loan and hence will enable the bank to have a higher credit limit for this borrower. It should also enable the bank to reduce the amount of (equity) capital that it must commit to the loan under regulations based on the Basel framework. According to Marsh:[16]

The benefits of NPIs for project finance lenders include:

1. *Risk appetite: NPI enables lenders to take on larger deal tickets and complete deals that would typically exceed the bank's credit limits. It also enables the lender to manage obligor group, sector, or country risk concentrations.*
2. *Competitive advantage: By not involving other banks, NPI provides a competitive advantage. Clients are not introduced to your competitors. The insurance enables you to lend amounts that maintain relevancy for sponsors and buyers that you may not have acting alone.*
3. *Revenue: Larger tickets equal larger upfront fees, meaning lenders with NPI behind them can increase their revenue.*
4. *Regulatory: NPI may help optimize the bank's use of regulatory capital, with many jurisdictions allowing the policy to count as tier-one regulatory capital under Basel III rules, providing capital relief for banks.*

It may seem somewhat strange for institutional investors to be buying loans and not just bonds. However, while there are some small legal differences between them, both are provision of credit and, provided the risk/ return profile and other features (eg, term, amortisation schedule) match their needs, institutional investors are generally as happy to purchase loans as bonds. Thus, it may be possible over time for markets to adapt to banks originating (arranging) loans, but with agreements with investors to buy the loans even before construction completion and possibly even at a pre-agreed price, which would hedge the return expected by the investor.

(c) PEBBLE – a possible solution to tailoring project bonds to investor needs

The credit rating problem has been substantially overcome in a very innovative approach developed in 2014 by Allen and Overy (a European law firm with expertise in project finance). This approach also has the potential to overcome the problem of a single drawdown at financial close on bonds compared with a drawdown to match cash outflows during construction. It can potentially also overcome the likely need to modify covenants (waiver requests) during the construction process – something bond investors are not generally willing to undertake.

This approach is named PEBBLE (Pan European Bank to Bond Loan Equitisation) and was adopted by the International Project Finance Association as a standard format for use by the market. The only project on which it has been used so far (by ING and NIBC) was for the Zaanstad Penitentiary. While the concept would appear

16 See Marsh website www.marsh.com/us/services/political-risk/four-benefits-non-payment-insurance.html.

to be sound, alternative lower-cost financing from the European Investment Bank would seem to have subsequently supplanted it. However, it is certainly worth exploring the logic behind it, as it is likely to resurface at a future date. A summary from Allen and Overy[17] is excerpted below:

PEBBLE is designed to boost liquidity for long-term project finance by facilitating the deployment of institutional capital from investors such as pension funds and insurance companies.

Institutional investors have historically struggled with two aspects of project finance:

- *the administrative burden of cash management and waiver requests, especially during the construction phase*
- *the credit rating of most projects, which is typically low investment grade, whereas investor appetite is much greater in the A range*

PEBBLE offers a solution to both of these issues and, as a standard form, is designed to streamline and simplify access for sponsors and procuring authorities to the capital markets. It is structured with a senior A Note and a B Loan, the latter designed to be provided by banks. The B Loan is a first loss piece. It pays down in advance of the A Note, with a maturity of 8 to 10 years, and so covers the riskiest phase of the project.

The B Loan both enhances the credit of the A Note and the B Lenders also act as controlling creditor, taking the more administrative decisions for all creditors, although key decisions affecting project economics will require A Noteholder consent.

The PEBBLE structure also incorporates a Construction Revolving Facility to smooth the drawdown profile of the A Note and B Loan. Importantly, the Construction Revolving Facility can be used to provide liquidity for construction cost overruns. Recent rating agency comment on project bond structures reveals a focus on construction liquidity in determining a whole-life project rating, so this is a key aspect of the PEBBLE structure.

(d) Tranching to transfer credit risk within the capital structure

Another way in which the credit rating of a bond may be increased from that of the underlying project is by internal credit enhancement through subordination by tranching (securitisation). This type of credit enhancement, by creating 'divided interests' in the cash flow of a financing, enables a junior debt tranche (loan or bond) to provide credit support to a senior tranche. An example of such a credit enhancement was the FHW Dalmore (Salford Pendleton Housing) Plc, as shown in the table on page 140.[18]

In this financing, the Class B notes give credit support to the Class A and, in exchange for this support, the nominal return on the Class B is much higher.

(e) Innovative government financial support package

The most innovative infrastructure (but not energy) financing of 2016 was, in our view, the Thames Tideway Tunnel (TTT), the elements of which may also be

17 www.allenovery.com/SiteCollectionDocuments/Pebble.pdf.

18 This is taken from AFME Guide to Infrastructure Financing 2015 www.afme.eu/en/reports/publications/guide-to-infrastructure-financing/.

Issuer	FHW Dalmore (Salford Pendleton Housing) plc
Project description	Refurbishment and management of social housing
Sector	Social
Country	United Kingdom
Project type	Greenfield
Issue type	Internal subordination of the class B notes
Issue rating	None
Amount	Class A: £17.7 million; Class B: 8.35%
Maturity	29 years
Coupon	Class A: 5.41%; Class B: 8.35%
Spread	n/a
Issue price	100%
Listing	Irish stock exchange

Source: AFME Guide to Infrastructure Financing 2015

applicable to the energy projects we consider toward the end of this chapter. The project (Figure 4)[19] is a good example of a highly structured project within the private sector financed with mainly private finance but with support (financial support package) from the UK government.

The tunnel (under the River Thames to take overflow sewage to a sewage works) was required by EU water quality regulations. At a cost of £4.2 billion, the risk to the sponsor's already highly leveraged balance sheet (Thames Water Utilities (TWU) who are responsible for fresh water and sewerage in London) was considered too great for its shareholders to accept. Thus, putting this large project on TWU's balance sheet was not possible. The alternative involved a project company being set up by Thames Water.

In this financing, the regulator, Ofwat, took an unusual approach by asking for bids for the project based on the weighted average cost of capital. On 24 August 2015

19 www.nao.org.uk/wp-content/uploads/2015/06/Thames-tideway-tunnel-early-review-of-potenial-risks-to-value-for-money.pdf www.nao.org.uk/wp-content/uploads/2017/03/Review-of-the-Thames-Tideway-Tunnel.pdf

Figure 4: Flow of money between different parties

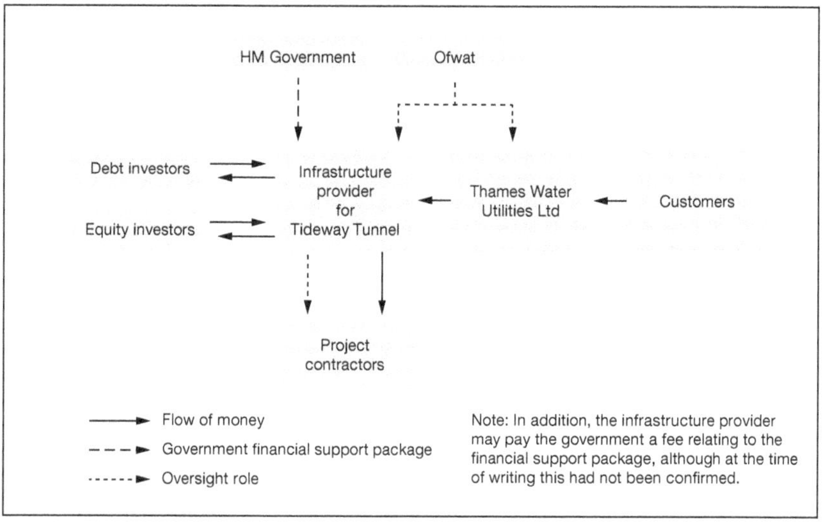

Source: National Audit Office

Ofwat confirmed the award of the project licence for the TTT to Bazalgette Tunnel Limited (BTL). BTL is a special-purpose company formed by a consortium of funds comprising Allianz Infrastructure (34%), Dalmore Capital (34%), INPP (16%), DIF (11%) and Bazalgette Investments Limited (5%).

This project, which is now under construction, had a surprisingly low weighted average cost of capital of only 2.497%. While leverage on the project has not been disclosed, estimates made by Oxera and CEPA suggest that the cost of equity on this project was between 4% and 5.5%.

The TTT has a government support package which is designed to mitigate high-impact/low-likelihood risks during the construction period, and includes insurance cover of last resort, short-term liquidity in the event of financial market disruption, and an additional equity contribution in the event of a significant construction cost overrun. These are among the features which have sufficiently reduced low-likelihood risks, to make this a highly attractive investment to institutional investors, while offering them what would appear to be a very low cost of financing.

However, in order to enable the project company to pay equity dividends to shareholders during the whole of the 10-year construction period, Ofwat also agreed that Thames Water could add a special charge to all London water bills. This made the equity much more attractive to investors by transferring the cost of servicing the equity to customers, prior to the asset coming into operation.

3. A case study: innovative engineering design, production techniques and project financing for generation IV nuclear

There are many who do not believe that we can have clean and green and safe nuclear as an alternative source of energy for power generation. That was the case with previous and some current generation reactors – in particular pressurised water reactors (PWRs), which are not failsafe as a number of nuclear catastrophes have demonstrated. They also cannot be financed using project finance as they have such a high technology risk, high construction phase risk, very high total capital cost and long construction times. These factors all make such power stations not amenable to private sector financing without considerable state support.

Generation IV, high temperature reactors (HTRs), of which the first commercial project will come on-line in China in 2018, are very different from PWRs. These employ passively safe technology which removes the need for redundant, active safety systems. According to the Wikipedia entry for this type of reactor, it can cool by natural circulation and still survive in accident scenarios. Its higher operating temperature allows higher thermal efficiency than is possible in traditional nuclear power plants (up to 50%). This enhanced safety is one factor that may make them financeable using project finance.

In addition to its use for power generation, its high temperature operation makes it very suitable for heat manufacturing processes and thus the production of hydrogen, ammonia (one of the most important chemicals manufactured in the world and used for fertiliser production), synthetic fuels and water desalination. The high safety factor also enables such reactors to be placed much closer to cities than traditional nuclear and thus to be a source of zero carbon space heating as well as power production (combined heat and power). These varied uses, which increase demand beyond just power stations and simpler manufacturing technology, make possible a mass production system in a factory which may give substantial cost reductions (and hence an increase in profit) as they transition from high-cost 'first of a kind' to mass production.

The role of passively safe nuclear in the energy mix arises from the fact that intermittent power (solar and wind) on its own is not, in the authors' view, suitable to provide all the power needs of a country. Even with storage, real issues remain that may not be overcome. Indeed, once we take into account what is known as 'buffering' to overcome output variability, this being the need for overcapacity and storage to enable on-demand dispatch (dispatchability) of the energy source, the efficiency and hence the true cost of utilising an increasing proportion of intermittent power becomes much clearer.

Once we allow for the need for buffering, and the energy losses that result therefrom, the economics of nuclear on the one hand and solar and wind on the other look very different.[20] The 'energy money return on investment' (EMRI) (which is one way of trying to make the economics of different forms of energy comparable) reveals that the cost of buffering does not result in any drop in the EMRI in the case of nuclear (no buffering is required), but a dramatic drop in the case of solar and wind. Wind, in particular, by this calculation drops below what the author defines as the 'economical threshold'.

---

20 Weissbach, D *et al*, Energy intensities, EROIs (energy return on invested), and energy payback times of electricity generating plants, *Energy* Vol 52, Elsevier, April 2013, https://doi.org/10.1016/j.energy.2013.01.029.

The Generation IV reactors provide dispatchable power as, unlike conventional nuclear, they can increase or reduce their output rapidly to help balance fluctuations in wind and solar supply. This makes it easier for the grid operator to manage the variable loads created by wind and solar, thus increasing grid stability. It also reduces the demand for energy storage and so makes wind and solar more attractive to power companies. While the need for dispatchable power provision is debated, it seems likely that if electricity is widely used for space heating and electric vehicles, such power stations will continue to be necessary in addition to intermittent sources such as solar and wind.

Generation IV reactors are generally constructed as small modular reactors (SMRs). They produce only 1/10 of the output of traditional power stations. However, a potentially great advantage is their financeability (ie, they are potentially more bankable than older technologies). The reason for this is that previous generations of power station are so large that the total amount of finance is such that even the capital markets strain to provide the necessary amounts despite huge subsidies from the consumer.

While the cost of power from SMRs per unit of output is still uncertain (as none is yet operational), they remain a potential option for project financing in a way that is not the case for previous and current generations of nuclear. In addition, they can produce hydrogen for use as a vehicle fuel (or to store surplus power) without using natural gas reforming, which is the current process and is not carbon free. Production of electricity and hydrogen can also be switched relatively quickly as demand for power changes. Hydrogen fuel may be necessary as part of the transport (automobiles, trucks, trains, buses) fuel mix as battery power may not be sufficient or appropriate for all electric vehicles currently expected to be on the roads by 2030.

In its 2017 annual update of its *Future Energy Scenarios*,[21] the UK National Grid states that the United Kingdom needs to build 14.5 gigawatts of new nuclear capacity by 2035 or it will fail to meet the two degrees scenario. The report suggests that the size and standardisation of SMRs made in factories and not on site makes them quicker and easier to build than traditional large nuclear plants. In turn, this ability to decentralise power with smaller nuclear is a key factor in facilitating its financing. We are therefore of the view that high temperature modular reactors may be the only financeable option for the generation of a considerable proportion of the United Kingdom's – and other countries' – power needs in the decades ahead.

One company which is developing such reactors is Terrestrial, a Canadian company which has started the licensing process for its molten salt reactor, and which offers an 'economic case' for its reactors based on the much shorter time to reach the end of the construction phase and start producing power (which is one factor in making conventional nuclear unfinanceable in the capital markets) and the much lower unit cost of constructing a single SMR compared with a large reactor (which is the other factor making conventional nuclear unfinanceable without very substantial government support). It also claims a total system cost of $60 per megawatt hour (MWh), which is lower than any other means of electricity

21 www2.nationalgrid.com/uk/industry-information/future-of-energy/future-energy-scenarios/.

generation based on US Energy Information Agency statistics (Capacity-Weighted Average LCOE 2016 \$/MWh). In the graphic below,[22] it also uses a construction cost for conventional nuclear of \$6 billion, whereas the cost of the United Kingdom's Hinkley Point C conventional nuclear station is currently estimated to be £20 billion.

Figure 5: IMSR® – the economic case

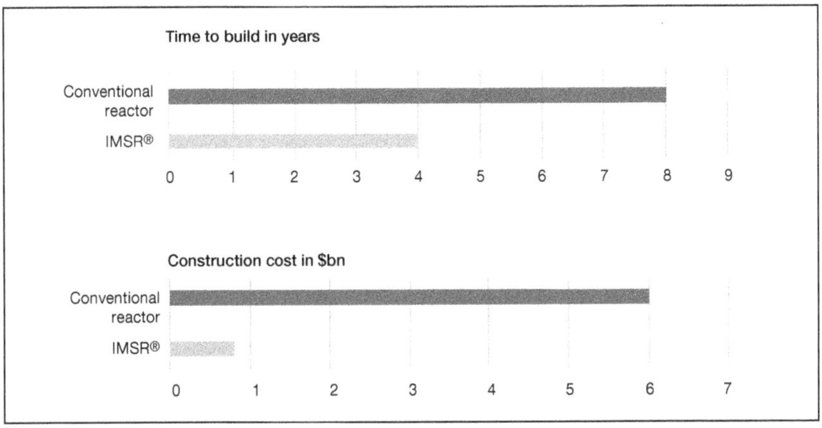

If Terrestrial's estimates or those of other SMR manufacturers prove to be correct, it is possible to conceive of nuclear power being financed almost purely privately through normal project finance techniques. This would, however, require some government support, at least initially, of a type similar to the innovative financing support for the TTT as provided by the UK Government. This, as we noted earlier, involved cover for high-impact/low-likelihood risks during the construction period and included insurance cover of last resort, short-term liquidity in the event of financial market disruption, and an additional equity contribution in the event of a significant construction cost overrun. Additional cover might include cost overrun for decommissioning – although in the case of most SMRs, these costs are expected to be much lower and less uncertain than for conventional nuclear. These support mechanisms are supposed to be priced by a government on an expected cost basis. If this were the case, the expected cost to the government of providing a portfolio of such guarantees (after premium income) would be zero.

A further feature of an SMR project financing would be the attraction to investors of a project with an estimated 55 to 60-year life. This would allow it to be financed using 50-year bonds, which can be highly attractive to some investors and yet still have a long 'tail' to reduce investor risk. The slow amortisation required on such bond financing would reduce cash outflow from amortisation each year and thus provide the potential for a larger annual equity distribution and hence a higher IRR for equity investors (as we noted in 2.4 above). Our conclusion, therefore, is that with an innovative financing solution and on the assumption that SMRs can be

22 www.terrestrialenergy.com/low-cost/.

constructed at a cost around the level being suggested by potential suppliers, that they may within a few years come to supplant CCGT and other uses of natural gas such as space heating.

4. Conclusion

Sustainability, which is where we started this chapter, is about adapting to change, whether in markets, companies, regulation or individual behaviour. What we have considered in this chapter specifically is how a financial system adapts to change to enable the minimum disruption to people's lives despite a changing environment, relative prices in markets and changing risks across the energy sector. Adaptation to enable sustainability will be achieved in financial markets in relation to the energy sector with the necessary push from legislation, regulation and the profit motive. Our final section on SMRs is a demonstration that science and engineering, along with innovative financing mechanisms and risk allocation and mitigation, are enabling an adaptation to the new reality for energy and related markets as we head towards 2050.

Security risk

Gabriel Carter
ALARYX

1. Security risk: context and relative assessment

In the simplest terms, 'security risk' can be differentiated from other risk categories as risk arising from hostile actions planned or carried out by a person or group (a 'security threat'). It is essential to define security risk clearly, to position it in the spectrum of risks affecting the energy sector. This permits effective planning of mitigation strategies and helps to avoid the common error of 'siloing' security management in isolation from other factors that impact upon it.

There are four key risk factors that are not obviously associated with security risk but nonetheless have a profound impact on it (in the context of the energy sector or other large infrastructure sectors). These are discussed in more detail in the following sections of this chapter, but can be understood most effectively by reference to the petal diagram below. A 'secure operating environment' – the fundamental goal for any project – is dependent on effective management of all the risks represented, which, if incorrectly managed, cause an increase in security risk and a corresponding deterioration of the secure operating environment.

Figure 1: Security risk in an holistic context

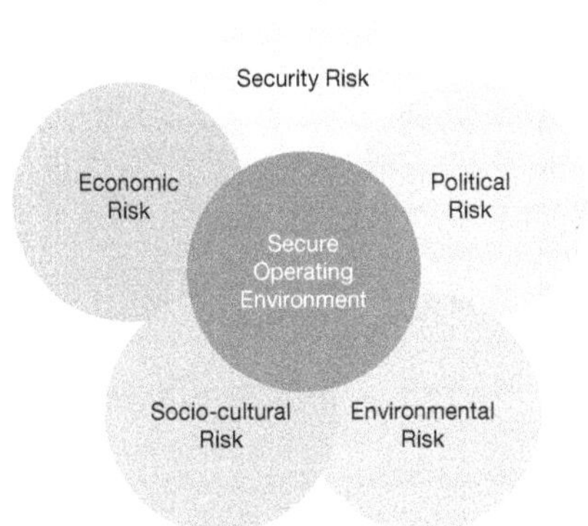

A further challenge facing the energy sector is the need to differentiate between a standalone risk rating and a relative risk rating. While it might be simple to assess the risk to a single facility (using the conventional square matrix of probability × impact), the range, variety and geographical spread of energy sector assets in any given country or region means that it is preferable to establish a relative risk index: to determine the level of risk affecting 'Asset A' relative to the level of risk affecting 'Asset B'.

Garcia (2001) provides an accepted industry standard methodology for comparative rating of threat, probability of attack, and risk. The following formula provides a useful means of comparative, standardised threat assessment:[1]

$$T = \frac{(G_S \times \sqrt{S_L}) + M + \sqrt{O}}{3}$$

$$\text{Threat} = \frac{(\text{Group Size} \times \sqrt{\text{Skill Level}}) + \text{Motive} + \sqrt{\text{Opportunity}}}{3}$$

Each value is represented on a decimal scale of 0.1 (lowest) to 1 (highest). In this way one can compare, for example, a highly motivated, but small and inexperienced hostile actor, with limited means and a relatively un-motivated, but large and capable hostile actor, with excellent means, and determine the relative threats posed by these two sources of threat.

From the threat it is possible to calculate the Probability of Attack (PA) – an essential variable in assessing comparable risk. The following simple formula provides a means of determining the Probability of Attack:

$$P_A = T \times V$$

Probability of Attack = Threat × Vulnerability

Using the same process as for a threat assessment, one can compare, for example, a high threat actor targeting a low vulnerability asset and a low threat actor targeting a high vulnerability asset, and determine the relative probability of a successful attack in each case.

Finally, the following formula allows comparative calculation of risk to deliver a relative risk rating for two or more assets:

$$R = P_A \times (1 - P_I) \times C$$

Risk = Probability of Attack × (1 - Probability of Intervention) × Consequence

This process enables meaningful comparison of, for example, a highly probable attack, strong response capability, low impact incident and a medium probability attack, weak response capability, medium impact incident, and allows the project

1 Garcia, ML, (2001) *Design and Evaluation of Physical Security Systems*; Woburn, MA, Butterworth Heinemann: Ch 1, p9.

operator to determine the relative risks from these potential security incidents. The table below illustrates a simple use case for this process, to determine the true security risk to two different project assets:

Table 1: illustrative T/PA/R analysis of relative risk for different asset categories

	During the first three years of project operations	
Threat Size (S) Skill Level (S_L) Motivation (M) Opportunity (O)	**Attack on export terminal**	**Attack on pipeline**
	0.90 0.70 0.50 0.20	0.40 0.50 0.90 0.80
	$T = \frac{(0.90 \times \sqrt{0.70}) + 0.50 + \sqrt{0.20}}{3}$	$T = \frac{(0.40 \times \sqrt{0.50}) + 0.90 + \sqrt{0.80}}{3}$
	Threat level = 0.60	**Threat level = 0.60**
Probability of attack Threat (T) Vulnerability (V)	**Vulnerability is low: secure location**	**Vulnerability is high: remote location**
	0.60 0.20	0.60 0.90
	$P_A = 0.60 \times 0.20$	$P_A = 0.60 \times 0.90$
	Probability of attack = 0.12	**Probability of attack = 0.54**
Risk to asset from threat P. Attack (P_A) P. Intervention (P_I) Consequence	**Probability of intervention is high; Consequence is very high**	**Probability of intervention is low; Consequence is medium**
	0.12 0.70 0.90	0.54 0.20 0.50
	$R = 0.12 \times (1 - 0.70) \times 0.90$	$R = 0.54 \times (1 - 0.20) \times 0.50$
	Risk from Threat = 0.03	**Risk from Threat = 0.22**

As this example illustrates, while the potential impact of a successful attack against an export terminal by a well-resourced and capable terrorist group might be extremely high, a greater security risk might in fact be posed by low-level pipeline attacks from aggrieved local populations. Similarly, while the potential impact of a deliberate act of cyber warfare on a nuclear reactor might be catastrophic, the risk level might in fact be higher from accidental contamination of non-critical systems by cyber criminal attack.

A clear understanding of risk assessment process is essential, since conflation of impact and risk is a common error in assessing the security challenges and requirements of a project, often leading to misallocation of resources. For example, looking at Table 1 above, while additional capital expenditure on security might provide incremental reduction of risk at an export terminal, the same spend allocated to pipeline security in vulnerable areas might provide an exponential risk reduction. Or in the case of a cyber threat, costly efforts to secure a network against external compromise might be defeated by process failures if staff can bring personal computers, which might themselves be compromised, inside the network.

This chapter addresses some of the key physical security risks confronting the energy sector, and discusses some of the emerging trends in cyber security, highlighting areas of overlap between physical and cyber. The aim is to present a range of tools and processes to manage security risk effectively – recognising not only the core security factors, but also the effects of political, environmental, socio-cultural and economic factors as they influence security risk.

2. Achieving a secure operating environment

As illustrated in Figure 1, a secure operating environment depends on control of various risk factors – not all of which are obviously 'security risk' concerns, but all of which have the potential to compromise security of the operating environment if mismanaged.

2.1 Security risk

Security risk is a natural and inevitable element of any enterprise and includes both internal risk factors, which are often directly controllable, and external risk factors, which may be directly controllable but equally may not be controllable at all.

In a medium- to high-risk environment, control of all feasible security risk factors is critical to sustaining effective operations. Failure to control security risk can have a crippling operational, financial and reputational impact – particularly where it can be shown, after a security incident, that there existed a possibility of controlling or reducing the risk.

The most fundamental and basic principles of managing security risk are as follows:

- Identify the Threats ("What hostile activity may occur?")
- Assess the Risks ("How likely is a threat to occur, and how serious would that be?")
- Analyse the Vulnerabilities ("How susceptible is this asset to the identified threats?")

- Develop a Mitigation Strategy ("How can we reduce the likelihood/impact of a threat?")

The appropriate mitigation strategy depends on the nature of the business and the assets at risk. The energy sector is generally regarded as a high-risk business, dealing with critical assets, often in high-threat environments, and thus particularly robust mitigation strategies are usually deemed necessary. In all cases, the aim of a mitigation strategy is to achieve four key effects in relation to security threats:

Deter:	• Demonstrate that the asset is not worth attacking; is too challenging to attack; or that easier and more attractive targets exist • Take measures to reduce the likelihood of attack: corporate social responsibility programmes, community stakeholder initiatives, local employment, etc
Detect:	• Utilise available resources to identify a potential attack as early as possible – ideally before it has moved beyond the planning stage • Provide intelligence on a forward-looking and real-time basis to those responsible for security
Delay:	• When a threat does in fact eventuate, create layered barriers between the source of the threat and the assets being protected • Take measures to enable the protection of personnel and assets, pending implementation of an effective response
Respond:	• React decisively and swiftly, in accordance with planned measures, to maintain/maximise the safety of all personnel and assets • Cooperate effectively with third parties, including any private or national security providers, and emergency services

The energy sector represents a high-value target to both criminal and terrorist actors, as well as to conventional military forces in the event of inter-state conflict, due to its complexity and economic significance, as well as direct considerations such as the financial value of infrastructure and raw product. Furthermore, many of the territories in which the energy sector operates are also developing or semi-developed countries, and are frequently either post-conflict or conflict-affected areas. It is therefore crucial that mitigation strategies to control security risk are well designed and implemented; however, it is also vital that the mitigation strategies recognise other factors that may influence security risk.

2.2 Political risk

While it is common to consider political risk in terms of the most obvious concerns, such as sudden nationalisation of assets or changes to the regulatory environment, von Clausewitz's observation that "war is the continuation of politics by other means" often holds equally true for manifestations of physical violence that do not meet the strict definition of 'war'.

In the context of its effect on security risk, political risk may be directly related, indirectly related, or unrelated to the energy sector. For example:

- *Directly related political risk:* MEND (Movement for Emancipation of the Niger Delta) identifies the energy sector as directly complicit with the Nigerian government in exploiting and oppressing the people of the Niger Delta region. Consequently, a security risk arises to the energy sector in this region, as it is targeted for violence by MEND as the group seeks to further its political agenda of localising control over the region's oil assets.
- *Indirectly related political risk:* the 2013 In Amenas attack on the Tigantourine gas facility in Algeria was carried out by an Al-Qaeda-affiliated group seeking to compel political concessions from the US and Algerian governments. The Tigantourine facility was selected as an opportune target to further this strategic goal, rather than being targeted because of any direct political opposition to the activities of the energy sector.[2]
- *Unrelated political risk:* Baiji Refinery, which at its peak produced over a third of Iraq's domestic fuel, was almost entirely destroyed in fighting between Islamic State (IS) militants and Iraqi forces between 2014 and 2015, with much of the damage caused by IS fighters' deliberate sabotage of the refinery as Iraqi forces were close to recapturing the site. The refinery was not itself a deliberate target, but was effectively collateral damage in an intensely violent political confrontation.

In all three examples, political factors manifested in violence that profoundly affected the energy sector in these areas. It may not be possible for the energy industry to prevent or alleviate political tensions that lead to such events; however, it is essential that the political context is taken into consideration when assessing security risk in order to implement the appropriate mitigation and response measures.

2.3 Environmental risk

Environmental risk is directly linked to the energy sector, since infrastructure of any kind has an inevitable impact on its environment. The risk is inherent to any infrastructure project during pre-construction, construction and post-construction phases – and is not limited to obvious industrial accidents or disasters (although the energy sector poses specific challenges, inasmuch as energy infrastructure is typically designed to transport or process fuel which, if released into the environment, poses an independent threat of environmental harm).

Environmental risk most commonly affects security risk during the construction

---

2 Hagen, T; Grung-Olsen, R; Fulcher, A; Riis, L; Bunn, J; Handal, EK, (2013) *Report of the investigation into the terrorist attack on In Amenas*, p26.

and post-construction phases. However, it is during the pre-construction phase that the potential impacts should be identified and mitigated to reduce or prevent the likelihood of environmental risk becoming (or contributing to) security risk. For example:

- *Pre-construction:* detailed environmental risk analysis should be undertaken at the earliest stages of the planning process to identify areas of particular sensitivity. Factors which, if not addressed appropriately, frequently cause or exacerbate security risk concerns include: water contamination, land access, livestock and wildlife impact, and human terrain impact.
- *Construction:* construction is usually the most evidently disruptive phase of any infrastructure project. Physical changes are made to the environment and the high tempo of construction activities has a substantial short-term impact. The factors most impactful on security risk are as outlined above: these factors should be identified during the pre-construction phase, in order that their inevitable impact during the construction phase can be minimised.
- *Post-construction:* post-construction normally sees a reduction in the day-to-day environmental impact, as compared to the construction phase, although once operation starts the risk of major contamination through accident or disaster naturally increases. As with the construction phase, it is vital that foreseeable impacts of operation are identified during pre-construction and (as far as possible) mitigated through design. Any environmental impacts that arose during the preceding phases are also likely to have a lasting impact, and where these have caused ill will to arise, it is during the post-construction/operation phase that the infrastructure is most susceptible to security risks arising out of earlier environmental harm.

In all three phases anticipation and prevention are key. Where environmental impacts are inevitable, ongoing dialogue throughout all phases is critical to obtaining and maintaining the consent of stakeholders who might otherwise come to represent a security risk.

2.4 Socio-cultural risk

Socio-cultural risk is inherent to any international activity, and consequently is a frequent concern for the energy sector due to its worldwide operations. The customs, lifestyles and values particular to any given region may well be unfamiliar to a foreign energy sector operator, and vice versa: tension or confrontation on the ground is often a reflection of limited socio-cultural awareness throughout the management chain.

Socio-cultural risk encompasses a wide spectrum of potential concerns. At the more obvious end, offensive behaviours rooted in a lack of cultural awareness (ie, behaving in a manner that offends local beliefs or customs) can cause both acute and chronic deterioration in community consent. On a more complex level, wider patterns of behaviour can undermine the legitimacy of a business operating in unfamiliar territory and erode community consent, without any single action necessarily being identifiable as a cause of this breakdown.

Socio-cultural risk can easily translate to or exacerbate security risk and, if inadequately managed, is perhaps the most corrosive risk factor when trying to establish a secure operating environment. Various key principles apply to effective mitigation, including but not limited to the following:

- *Free, Prior and Informed Consent:* the principle of Free, Prior and Informed Consent (FPIC) is critical, and should in all cases be a defining standard in the planning of any infrastructure project. The foundation of FPIC is a commitment to non-coercive negotiation between investors, companies and/or governments, and host populations at the early stages of any project.
- *Consultation, disclosure and grievance processes:* continuing dialogue is key to preventing any concerns from escalating, and therefore a structured framework for regular communication with host community representatives is essential. Similarly, a transparent and equitable system for addressing and, where necessary, remedying grievances is crucial; it is particularly important that this system is accessible to all members of the host community.
- *Community engagement:* positive engagement with host communities is self-evidently a desirable policy. As a rule, impact projects such as creating training or employment opportunities are preferable to large and expensive infrastructure projects (eg, building hospitals), since the latter very frequently become a long-term cash trap for the company, regardless of any host government assurances to the contrary.

The scope of socio-cultural risk is broader and 'fuzzier' than the other categories of security-related risk, reflecting the complexities of different operating environments, and it is therefore hard to be prescriptive as to all-purpose mitigation strategies. Instead, it is highly desirable to take expert advice from the earliest stages (eg, from anthropologists, social impact specialists and NGOs), and to engage from the outset and on a continuing basis with local community leaders, as well as host governments.

2.5 Economic risk

Economic risk in this context refers particularly to the distorting effect of a highly skilled and (relatively) highly paid industry on the local economy. The impact is felt both in terms of localised price inflation/purchasing power deflation, and often also displacement of or damage to pre-existing local economic activities. While these effects are rarely intended, the energy sector is particularly prone to causing this effect due to (i) its tendency to import external skilled labour and (ii) the inevitable disruption of the local area caused by any major infrastructure project.

Economic risk manifests early in a project – usually not later than the construction phase – and often becomes increasingly noticeable as the project matures. Therefore, it is possible for considerable harm to occur to local populations before this is noticed by the industry that has caused it, by which time tensions have often built to a level that spills over into security risk concerns.

Nevertheless, various measures can be undertaken to mitigate economic risk and reduce its potential to translate into security risk, including but not limited to the following:

- *Local skills development programmes:* one of the most beneficial long-term strategies is investment in developing core skill sets within the local population. This has multiple advantages, including (over a project lifecycle) the potential to reduce costs through local hiring, once a sufficient skill-base has been achieved. In the short- and medium-term, such programmes also demonstrate a clear commitment to the local community and offer a means of bringing the local population on board as stakeholders in the project.
- *Local employment in low-skilled roles:* any major infrastructure project requires a significant level of low-skilled employment in non-core roles – from catering and sanitation to refuse management and haulage. Sourcing local vendors or directly employing from the local population in these roles is a highly beneficial measure, offering (usually) reduced costs and more accountability, and simultaneously creating value in the local economy.
- *Local purchasing arrangements:* it is advisable to establish local purchasing arrangements, to include as much in terms of goods and services as can be achieved with acceptable levels of quality and cost-effectiveness. Simple measures such as purchasing groceries from local rather than national suppliers creates a beneficial ripple effect within the local economy, and further integrates the project with the local population.

Where possible, economic impacts on host populations should be minimised and positive value should be created. It can, however, be challenging to measure some of these outcomes. It is therefore highly desirable to monitor localised economic distortions on an ongoing basis (this can be carried out most simply by periodic 'shopping basket' assessments of local goods and services). Where distortions are identified, liaison with community leaders and in some cases local or national government may offer insight into alternative methods of reducing the adverse impact of such distortion.

3. Physical security risk to energy infrastructure

The physical security risks of main concern to the energy sector are those which potentially disrupt or damage infrastructure, or harm the operating company's (or its contractors') personnel. In essence, while criminal activity may be markedly more common than terrorist activity, it is the latter that represents the most serious risk due to the potentially catastrophic, versus superficially disruptive, impact if a security incident occurs.

3.1 Infrastructure at risk

In the context of physical security risk, energy infrastructure can be grouped broadly into three categories:

- *point assets* (production facilities, refineries, tank farms, power stations, man-camps etc – primarily upstream or downstream assets);
- *linear assets* (pipelines, road/rail haulage routes, communications networks, power networks etc – primarily midstream assets); and
- *remote assets* (surface-level features on an otherwise buried midstream asset,

such as pumping or heating stations, pressure reduction stations, block valves etc; also surveying vehicles and personnel, logistics camps and stores, construction machinery etc – primarily upstream assets).

The level and nature of security risk differs between point assets, linear assets and remote assets.

On the whole, the security risk level assigned to a point asset tends to be driven by the severity of impact should a security incident occur; whereas the risk level assigned to a linear asset tends to be driven by the high(er) probability of a security incident occurring. The risk level assigned to a remote asset will vary substantially, dependent on the nature of the asset.

The high potential impact of disruption or damage to upstream/downstream infrastructure resulting from a security incident (in terms of complexity, cost and time to repair, and increased likelihood of human losses) means that the energy sector tends to focus its efforts in the physical security sphere on controlling these point assets. By contrast, linear assets tend to be substantially less complex and expensive to repair, as well as far more challenging and costly to protect, and are often therefore considered a lesser priority for protective physical security measures.

The impact of accidental or deliberate interference with remote assets varies considerably, dependent on what exactly is being targeted, and for what reason. Criminal activity, such as pilfering of construction equipment, carjacking of inspection vehicles or metal theft is common, but generally has a limited impact, except where the frequency of occurrence exceeds the rate of replacement. Terrorist activity is less common than criminality, but remote assets are consistently one of the more common energy sector targets for terrorist activity, due to their weaker protection (compared to point assets), their accessibility (compared to hardened linear assets), and their remote nature, which facilitates access and escape for an attacker. Again, dependent on what exactly is being targeted, and for what reason, the impact may vary considerably, but it is often relatively high due to the vulnerability of remote assets and the challenges of accessing them for repair.

3.2 Controlling physical security risk

Proper management of the physical security risks affecting point, linear and remote assets relies on a combination of physical, procedural and technical measures.

(a) Point assets

In the case of point assets, conventional response measures focus on three main mitigation strategies:

Reduce:	• Establish a business unit responsible for security management • Develop and apply a security policy and security plan • Negotiate a level of support from the host government • Contract private security where needed to protect the site • Build or enhance physical defences
Transfer:	• Insure against identified threats • Outsource and/or sub-contract higher risk elements • Employ low(er) cost and risk personnel: third country or local
Concentrate:	• Centralise functions and critical assets for ease of protection • Define and establish a perimeter 'safe zone'; limit travel outside

Security response measures at a typical point asset (regardless of the level of threat) usually comprise several layers of physical security protection, and broadly similar security procedures to maximise the effectiveness of security infrastructure. Individual elements may be hardened, dependent on the level of threat.

A typical point asset is likely to resemble the diagram below:

Figure 2: Typical security design of a high-risk point asset

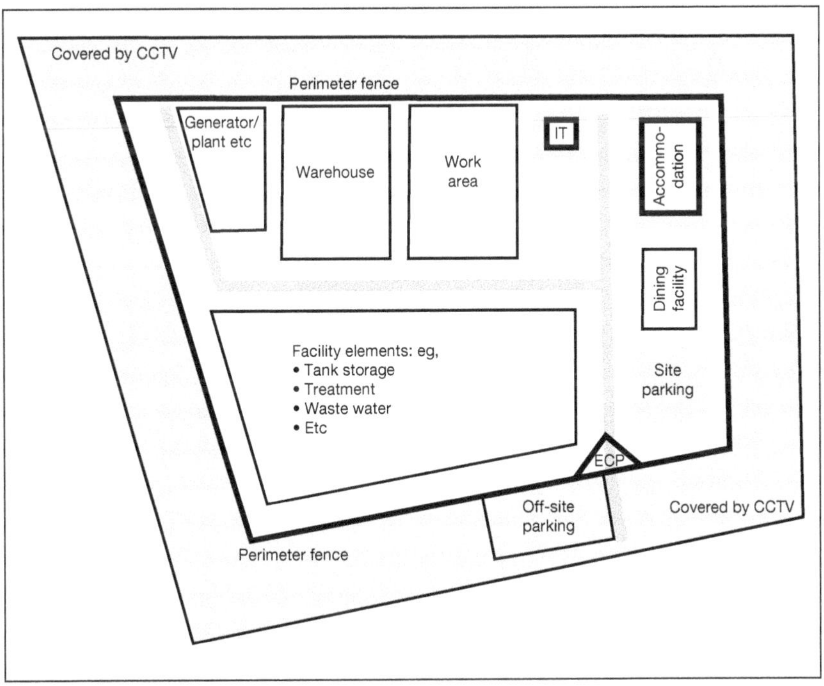

The most common security design for point assets, from major refineries down to comparatively small man-camps, engineering stations or logistics hubs, consists of a blended layer system, as per Figure 2 above:

- *Outer layer:* CCTV monitoring, lighting and maintenance of a clear area around the perimeter;
- *Mid layer:* perimeter fence, wall or berm; one or more controlled entrances; intermittent patrolling from a security guard force;
- *Inner layer:* building access control, locked doors, zoned permissions; and
- *Critical layer:* internal CCTV, restricted zones, hardened doors/windows.

As can be seen in Figure 2, the effectiveness of the security design for point assets is inextricably linked to a concentration strategy. In other words, everything that needs protecting is in a relatively small, easily controlled space, and particularly high-risk elements are treated in the same way, with their own layered security design within a wider security envelope.

While this form of mitigation strategy presents an increased risk in some senses – effectively, the potentially disastrous impact of massive losses in a single security incident – the increased ease of control generally renders it an effective approach for standalone facilities of medium size or larger.

Point assets are a consistent target for hostile activity (particularly terrorist activity), but are also consistently 'hard' targets. Historically, the most common form of attack on point assets in the energy sector has been sabotage, often covered by a conventional ground attack. The most common actors in these attacks are well-established militant groups (recently Al-Qaeda, affiliated Islamist groups and militias).

To protect more effectively against the threat of sabotage and/or ground attack, conventional security measures are commonly employed, including:

- use of armed guards and physical security infrastructure to deter attack;
- use of CCTV systems and alarm systems to identify an attack as early as possible and trigger/inform a security response;
- fencing, gates and controlled zones to prevent or delay entry; and
- use of on-site armed guards and coordination with host country security forces to provide an effective response to any attack

While these measures cannot guarantee the integrity of a point asset, they are generally effective and sufficient to prevent most attacks. The substantial cost of security infrastructure and manpower is justifiable and achievable for concentrated point assets, particularly given the potentially critical impact of a successful attack.

However, the same level of protection cannot feasibly be provided to linear assets, due to their scale and location.

(b) Linear assets

Linear assets may extend for hundreds or even thousands of kilometres, and their decentralised nature makes it impossible to manage risk by concentration in the same way as point assets. The key principles of security risk management (deter, detect, delay, respond) remain at the core of physical security strategy, but are substantially more challenging to achieve:

- *Deterrence:* not all sectors can be protected all the time; creating effective physical deterrents over long distances may be cost prohibitive.
- *Detection:* reliant on technology more than human observation.
- *Delay:* the period of delay needs to be substantially longer, to compensate for the reduced deterrent and detective capacity, and the longer time required to mobilise an effective response.
- *Response:* it is practically and financially challenging (often impossible) to have an evenly distributed response capability that affords rapid and effective reaction to an incident, due to the scale involved.

Conventional response measures to mitigate the risk to linear assets therefore focus on three main mitigation strategies:

Reduce:	• Establish a business unit responsible for security management • Develop and apply a security policy and security plan • Negotiate a level of support from the host government • Maximise detection capability: seismic, optic, radio frequency (r/f), etc • Harden the asset: bury or conceal the pipeline/cabling • Build or enhance physical defences: fencing and berms
Retain:	• Invest in assets to repair damage as quickly as possible • Provide support to host country security forces, to assist reaction
Transfer:	• Insure against identified threats • Outsource and/or sub-contract higher risk elements • Employ low(er) cost and risk personnel: third country or local

Conventional security measures used to protect linear assets are somewhat effective, but substantially less so than measures applied to single-site assets, whether in permissive or hostile environments. To illustrate the difficulty of securing linear assets even in permissive security environments, between 2000 and 2003, the Trans-Alaska Pipeline System in the United States was affected by more than 50 partial or total interruptions to availability, resulting from hostile acts, including: two bombings, 45 instances of damage resulting from small-arms fire, and six miscellaneous instances of sabotage not linked to explosives or firearms.[3]

Security response measures for a typical linear asset generally vary more in line with perceived threat levels than is the case for single-site assets. Measures usually consist of a range of detection and control systems to identify an attack as early as possible,

3 Luft, GL, Korin, A, (2003) *The Journal of International Security Affairs*, (December), "Terror's Next Target", available online at www.iags.org/n053004a.htm.

expedite a response, and minimise disruption and damage. Individual elements may be prioritised, dependent on practical and environmental constraints, or other factors.

A typical linear asset is likely to be protected at least to the standard indicated in the diagram below – in other words, buried for basic protection:

Figure 3: Typical security design of a pipeline in a medium/high-risk area

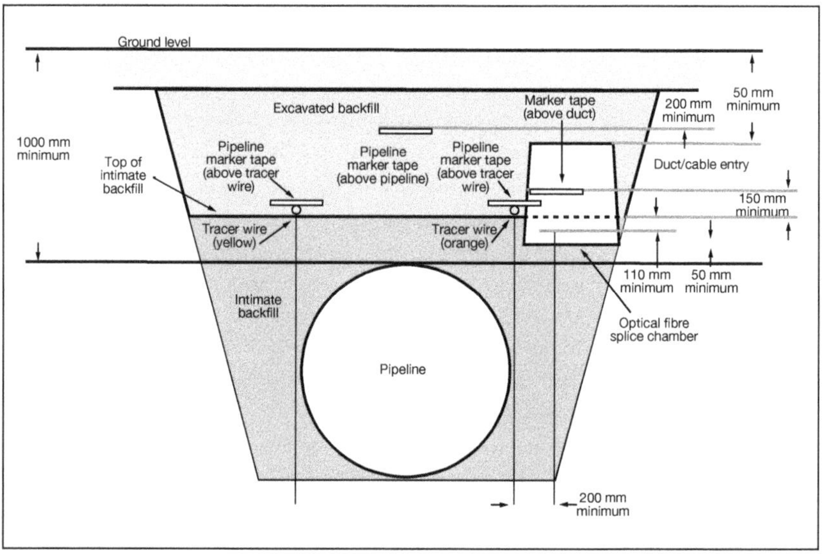

The most common security design for linear assets, from main export pipelines down to single-core fibre optic communications lines, consists of simple target hardening – often burying the pipeline, cable or other asset as per Figure 3 above. It is generally not possible to protect all sections of a linear asset to the same degree or in the same manner as a point asset, since the resources required to achieve this effect are usually cost prohibitive over a long distance.

Where a specific threat to the asset exists – for example, terrorism or criminality – it may be necessary to increase levels of protection further. Typically, this entails deployment of additional detection infrastructure (distributed acoustic sensor, aka fibre optic seismic sensor; use of manned or automated surveillance systems, etc) to trigger a security response to any identified tampering, and may entail further hardening, including:

- burying at greater depth;
- installation of concrete shielding;
- installation of armoured conduit (for cable); and
- deployment of additional detection infrastructure: optic, r/f, etc.

Conventional surface or elevated pipelines are acutely vulnerable to attack using explosives, and indeed are substantially more vulnerable to criminal damage (eg, hot-tapping) or even accidental damage than a buried pipeline. However, even conventional buried designs can be defeated relatively quickly and easily, using techniques that are becoming increasingly commonplace. Due to the vulnerability of even conventional buried linear asset protection (usually around 1 metre depth), additional depth and/or other hardening measures are generally deemed necessary in high-risk environments, or where a known specific threat to the asset exists.

(c) Remote assets

Remote assets are frequently associated with linear assets. For example, pipelines and communications cable commonly require surface infrastructure at predictable intervals to function correctly. Over the long distances common in such situations, remote assets are affected by many of the same fundamental challenges as the linear assets they serve: their decentralised nature makes it impossible to manage risk by concentration.

Conventional response measures to mitigate security risk to remote assets therefore focus on four main mitigation strategies:

Reduce:	• Establish a business unit responsible for security management • Develop and apply a security policy and security plan • Negotiate a level of support from the host government • Maximise detection capability: seismic, optic, r/f, etc • Conceal, disguise or reduce the apparent value of the asset • Build or enhance physical defences: fencing and shielding
Retain:	• Invest in assets to repair damage as quickly as possible • Provide support to host country security forces, to assist reaction
Spread:	• By nature, remote assets are dispersed: risk is spread somewhat • Ensure redundant capability in the event of single asset failure
Transfer:	• Insure against identified threats • Outsource and/or sub-contract higher risk elements • Employ low(er) cost and risk personnel: third country or local

Remote assets are by definition isolated: consequently, the deter/detect/delay/respond process is substantially harder to achieve. Deterrence is compromised, as remote assets often stand out rather than blending in, and security infrastructure is usually quite rudimentary. Detection is more challenging as the remote nature of the assets prevents effective control and detection capability in the immediate surrounding area. Delay is harder to effect because of the practical and financial implications to erecting adequate delaying barriers. Further, response times are usually considerable, given the late detection and the travel time from the nearest reactive force location.

Remote assets in the energy sector are vulnerable to similar threats to linear assets: terrorist or criminal sabotage, damage or theft. In certain cases (eg, remote workers) the threat of kidnap or assassination also exists. Generally, remote assets have substantially lower levels of security measures than single-site assets, as their unit value and unit risk are lower. Similarly, where they are required by design to exist as surface infrastructure, they are less effectively protected than pipelines, cables or other buried infrastructure.

Consequently, remote assets are some of the easiest targets for either criminal or terrorist activity, and the risk to them and their operators should not be discounted.

4. Cyber security risk to energy infrastructure

Cyber security risk is a rapidly evolving feature of the security risk landscape, and one that is far less clearly defined than physical security risk. The widespread (and increasing) networking of operations in all business sectors – from communications to data storage or control systems – means that the range of potential vulnerabilities is ever increasing. As networked operations continue to expand, the range of hostile threats increases rapidly, and the potential severity of such threats is increasing in correlation to the critical nature of networked systems.

Cyber security risk is a particularly challenging field because the range of potential hostile actors (and the nature of their capabilities) is in many cases much wider than is the case for physical security risk. A successful physical attack against energy infrastructure is likely to require not only opportunity and motivation, but also a degree of resource scale on the part of the attacker. In contrast, cyber threats can originate from 'lone wolf' activists, state-controlled cyber warfare agencies or anything in between: a catastrophic attack might originate from a hobbyist's basement. Furthermore, in many cases the threat may not even be targeted deliberately against its actual victim: potentially damaging malware or other cyber attacks often seek to compromise systems indiscriminately, without deliberately targeting any specific organisation.

4.1 Forms of cyber threat

In broad terms, cyber threats can be grouped into four main categories:[4]

- cyber crime;
- hacktivism;
- cyber espionage; and
- cyber warfare

All of these categories represent potential risks to the energy sector: even an untargeted cyber breach may have a serious impact on industrial control systems (ICS), for example, and targeted cyber attacks may have catastrophic consequences. As the sophistication of hostile cyber actors increases, the energy sector is ever more exposed to cyber security risk: the prevalence of unpatched legacy systems, and the difficulty in achieving network-wide downtime to update systems without compromising operations, means that the energy vertical is an increasingly attractive target for cyber attack.

---

4 US Department of Homeland Security (2015) report on cyber security concerns.

(a) ***Cyber crime***

Cyber crime is commonly indiscriminate in nature. The intent is to obtain value opportunistically from compromising individual computers or systems. Ransomware (designed to deny access to data on a victim computer until a ransom payment is made) has been the most rapidly growing threat in this category since 2015, closely followed by data theft.

Currently, ransomware attacks are unlikely to have a catastrophic impact on the energy sector: ransomware attacks have mainly targeted individual computers rather than networks, meaning that a compromise is likely to have a limited effect. However, it is probable that industrially/commercially focused ransomware will start to be deployed, seeking to deny networks or control systems, and potentially extort far larger ransom payments (as seen in a small number of targeted ransomware attacks against hospitals in 2016).

Data theft attacks, on the other hand, are potentially of very serious concern to the energy sector. For upstream operators, the possibility of sensitive commercial information theft is a serious concern. For consumer suppliers in the energy sector the reputational consequences of losing customer data are potentially enormous, and the possibility of punitive regulatory action by governments and/or class action lawsuits in the event of a data breach must also be taken into consideration.

(b) ***Hacktivism***

Hacktivism is usually targeted against specific organisations or individuals for idealistic reasons: hacktivist attacks generally seek to cause embarrassment and/or disruption, usually with the stated aim of righting (real or imagined) social wrongs. Hacktivist attacks are most commonly associated with perceived infringements of free speech, human rights or freedom of information.

Vandalism or takedown of websites have been the most common threats in this category since 2015, although more seriously disruptive attacks are not unknown. At the most prominent end of the hacktivist spectrum, groups such as Wikileaks and Anonymous have engaged in widespread hacktivism against governments, private sector organisations, terrorist networks, paedophile groups and other targets.

The energy sector has so far been minimally subject to hacktivist activity. However, any activity attracting unusually high controversy (eg, fracking, disputes over pipeline routing, industrial accidents or disasters, allegations of human rights abuse, etc) increases the risk of energy sector operators being targeted by hacktivist groups.

(c) ***Cyber espionage***

Cyber espionage refers to the use of computer networks to gain illicit access to confidential information. Historically, cyber espionage has on the whole been confined to nation-state level actors, and is closely linked to cyber warfare. Cyber espionage usually seeks to compromise networks as widely as possible, with as little disruption as possible, in order to harvest data over a long period of time and potentially act as a dormant back door for any future act of cyber warfare. By virtue of its often-covert nature, trends in cyber espionage are typically harder to identify.

Generally, cyber espionage has two motivations: data gathering (for economic or other purposes) and human targeting (seeking to develop a coercive hold over an individual with privileged access to information or control systems).

Cyber espionage is a significant threat to the energy sector, and closely related to cyber warfare. The energy sector may be targeted for cyber espionage for multiple reasons, including but not limited to:

- economic exploitation of sensitive or commercial data (eg, the Dragonfly cyber espionage group, which penetrated and stole data from over 300 energy sector firms in the United States and Europe between 2011 and 2013);
- indirect state-on-state influence operations (eg, the extensive cyber espionage penetration of Ukrainian energy sector organisations, which opened the door for a major cyber warfare attack in 2016); or
- gaining intelligence on unknown capabilities and activity (eg, credible allegations of cyber espionage against the Iranian nuclear power sector by Israeli and US intelligence agencies).

(d) Cyber warfare

Cyber warfare is almost exclusively the preserve of national intelligence and/or military agencies, and aims to achieve widespread degradation, disruption, denial or destruction of critical infrastructure. While comparatively rare, cyber warfare attacks are not unknown – and the energy sector is a high-probability target in the event of a cyber warfare attack being carried out, due to the major disruption caused by knocking out elements of a country's energy infrastructure.

Examples of cyber warfare include:

- the December 2015 attack against the Ukrainian power grid, generally attributed to the Russian intelligence services (although this has not been proven);
- the crippling of North Korea's internet capability in December 2014, believed (although again not proven) to have been the result of a cyber warfare attack by the United States;
- the 2012 hacking and destruction of 30,000 computers within Saudi Aramco's corporate network – albeit not affecting production systems – believed (although again not proven) to have been a cyber warfare attack by Iran; and
- the partial destruction of Iran's Natanz nuclear reactor, and other elements of aerospace and defence systems, in late 2009/early 2010 by a US and Israeli cyber warfare attack (Stuxnet Worm).

Cyber warfare, like cyber espionage, represents a very serious threat to the energy sector. Energy infrastructure and its owners/operators may not be the primary target of a cyber warfare attack (which is more likely to be targeted against the host country), but the impact on the host nation of a cyber attack against energy infrastructure is likely to be of sufficient strategic value that the attacker may view energy infrastructure as acceptable collateral damage, or indeed as a viable strategic target in its own right.

4.2 Cyber security vulnerabilities

The cyber vulnerabilities of the energy sector are concentrated in, although not limited to, networked systems: industrial control systems (ICS) in general, and particularly supervisory control and data acquisition (SCADA) systems and distributed control systems (DCS).[5] Among these vulnerable infrastructure components, open software systems and communication protocols are more commonly targeted than proprietary systems. The open standard makes it significantly easier for cyber attackers to gain in-depth knowledge of the systems' strengths and weaknesses.

Vulnerabilities are particularly acute in older systems. Hostile cyber actors are more likely to have a developed understanding of the code weaknesses in these systems, and countermeasures are likely to be outdated. Compounding this problem, the increasing trend to integrate as many systems as possible means that access may be gained to a SCADA network via peripheral devices. Although these devices may not themselves be critical, they can act as a stepping stone to more critical system components.

While critical infrastructure control networks are normally – and should always be – air gapped from unsecured public or local networks, there are still vectors that can be used to jump this gap. There are several known examples already in the cyber ecosystem of malicious code that seeks to defeat air gap isolation, including methods of hijacking a cell phone and using it as an unwitting bridge to an air-gapped computer.[6] As with any form of security threat, a continuous arms race persists between the defenders and the would-be attackers, and it is highly probable that efforts to defeat air gap isolation will remain a key priority for cyber espionage and cyber warfare agencies in particular.

Countering these vulnerabilities is highly challenging, as the threat is continuously evolving and very often undetected until an attack has been carried out. It is therefore essential to understand the interconnection of cyber and physical security risk, as far as possible, since this provides some ability to: (i) look 'over the horizon' at the potential origins of cyber security threat; and (ii) recognise the potential physical impacts of a successful cyber compromise.

4.3 Where cyber security meets physical security

The factors that influence a secure operating environment (discussed earlier in this chapter) are as relevant to cyber security as they are to physical security. Likewise, the increasing connectivity of systems, processes and data mean that a cyber security incident is increasingly likely to have physical consequences and vice versa, as illustrated by the examples below.

- *Political risk creating a high cyber security risk:* a hypothetical international energy operator in Saudi Arabia should recognise that political risk represents a key source of physical and cyber security risk. The persistent tension in Saudi/Iranian relations might present only a low risk of conventional warfare

---

5 Robles, Choi, Kim, Park, 'Vulnerabilities in SCADA and Critical Infrastructure Systems' (2015) *International Journal of Future Generation Communications and Networking*, Vol 1.

6 Guri, Mordechai, Kedma, Gabi; Kachlon, Assaf; Elovici, Yuval: 'How to leak sensitive data from an isolated computer (air gap) to a nearby mobile phone' (2014) *BGU Cyber Security Labs White Paper.*

(in a conventional war the energy sector would be a key target for attack, but the likelihood of conventional war is low). However, the cyber security risk is far higher. Iran is known to have highly advanced cyber warfare capabilities: its antagonistic history with Saudi Arabia indicates a high level of cyber threat, and a very credible risk of attempted cyber espionage, back-dooring, and potentially cyber warfare attack in the event of escalating political tensions. In this case the 'victim' energy sector operator would be merely a strategic target in a wider confrontation, rather than a target per se.

- *Socio-cultural and environmental risk creating a medium cyber security risk:* a hypothetical European infrastructure contractor consulting on the construction of a controversial pipeline (eg, the Keystone pipeline) might conclude that its physical security risk exposure is minimal; but might equally conclude that a medium level of cyber security risk exists, focused on hacktivist vandalism of the company's reputation, communications systems or data.
- *Cyber security risk creating a physical security risk:* a hypothetical guard-supervisor at an oil and gas services man-camp in Algeria suffers from an opportunistic criminal email hack, which reveals not only his name, his job and his home address, but also evidence of an extra-marital affair. This information is sold by the cyber criminals to a terrorist group, which blackmails the guard-supervisor into allowing the group access to the camp, where a mass-casualty attack is carried out.
- *Physical security risk creating a cyber security risk:* a hypothetical upstream operator in North Africa allows members of staff to access the company intranet via a VPN installed on their personal laptops. A staff member leaves his non-password protected laptop in his hotel room, from where it is stolen. Details of the company's network and communications systems are exposed, and substantial amounts of data and confidential information are stolen. This leads to the release of inside information and a huge loss of market advantage.

5. Conclusion

The basic tools commonly used to assess security risk are insufficiently complex to reflect accurately the range and variety of physical and cyber security risks to the energy sector. More sophisticated assessment methods are called for, and these should be deployed with due consideration to less obvious peripheral factors that may influence security risk.

Physical security risk rarely, if ever, arises in a vacuum. And, almost invariably, where a physical security risk becomes a physical security incident, subsequent analysis shows early warning signs or other intelligence which could have prevented or mitigated the impact of the incident. Consequently, it is imperative to devote appropriate resources to: monitoring for such warning signs; de-escalating potential triggers; and developing and sustaining a secure operating environment with more than just barbed wire and armed guards.

Particular to the energy sector and other large distributed infrastructure sectors, the physical security risks vary considerably between specific assets. As well as reinforcing the need for more sophisticated risk assessment processes, this variation in security risk requires a clear understanding of the different methods of mitigating security risk for each class of asset, and a strong strategic grasp of the principles of security to integrate these different mitigation measures effectively.

Cyber security is an extremely fast-evolving arena, and the 'arms race' between would-be attackers and defenders shows no sign of slowing down. It is rarely possible to prove definitively the origin of a cyber attack. National agencies are increasingly taking advantage of this opacity to carry out semi-covert (or at least deniable) cyber attacks in furtherance of national policy: the energy sector, which often falls into the critical national infrastructure category in its host country(ies) has been targeted for cyber attack in the past and is highly likely to be so targeted in the future.

In today's increasingly networked world, it is increasingly challenging to isolate cyber and physical security risk even at the micro or consumer level. For any complex industry, and particularly for the energy sector (which typically operates connected infrastructure over long distances and wide areas), it is impossible to disentangle cyber security and physical security concerns. Consequently, there are clear advantages to assessing the risks posed by each on a comparative rather than standalone basis, and to treating both the causes and symptoms of security risk (be they cyber or physical) within an holistic framework for security management.

Black swans and disruptive change

Sir Mark Allen

Troy Edwards
Allen & Overy LLP

Sir Mark Allen:

A friend this morning brings to mind our conversation about risk. He tells me he advises a major bank which has a 'risk department' employing 7,000 people... After a few moments chewing this information, I reflect that risk is indeed, as Mary Douglas taught, a 'social construct'. Our attitudes to risk are conditioned by social and cultural influences, as well as by individual factors. By collectively talking up risk, we increase our perception that there is risk out there. A proliferation of 'risk talk' promotes the growth of an industry of risk analysis. In no time you need a fair sized department to do it all. Is it that simple?

Clearly there are a number of categories of risk which it may be useful to comb out. There is, for instance, statistical risk which presumably lies behind the techniques of life insurance companies who have to make a judgement about the likelihood of death, as people age. The insurers may take a detached view of this, but it probably sounds like risk to the policy holder. Political and economic risk assessments genuflect to the doctrine that we cannot foretell the future, but then go on to retail forecasts. These are usually built on the evidence or argument of so-called underlying trends. The subjective selection of these and the way other possible underlying factors are excluded are another matter. There are risks posed by 'unknowables' like technological breakthroughs, or the outbreak of epidemic or pandemic diseases – Spanish 'flu or bird 'flu. There are risks latent in the unpredictable connections between events, like the eruption of a volcano in Iceland engaging with particular weather conditions – and the result? The grounding of commercial air travel across much of Europe and Western Asia. There are risks which seem particularly to be conjured up by ignorance – early popular anxieties about the nuclear power industry were a good example of this. It is not hard to imagine the teams one might like to have researching and getting a grip of risks like these.

Mary Douglas's point was that there are social factors at work here and not simply individual choices. Subliminally or not, these factors could point in the direction of groupthink. Her often-used example was the perception that New York was a dangerous city. She showed that the strength of the perception bore little relation to the statistics for violent crime and murder in the city, which latterly showed a clear improvement in security. She was always careful to emphasise that her 'cultural theory' model for showing the relationships between group characteristics and behaviours was only indicative and slight, not meant to be inflexible or all embracing.

In the 10 years since Mary died, so much has happened in the fields of information and communication that one can only speculate how she would have interpreted these changes. An immediate question arises about how Western society is using information and communications. The social glue of agreed 'common sense', itself a powerful contributor to groupthink, seems to be diminishing as hierarchical influences over attitudes get weaker. On the other hand, the individualistic quality of social media, together with the corresponding empowerment of opinion and news, gives us the phenomenon of information (of whatever kind) 'going viral'.

Our society increasingly conforms to an egalitarian culture characterised by weak regulation and strong integration, at the expense of the hierarchical type, strong on both regulation and integration. Both types, being strong on integration, suggest an inclination to conform, although in different ways.

The information revolution may suggest we can have more confidence in our cognitive powers. Purposeful data mining and online sources like Wikipedia appear to give us greater mastery, but the integrative factors still point in the direction of groupthink. Whether we understand society to be still hierarchical in nature or (increasingly) egalitarian, we find that we are keyed into patterns of conformity. Whether the explicit exclusiveness of sensitivity about 'people like us' or the coercive inclusiveness of political correctness, the outcome is similar: there is an infectious quality to our sense of risk. Fear is at its most effective when it speaks in the present tense.

Groupthink contains its own surprises. Consider for a moment those wonderful documentary films about migration on the Serengeti. In the aerial shots, long lines of gnus stretch across the screen. We can scarcely hear the insistent lowing and grunting from the herds. This comes suddenly as the camera pans in and we see the stoic expressions on the beasts' faces. Then to one side we see the lions... they are watching the parade. The gnus are aware, they must be, of the lions, but are not twitched by them. A lion stands, walks, breaks into a trot and then a focused run. She has spotted a calf and is charging. The calf outruns the lion. The calf's parents and relations make feints and minatory gestures at the lion who retires back to the side of the parade. No other drama.

The point here seems to be that the gnus' groupthink has calculated that the fear of lions is outweighed by the knowledge that there is safety in numbers; that the lions will only go for weaker prey, but that at this season the calves are strong enough to outrun the predator, give or take some distracting anti-lion antics from the relations.

Similarly, years ago when I was a falconer and going rook hawking on Salisbury Plain, I remember being struck by the speed at which a flock of rooks, thrown into turmoil and extreme exertion by the sight of the hawk (and they could always tell a hawk intent on prey, as opposed to one just flying around), would then resettle quite quickly on the ploughed field when one of their number had been taken by the hawk. They would begin feeding again.

The robust resilience of these natural risk analysts is very striking. Their discipline in fitting their capacity for groupthink into useful and pragmatic purposes is impressive. And how different are impressions of groupthink in our own species when it often signals a resignation from the robust and purposeful. It seems very likely that the filmmaker's hunch was that the viewers would be more disturbed by the lions than were the gnus. If a lion charge was a point of high drama on the migration, the gnus were not showing it. The safari set, however, were.

So what is to be said about the psychological dimension of our perception of risk – collectively as much as individually? Does certainty (itself a social construct) offer some prophylactic stability in how we see risk? Does uncertainty, in contrast, seep from one sphere into another (what about all those prognostications of economic dip following the Brexit vote?), increasing the velocity of 'actual' risk as things fall apart?

Troy Edwards:

There is, in certain parts of the advisory community, a consistent undercurrent of concern as to whether our clients' approach to risk is, as you say, driven by a level of groupthink that derives comfort from the fact that a particular risk has always been acceptable before, so why would there be any need to change that now? This approach with some adaptation from transaction to transaction has served investors and financial institutions well for the vast majority of risks and projects. Why would a trader revise his model for future oil prices if that same model has generated reliable predictions, and reliable returns, for the past five, 10 or 20 years?

However, what those models and approaches will generally fail to account for properly is disruptive change, which in our current epoch has been largely driven by incredible technological advances, environmental changes and social developments.

In this respect, it is worthwhile differentiating between short-term investments that are much less susceptible to disruptive change, and long-term investments where the return on that investment, including the initial principal, requires certain consistent conditions to be maintained over a prolonged period. The types of projects and investments discussed in this book for the most part fall into this second category. For example, the enormous capital cost of a new liquefied natural gas (LNG) facility, upstream oil and gas development or utility-size power plant necessarily means that the investors in those projects, including the governments that are relying on those projects to deliver outcomes for their populations, will require a range of assumptions to remain correct so as to generate their expected returns.

When establishing those assumptions, those investors will have considered and weighed the risk factors applicable to the investment. This is where the benefits and risks of groupthink arise, with classical risk factors including:

- Credit risk – will the person that has promised to pay for the generated product (and therefore ultimately to fund the project) actually have the means to make those payments over a prolonged period?
- Market risk – will the price of the product in the market over the same prolonged period produce sufficient cash flows to repay the project's investors?
- Construction risk – will the project be built in the required time period? Will the constructed asset actually be capable of operating at the assumed and

required levels? Will the cost of the construction be consistent with the assumptions that underpin the investment?

- Political risk – will those governments with jurisdiction over the project act in a manner which is consistent with generating the required return on the investment throughout the life of the project?

However, the question in a changing world must be whether these standard lists of issues remain the critical factors for assessing a project. Or, alternatively, do questions of credit, market, construction and political risk need to be viewed through a prism of potentially disruptive change in social, technological, environmental and political areas?

Arguably, this is a question which industries and their supporters have always faced, yet it is today's pace of change which brings the need for a reassessment of project risk analysis to the fore.

A relatively recent example of an industrial sector which has had disruptive change thrust upon it is the coal industry. The environmental and health and safety risks associated with the coal value chain have been known for a long time, yet it is only recently that investments in coal sector have come under significant pressure, including due to the following factors:

- a rising political and public focus on climate change, an acknowledgement of the critical role that energy production plays in climate change and the incompatibility of coal-generated power production with the various climate change objectives adopted by sovereign states, either independently or through multilateral treaties and regional agreements;
- the growth of the natural gas sector, including through LNG technology and shale gas developments which have changed the United States's energy markets with significant knock-on effects for global energy markets. Natural gas reflects and has been adopted as a viable alternative means for the production of baseload power, with negative implications for both coal and nuclear investments (albeit that nuclear has at least superior climate change credentials). Indeed, the cancellation of troubled new-build nuclear power plant projects in the United States and the early closure of operating nuclear assets, notwithstanding the promise of nuclear electricity that would be 'too cheap to meter', underlines the fundamental disruption that the rise of natural gas has caused;
- the significant technological, cost (particularly when coupled with government support arrangements, driven largely by climate change objectives) and reliability advancements made in renewable energy, especially solar and wind power, which have enabled renewable energy to become a realistic complement, and in some jurisdictions an alternative, to traditional fossil fuel power production. The next logical disruptive event in this respect is likely to be the development of industrial scale battery technology which mitigates the intermittency limitations associated with renewable energy so as to allow renewables to operate as, or close to, base load production.

A consequence of these developments has in many, although certainly not all, jurisdictions been either an economic sidelining of coal-fired generation or a politically imposed moratorium on new coal-fired power plants and the shutdown of existing assets. Investors in coal-fired plants may or may not have foreseen these changes and, indeed, may have fully amortised their investments ahead of them. However, the lesson is clear: just because a particular technology is dominant now (as coal once was), today's cutting edge solution is inevitably at risk of becoming tomorrow's mothballed and retired plant.

This has always been true; what is different now is that the time until tomorrow is much shorter, but the investment horizon for developers and governments has not changed. The result is that today's investments are exposed to disruptive change to an extent and in a manner that has perhaps never before existed.

The difficulty with disruptive changes, with 'black swans', is of course that by definition they are not predictable. However, playing clairvoyant and looking at recent events for inspiration as to what the future might hold, we can speculate as to the factors which are likely to play a material role in our future and could, therefore, form a basis for an adjusted approach to project risk assessment that goes beyond today's current methodology.

- Technological developments remain the most obvious initiator of disruptive change, particularly in the energy sector. As mentioned above, the rise of battery storage coupled with enhanced renewable power options and improved extractive methodologies in the hydrocarbons sector are all very relevant factors for assessing what the future world's global energy mix will be, and therefore what will represent a sound investment today. More dramatically, should nuclear fusion be mastered and become available for commercial use (with the ITER fusion project being among the most exciting developments under way in any sector), then our current energy technology will likely seem primitive by comparison. Similarly, the rise of electrified transportation, smart networks, the 'Internet of things', blockchain technology and a range of comparable developments all have the potential to alter materially our demand-side requirements.
- Environmental change is (notwithstanding the views of those that seem, whether through self-interest or ignorance, to disregard the startling evidence) upon us. Droughts, hurricanes, rising temperatures, as well as, among other things, dwindling fish stocks, pesticide-resistant insects, the effects of clear-felling rainforests, mass production of cattle and increasing urbanisation are, either individually or collectively, matters that are very likely to affect the nature and need for industrial developments in the future.
- Finally, the change in the way we interact with each other and the availability of information across social, cultural, physical and nation-state boundaries through Twitter, Facebook and other social networks underlies the potential for enormous social and political upheaval with knock-on effects to virtually all endeavours. The Arab Spring, as well as recent elections in the West, are examples of this, with rising populations in Africa and other emerging jurisdictions and growing middle classes in China and India

> presaging potential future social adjustments on a vast scale. How our politicians adjust to this and how we are able to manage our natural resources to feed, power, water and meet the aspirations of this and future generations may perhaps generate the biggest disruptive change of all.

We certainly live in interesting times and predicting the future has never been more challenging.

Sir Mark Allen:

An Arabic proverb runs, "Your grandfather's enemy doesn't like you, seem though he may, like the water of Qubaisa, every moment a different colour." The point is that the water at Qubaisa in western Iraq has such a strong mineral content that colours merge, change and swirl on its surface in the sun, rather as we see in petrol spilt on a puddle. So this is an evocation of a profound human truth about the intractable prejudices of politics in a tribal society and also a striking metaphor for change – we would say, 'it's like petrol on water'. It seems to me that our exchange about risk is really about change and our capacity to see and cope with it – the human factor.

I tried to bring out the riddles in our perception of our world – the way we are caught at once in the reflexes of group behaviours and the wilfulness of individualism, the atomisation of communications through the internet. In your reply you traced these themes in the field of energy, tracking factors for uncertainty through technology, the environment and the turbulence (increasingly) affecting politics and the context for investment and commercial decisions. You ended by underlining the vital links between the need to manage natural resources and political responses to the currents of change which are confronting society.

No wonder, then, we are fascinated, like the safari set, by ambush and disruption, intravenous change. How we love drama. And you are right in showing that part of the big drama in risk assessment is really seeing how change itself changes.

It is easy to see how change marches on in straight lines, particularly when we are watching in retrospect. For all sorts of reasons, it is now possible to make rational forecasts about the future course of certain diseases. A chain reaction in cognitive advances delivers progress.

The acuity of the Arabic proverb is to remind us how change, 'every moment a different colour', does not have to move straight ahead in deductive, logical sequences. Instead, like petrol on water, the colours slip and shift. To our eyesight, it all seems beyond rhythm and pattern. Correspondingly, the changes surprise and fascinate us. Changes in one department of life cause collateral changes in others, which can seem mystifying. The application of nano physics to medical procedures may prove to be a case in point. The impact of forex shifts or step changes in financial conventional thinking can amount to others, as we saw in 2011. Suddenly the effect is felt in the midst of an energy sector project – the risk analysts are quickly wise after the event; consultants go Panglossian; and corporate culture, like the rooks on the plough or the gnus on migration, determines stoically to press on. The commentariat, meanwhile, revels in a perceived crisis.

So I quite agree with your critique of those who hold fast to the judgements of the past, in assessing future risk. Facing up to the challenge of exploring change takes good nerves. We do need to remain open to new connections and patterns, new science and new thoughts about our natures, else we shall assuredly get behind the game.

You point to the contrasting timescales of technological change and major industrial projects in the energy sector. The tension in the investor community is a reflection of an impatient culture, vulnerable to short-term performance worries. In the end, the problem comes back to ourselves and how we are. The theme in the proverb is the important one: the enduring characteristics of human nature. It is a good rule, particularly in times of change, not to lose sight of human nature. We may improve in our understanding of change (chaos theory is part of our colloquial now), but the key thing is how well we are doing, both individually and collectively, in coping with ourselves in the face of change. Recognising that we are ineluctably part of it is in the nature of the challenge. Black swans are not just alien incomers, but also represent the blind spots in our imagination and perception. The oracle at Delphi was ace at risk assessment: 'γνωθι σεαυτον' – 'Know thyself'.

About the authors

Sir Mark Allen
mjsa@btinternet.com

Sir Mark Allen has been a special adviser to BP plc since 2004. He studied Arabic and Turkish at Oxford and joined the Foreign Service in 1973. With postings in Abu Dhabi, Cairo, Belgrade and Amman, his career was divided between Middle Eastern, African and East European affairs and with global issues such as counter-proliferation and counter-terrorism.

He has written four books and his latest, *Arabs*, was published in June 2006. He is a director of St John and St Elizabeth's Hospital in London and sits on a number of advisory boards and councils. Mark is an honorary fellow of St Antony's College, Oxford. He was appointed CMG in 2002 and knighted in 2005. He received a papal knighthood in 2009. He is married with a grown-up son and daughter.

David Baker
Partner, White & Case
dgbaker@whitecase.com

David Baker is a partner in the Energy, Infrastructure, Project and Asset Finance Group at White & Case based in London. He has advised governments, national oil companies, oil companies, trading houses and lenders on oil and gas projects for over 20 years. He has particularly extensive experience in the UK upstream and energy business and the international gas market, including LNG project financing in various jurisdictions covering Europe, the Middle East, Africa and Asia.

David is recognised for the depth of his experience for energy, oil, gas and electricity. He is ranked regularly in the Chambers UK as well as in the Legal 500 UK directories for projects, energy and natural resources.

Deyber Cano
Consultant, Project Financial Modelling
deyber.cano.14@alumni.ucl.ac.uk

Deyber Cano is an economist specialising in infrastructure finance and financial modelling. He graduated from University College London with a distinction in his MSc Infrastructure Investment and Finance. He was the co-author with Brian Scott-Quinn of the *AFME Guide to Infrastructure Financing*.

Gabriel Carter
Chief executive officer, ALARYX
gc@alaryx.com

Gabriel Carter is the chief executive officer of ALARYX, a security company working chiefly in the Middle East and North Africa region (MENA) and South Asia. Since 2008 he has worked extensively in the security industry both on operational deployments and providing strategic consultancy support across a wide range of fields.

He has delivered numerous security projects for the oil and gas and infrastructure sectors, including global and regional audits, strategic route selection, security strategy and policy development, and crisis management capacity building programmes. He has also been heavily involved in technical/physical security design for several major pharmaceutical companies, defence manufacturers and development-focused NGOs.

A graduate of Cambridge University and a member of the Special Forces Club, he has written articles for numerous industry publications and has spoken on television and radio about the challenges facing the security industry and other sectors operating in high-risk environments.

Thomas Dimitroff
Partner, Infrastructure Development Partnership;
Senior adviser, Roland Berger GmbH
tdimitroff@infradev.co.uk

Thomas Dimitroff has over 20 years' experience in the energy sector. He has functioned as a core member of multiple negotiating teams that have delivered globally significant energy projects, including the one million bbl/day Baku-Tbilisi-Ceyhan oil pipeline, the 10 billion cm/year South Caucasus gas pipeline, the 6.8 bcma gas sales agreement between Turkey and Azerbaijan and the 10 bcma Trans-Adriatic Pipeline Company. He has advised governments including the Azerbaijan Republic during its multilateral Energy Charter Transit Protocol negotiations, and he has led cross-functional teams in delivering multiple feasibility studies and strategy advice to governments and developers for conventional and renewable projects in the former Soviet Union (FSU), Africa, the Middle East, Asia and North America. Tom has also developed and negotiated arrangements for the acquisition and sale of upstream oil and gas assets in the FSU and the Middle East on behalf of oil and gas companies and private equity funds. Prior to joining the Infrastructure Development Partnership, he was regional advisor to BP plc for Africa, the Middle East, Russia, the Caspian and Turkey, advising on non-technical risks posed to new ventures and existing operations across the region.

Tom was consulting editor for *Risk and Energy Infrastructure: Cross-border Dimensions* published by Globe Law and Business in 2011.

Troy Edwards
Partner, Allen & Overy LLP
troy.edwards@allenovery.com

Troy Edwards is a partner in Allen & Overy's Projects, Energy and Infrastructure Group based in London. He has extensive experience acting for sponsors, governments, lenders and contractors on a large number of privately and publicly financed energy and infrastructure projects with a particular focus on first-of-a-kind transactions.

Troy has worked in a variety of sectors with his recent focus including the power sector (thermal, nuclear and renewable), oil & gas (upstream, pipelines and petrochemical facilities) and the transport and water infrastructure sectors. He acts across a broad range of jurisdictions, including throughout Europe, Africa, the Middle East and Central Asia and on all types of commercial arrangements, including revenue and offtake agreements, governmental agreements, joint ventures, concessions and EPC contracts.

Troy is additionally a contributor to the 4th edition of the leading text *Project Finance, A Legal Guide* and the construction textbook *EPC Contracts and Major Projects*.

Kevin Gardiner
Senior investment strategist

Kevin Gardiner is a City-based senior investment strategist at a private bank. Previously he was chief investment officer (Europe) at Barclays Wealth Management, and worked at several investment banks and the Bank of England in a financial market career spanning more than 30 years. In 1994, while at Morgan Stanley, he wrote the 'Celtic Tiger' report on the Irish economy. He was educated at Atlantic College, the London School of Economics and Cambridge, and is a governor at Atlantic College and a member of the Welsh Government's Financial and Professional Services Advisory Panel. His book, *Making Sense of Markets,* was published in July 2015 by Palgrave Macmillan.

Paul Griffin
Lawyer, arbitrator and mediator
Special adviser – oil and gas, White & Case;
University of Dundee
paul.griffin@whitecase.com

Professor Paul Griffin is an English lawyer and has more than 35 years' experience of practising in the international oil and gas business. Paul was a partner in leading international law firms for some 25 years until his retirement from Allen & Overy in 2016. During that time, he led the oil and gas teams at those firms and worked on many of the significant deals and disputes of the global oil and gas business, as well as being involved in related matters of public law and competition law. He has been recognised as the 'World's Leading Energy Lawyer' in the *Expert Guides: Best of the Best*, and as the 'World's Leading Oil and Gas Lawyer' in *Who's Who Legal*.

In addition to his role at the University of Dundee, Paul is special adviser to the global oil and gas group at White & Case. He is also now active in the resolution of disputes in the international oil and gas sector, where he works as an arbitrator, an expert and a mediator.

Paul writes and speaks regularly on issues and developments in the law in the context of the global oil and gas industry.

Paul is vice-chair of the Oil and Gas Law Committee of the International Bar Association and a member of the Association of International Petroleum Negotiators and the Institute of Energy Law. He is also a member of the Chartered Institute of Arbitrators and a CEDR accredited mediator.

Mark Podlasly
Trustee, Nlaka'pamux Legacy Trust
mark@nlxlegacytrust.com

Mark Podlasly is a member of the Nlaka'pamux First Nation, an indigenous community located in British Columbia, Canada. A graduate of Harvard University, he holds degrees in business and public administration. He has over 20 years of international experience in the planning, permitting and construction of large capital projects related to energy, resource development and community infrastructure.

Mark advises the Canadian Assembly of First Nations and the First Nations Energy and Mining Council on energy and mining issues and their impact on indigenous lands and communities. In addition, Mark counsels indigenous governments across Canada on the establishment of sovereign wealth funds to capture and invest revenues from resource development.

He is a founding Trustee of the Nlaka'pamux Legacy Trust, managing and operating a seven-figure sovereign wealth fund shared by eight indigenous communities in British Columbia.

Brian Scott-Quinn
Chairman, ICMA Centre for Financial Markets
Henley Business School, University of Reading
bsq@icmacentre.ac.uk

Brian Scott-Quinn originally worked as an investment banker in the Eurobond market before setting up the ICMA Centre at the University of Reading with the help of £8 million in gifts from the International Capital Market Association (ICMA), the trade association and market regulator for the international capital market.

He has published extensively and is the author of *Commercial and Investment Banking* published by Palgrave Macmillan. He has also co-authored (with Deyber Cano) the Association of Financial Markets in Europe (AFME) *Guide to Infrastructure Financing*.

He is a non-executive director of Civilised Bank Plc and chairman of its Audit and Assurance Committee. He is also a director of Madiston Plc, a peer-to-peer software company. He is currently examining how private project finance could enable the deployment of high temperature small modular reactors (HTSMRs). He is on the advisory board of Penultimate Power UK Ltd.

Antony Skinner
Partner, Ashurst LLP
Antony.Skinner@ashurst.com

Antony Skinner is a partner in the energy and infrastructure team at Ashurst. Antony has worked in the power and renewables sector for 20 years. He specialises in renewable and thermal power with respect to development, financing and M&A in the UK, Europe and Africa. He has advised sponsors and lenders, purchasers and vendors in a range of transactions in relation to renewables and power generation developments and in connection with a number of renewable portfolio acquisitions and financings.

Drew Slaton
Senior project manager
drewslaton@yahoo.com

Drew Slaton has over 30 years' experience in the engineering and construction industry involving power generation, infrastructure and petrochemical-related projects in the commercial and government sectors. He completed two business management degrees in the United States, a master's degree in technology management in Australia, and is currently pursuing a doctoral programme.

Drew has worked in 30 countries spanning five continents supporting high risk, hardship, multi-billion-dollar mega-projects and has extensive experience working on joint venture projects with multi-national companies.

An active member of the Project Management Institute (PMI) since 1995, Drew earned internationally recognised Project Management Professional and Risk Management Professional certifications, as well as a Construction Risk and Insurance Specialist certification through the International Risk Management Institute. He has chaired the 40K+ member PMI Project Risk Management Community of Practice and served as the co-chair on a joint Risk Management Working Group formed between the International Council on Systems Engineering, the Massachusetts Institute of Technology and PMI.

David Wadham
Partner, Ashurst LLP
david.wadham@ashurst.com

David Wadham is a partner in the utilities and resources group of Ashurst LLP, based in London. He is global head of the firm's utilities practice and has previously worked in the Middle East and Paris. David specialises in the acquisition, development and financing of large-scale energy and infrastructure projects.

In particular, David advises sponsors, funders and governments on the acquisition, development and financing of independent power projects (IPPs). He advises on commercial agreements, such as power purchase and fuel supply contracts, construction and operating sub-contracts, as well as on conventional and Islamic financing.

David has advised on power and renewables projects across Europe, the Middle East and Africa and has become increasingly involved in nuclear projects, advising China General Nuclear on the Hinkley Point C project and acting as counsel to the project company on the NuGen (Moorside) project (both in the UK), as well as on nuclear new-build projects in Romania, Turkey and the UAE.

New journal – Modern Legal Practice

Globe Law and Business

Modern Legal Practice

Business • Strategy • Leadership

Editorial
Katherine Cowdrey

Opinion The effect of Brexit on London as a centre for dispute resolution
Deborah Finkler
Robert Brittain

Strategy The new normal lawyer – legal practice in the 21st century
Tony King

Remuneration Table manners: rewarding performance without 'eat what you kill'
Norman Clark

Technology and innovation in the in-house context
Bjarne Tellmann

Procurement Why you need to know about legal procurement
Dr Silvia Hodges Silverstein

Diversity Retaining women lawyers: the need for new perspectives
Ida Abbott

Finance and strategy Finance issues facing firms
Brian Dunlop

Interpersonal skills Finding a new way through difficult conversations
Alison Nolan

GC Perspectives Who should be the culture and ethics guardian?
Jeremy Barton

Meet the board
Tony King

Book review
Brighter thinking for law firms by Peter Noyce
Reviewed by Professor Stephen Mayson

July 2017 • www.globelawandbusiness.com

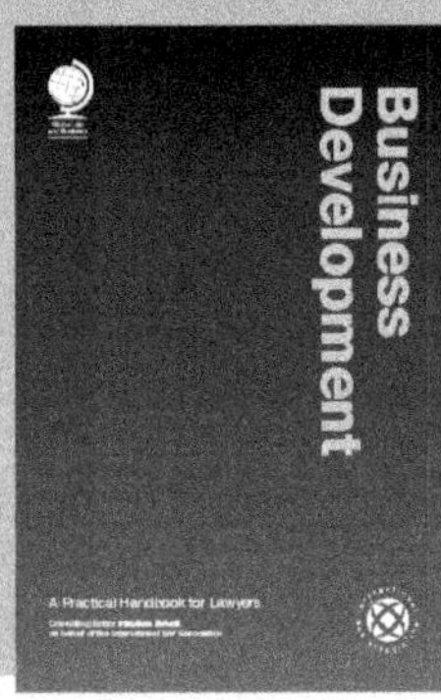

Founder Subscriber Offer

Subscribe today as a founder subscriber, and receive:

- Your first issue free of charge
- Over 20% discount on your first year's subscription
- A free ebook copy of our best-selling, 240 page book, *Business Development: A Practical Handbook for Lawyers* (usual retail price £130/$220)

Publication dates: Quarterly
Hard copy ISSN: 2398 - 5410
Hardcopy only: £295 per annum
Discounted price: £236 per annum

Go to **http://modernlegalpracticeoffer.globelawandbusiness.com** for full details and subscription offer.

About Globe Law and Business

Globe Law and Business was established in 2005 as an imprint of Globe Business Media Group. We set out to create law books which are sufficiently high level to be of real use to the experienced professional, yet still accessible and easy to navigate. Most of our authors are drawn from Magic Circle and other top commercial firms, both in the UK and internationally.

In autumn 2015, we had an exciting turn in our history when Globe Law and Business was bought by a management team which includes my colleague Jim Smith and me, Sian O'Neill.

We love books, and our hardback titles are carefully produced, with the utmost attention paid to the editorial, design and production processes. We hope this results in high-quality titles which are easy to read, and a pleasure to own.

Our customers and authors are of paramount importance – we are committed to devoting time and attention to each book as well as everyone involved in the publishing process.

We'd very much like to hear from you with your thoughts on our titles or ideas for improving what we offer. Please do feel free to email me at sian@globelawandbusiness.com with your views.

Sian O'Neill
Managing director
Globe Law and Business

www.globelawandbusiness.com

Globe Law and Business

Related titles in energy

Go to **www.globelawandbusiness.com**
for full details including free sample chapters